The Highlands and Islands

A Nineteenth-Century Tour

John Eddowes Bowman; drawing by his son, Eddowes Bowman.
John Freeman Milward Dovaston; silhouette by Thomas Bewick, c. 1825.

The Highlands and Islands
A Nineteenth-Century Tour

J.E. Bowman

ALAN SUTTON · Gloucester
HIPPOCRENE BOOKS, INC. · New York

First published 1986

Copyright © in journal, Sir John P. Bowman, 1986
Copyright © in note on J.E. Bowman and J.F.M. Dovaston, Elaine M.E. Barry, 1986
Copyright © in note on historical setting, Celia Miller, 1986

First published in Great Britain 1986
Alan Sutton Publishing Limited
30 Brunswick Road
Gloucester GL1 1JJ

British Library Cataloguing in Publication Data

Bowman, J.E.
The Highlands and the islands : a nineteenth century tour.
1. Highlands (Scotland)—Description and travel 2. Scotland—Description and travel—1801–1900
I. Title
914.11'10474   DA880.H7

ISBN 0-86299-275-3 (case)
ISBN 0-86299-236-2 (paperback)

First published in the U.S.A. 1986
Hippocrene Books, Inc.
171 Madison Avenue
New York, N.Y. 10016

ISBN 0-87052-316-3 (case)
ISBN 0-87052-343-0 (paperback)

Cover picture: detail from
Kindred Spirits by Asher Brown Durand, 1849.
Courtesy of The New York Public Library, Astor Lenox and Tilden Foundations.

NE/110/1280–900/R/040986/3500

Printed in Great Britain

Preface

THE ORIGINAL MANUSCRIPT of this journal, beautifully bound and illustrated, with nearly 800 pages of the author's elegant copper-plate script, has been kept in the Bowman family as an heirloom (together with a mass of other papers and diaries) for five generations, and is still in the possession of my uncle by marriage, Sir John Bowman of Newbury.

During the writing of it, in the winter of 1826–7, Bowman came under some pressure to publish, both from his fellow-traveller and journal-writer Dovaston, and from the engraver Thomas Bewick, whom the friends visited on this tour and also two years earlier on their Lake District one. He refused, however, on the grounds that there was 'not a sufficient portion of new matter to justify', and hoped that his 'children would never be persuaded to do so' after his time (diary, 30 March 1827). One hundred and sixty years later, however, this argument hardly seems valid, and Bewick's comment: 'The writing of your Tour in the Highlands, with a determination not to publish it, is like "hiding the Talent in a Napkin" – at that rate the world will know nothing about it,' (letter to Dovaston, 21 December 1826) – is surely to be more regarded.

I first saw the volume early in 1984, when visiting my cousin, David Bowman, great great great grandson of the author, in hospital. David was a victim of polio, which he contracted while working in Zambia in 1970 and which immobilised from the neck down; his father, Sir John, had brought him the book in 1982 as a focus of interest and potential source of gain; several publishers had been contacted at that point but little had come of it. I felt sure that with the current interest in travel writing the book had a future and we decided to renew the search for a publisher. This, together with all the research into the family background was to have been a joint project, and one which interested David greatly. The present publisher reacted favourably, but sadly David died in April 1985, before negotiations were fully concluded, so that he never had the chance of contributing from his specially adapted typewriter to the background material which follows.

Thanks are due to my uncle, Sir John Bowman, for allowing me to peruse his family papers so frequently; also to Iain Bain, of the Tate Gallery, who has given me invaluable assistance with Dovaston's background, and allowed me to quote from his parallel journal of the Tour.

ELAINE BARRY

Contents

INTRODUCTION
   1. J.E. Bowman and J.F.M. Dovaston   ix
   2. The Historical Background   xvii

THE TOUR
   Volume I   1
   Volume II   129

INDEX   206

FAMILY TREE OF THE AUTHOR, JOHN EDDOWES BOWMAN

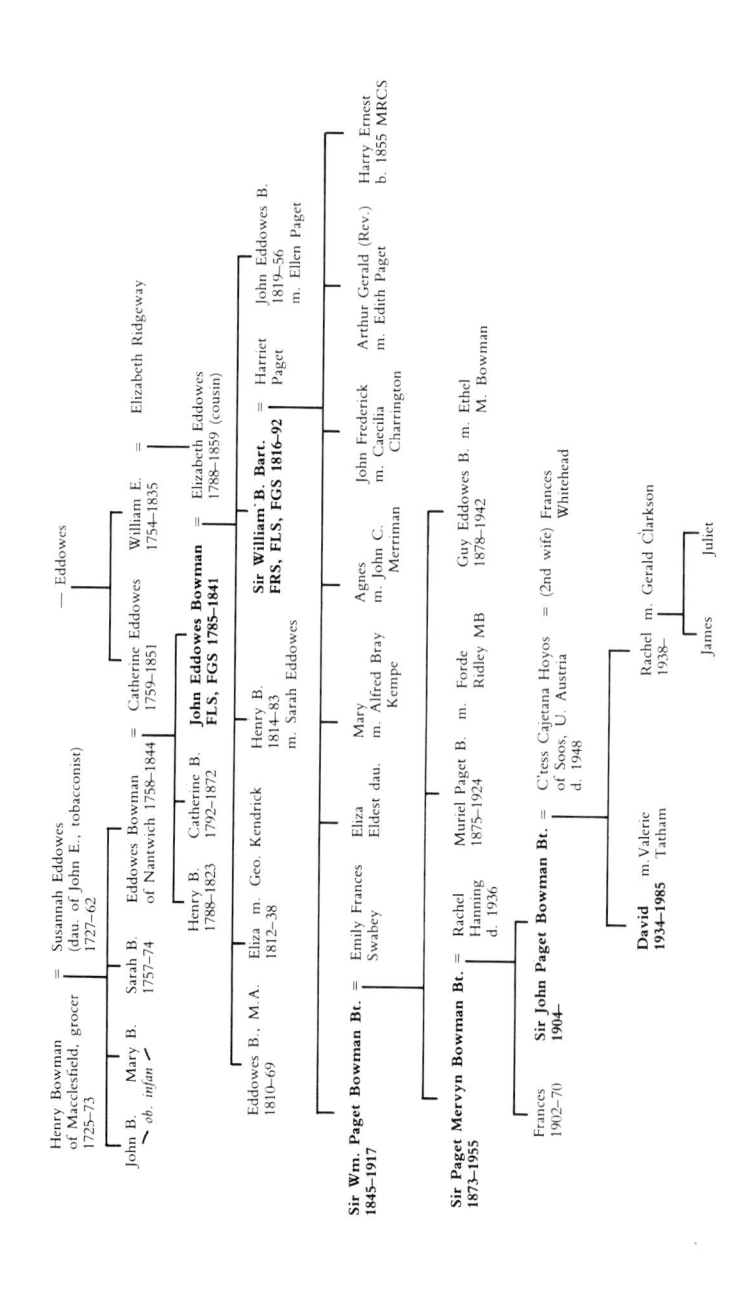

Henry Bowman = Susannah Eddowes
of Macclesfield, grocer (dau. of John E., tobacconist)
1725–73 1727–62

- John B. / Mary B. *ob. infan*
- Sarah B. 1757–74
- Eddowes Bowman of Nantwich 1758–1844 = Catherine Eddowes 1759–1851
- — Eddowes
- William E. 1754–1835 = Elizabeth Ridgeway

Eddowes Bowman of Nantwich children:
- Henry B. 1788–1823
- Catherine B. 1792–1872
- **John Eddowes Bowman FLS, FGS 1785–1841** = Elizabeth Eddowes 1788–1859 (cousin)

Children of John Eddowes Bowman:
- Eddowes B., M.A. 1810–69
- Eliza m. Geo. Kendrick 1812–38
- Henry B. 1814–83 m. Sarah Eddowes
- **Sir William B. Bart. FRS, FLS, FGS 1816–92** = Harriet Paget
- John Eddowes B. 1819–56 m. Ellen Paget
- Arthur Gerald (Rev.) m. Edith Paget
- Harry Ernest b. 1855 MRCS

Eddowes B., M.A. = Emily Frances Swabey

- **Sir Wm. Paget Bowman Bt. 1845–1917**
- Eliza Eldest dau.
- Mary m. Alfred Bray Kempe
- Agnes m. John C. Merriman
- John Frederick m. Caecilia Charrington
- Guy Eddowes B. 1878–1942 m. Ethel M. Bowman

Sir Paget Mervyn Bowman Bt. 1873–1955 = Rachel Hanning d. 1936

- Muriel Paget B. 1875–1924 m. Forde Ridley MB

- Frances 1902–70
- **Sir John Paget Bowman Bt. 1904–** = C'tess Cajetana Hoyos of Soos, U. Austria d. 1948 = (2nd wife) Frances Whitehead

- **David 1934–1985** m. Valerie Tatham
- Rachel 1938– m. Gerald Clarkson

- James
- Juliet

Introduction

1. J.E. BOWMAN AND J.F.M. DOVASTON

The Banker and the Barrister together they did ride,
To gaze on bonny Scotland's rocks and lakes from side to side.

This was the verse sung by Dovaston (and recorded in his parallel journal of the tour) as he and the author of this present text jolted along in a lime cart on the road from Fort Augustus to Inverness on the 25 July 1825, and it strikes just the right tone of happy unanimity that characterized their partnership.

John Eddowes Bowman (1785–1841) and John Freeman Milward Dovaston (1782–1854), the Banker and the Barrister, were in the prime of life when they undertook their month-long tour of nearly 1700 miles through Scotland, but for all that they pelted each other with snowballs on the summit of Ben Nevis, invented nicknames for disagreeable fellow travellers and approached every encounter with youthful enthusiasm. Bowman was in fact only a few months short of forty and Dovaston was three years his senior. They had first met only four years earlier and found their tastes and interests very similar, although their situation in life fairly different – Bowman being a family man and a banker, Dovaston a bachelor retired early from the law to a life of cultured leisure. The success of their tour, and the writing up of the journal which followed, owes everything to their genuine friendship and ability to co-operate.

Bowman was born in Nantwich, the elder son of Eddowes Bowman, tobacconist-grocer, and Catherine Eddowes of Shrewsbury. Eddowes Bowman had moved to Nantwich in 1759 from Macclesfield, where his father, Henry Bowman (1725–73) was a grocer; he married Susannah Eddowes, daughter of John Eddows, tobacconist (1727–62). The families had been intertwined therefore for several generations and assisted each other in trade. Eddowes Bowman took over his father-in-law's business on arrival in Nantwich, but retired in 1812 to become a partner in a banking concern.

John Eddowes Bowman, with whom we are concerned here, had a younger brother, Henry, who died in 1823 and a younger sister, Catherine, who lived to be 79. He went to Grammar School and was known as a studious boy, fond of reading. From his father he got a taste for botany and a lifelong habit of temperance – this he attributed to his father's telling him of the family tendency to consumption and his efforts to overcome it.

At the age of sixteen Bowman entered his father's shop; the long hours behind the counter were completely uncongenial to him and in his diary, which he kept from 1812 to his death in 1841 he comments, somewhat bitterly, when reviewing his situation at the age of 35: 'For the first six or seven years after leaving school I was in the shop with my father, which I could never bring myself to like . . . it is somewhat surprising he could never be prevailed upon to think of some way of life more congenial to my natural cast of mind and to the tenor of my pursuits.'

Determined not to be cheated of his true interests, at the age of sixteen he had a small table fitted to his bed and rose between 3 and 4 a.m. winter and summer, so that he could study before starting work each morning. One result of this industry was a minute analysis of Gibbon's *Decline and Fall*, filling a thick octavo volume. He was obviously a natural student and showed an unquenchable appetite for knowledge over a wide area. His early friendship with the antiquarian Joseph Hunter (1783–1861) gave him an interest in genealogy and antiquity and it was with Hunter that he made his first major tour from home in the summer of 1814. They visited Paris and most of northern France and Bowman afterwards wrote up their travels under the title *The United Notes of the Rev. Joseph Hunter and J.E.B., . . . incorporated together and arranged in form of a journal by the latter.* They form a handsome illustrated volume in much the same style as the Scottish tour, and are also in the possession of my uncle.

In 1809 he married his cousin-german, Elizabeth (1788–1859), daughter of W. Eddowes of Shrewsbury. It was a happy marriage – the diaries of both husband and wife are full of expressions of esteem and affection for each other. Five children were born to the couple: Eddowes, Eliza, Henry, William and John. Eddowes (1810–1869) became professor of classical literature and history at Manchester New College in 1846; Eliza (1812–1838) died tragically in childbirth; Henry (1814–1883) became an architect and author; William (1816–1892) became a distinguished ophthalmic surgeon and was created a baronet in 1881; while John (1819–1854) became the first professor of practical chemistry at King's College, London in 1851.[1]

---

1. Biographical details have been based on information in the *Dictionary of National Biography* (*DNB*).

Introduction xi

Bowman was a devoted family man, a painstaking educator who cared for his children's welfare above all else. Their success was a tribute to his paternal devotion.

Bowman became greatly dissatisfied with his working life – at one time he thought of becoming a Unitarian minister, but his father dissuaded him. The tobacco trade was bad and he could not face the thought of continuing in the retail grocery trade. In 1813 therefore, he joined, as junior partner, the banking business which his father had entered. Its failure early in 1816 left him, with a wife and three children, quite without resources. Reviewing this in 1820 he wrote '. . . I was without employment for a whole year and knew not what to turn to for subsistence – but I thank God, I always kept up my spirits.'

Soon after, he moved to Welshpool to become manager of the bank of Beck and Co. of Shrewsbury and in 1824 took up a managing partnership of a bank at Wrexham, and established himself as a country gentleman by moving to The Court, a pleasant house with grounds and garden which gave him endless scope for his horticultural and botanical interests. The Court adjoined the woods of Erddig (now a National Trust property) and he derived much pleasure from strolling in the woods in the early mornings 'seldom returning without something curious or interesting to lay on the breakfast table for the instruction and entertainment of his family.'[2]

In both Welshpool and Wrexham he was developing his interests in botany and geology in all the spare time available, although as yet without any direct contact with any professional or academic society. He became an expert on grasses and made minute observations of insects, fungi and parasitical plants; his first communication with the Linnaean Society was in 1828, when he gave an account of a minute species of fungus found in Erddig woods and which he was able to name, as the first recorder, *Enerthenema elegans*. Later he detected a minute fossil in Derbyshire which is name after him, '*Endothyra Bowmannii*'. In 1830 he was able to retire from the bank and devote himself entirely to science, particularly geology. He became a Fellow of the Linnaean and Geological Societies, and the Manchester Philosophical Society, and presented a number of papers to them and to the British Scientific Assocation. His chief work was on the origin of coal and Sir Charles Lyall, the geologist, wrote of him in 1871: 'The late Mr. Bowman was the first who gave a satisfactory explanation of the manner in which distinct coal seams, after maintaining their interdependence for miles, may at length unite, and then persist . . . with a thickness equal to that (of) the separate seams.'[3]

---

2. J.J. Tayler, Sketch of the Life and Character of J.E. Bowman, in *Memoirs of the Manchester Literary and Philosophical Society*, second series, vol. vii pt. i (read 4 October 1842).
3. Sir C. Lyall, *Elements of Geology* (1871), p. 382.

In 1837 he moved to Manchester, where he found a larger circle of men with similar tastes, and enjoyed the membership of the Philosophical, Literary, Natural History and Geological Societies of the city. His death came early on December 4 1841, as a result of a chill caught while geologizing in North Wales. For some time prior to this trip he had been preparing for a meeting of the British Association, by arranging his collection of fossils and botanical specimens in the house he had recently built. He was undoubtedly a distinguished and talented man, possessed of enormous mental energy and reaching the highest standards of scientific achievement, made all the more remarkable by the fact that he had worked in isolation and without the benefit of an academic training.

John Freeman Millward Dovaston was born into a landed family at West Felton, near Oswestry in Shropshire, he was educated at Oswestry School, Shrewsbury School and Christ Church, Oxford, where he gained his B.A. in 1804 and his M.A. in 1807. He was called to the bar on 12 June 1807 at the Middle Temple but found the life uncongenial and swiftly took advantage of his succession to the family estate on his father's death in 1808 to retire.[4]

The West Felton estate, although it had been in the family for generations, was largely the creation of his father, John Dovaston (1740–1808), who had built it up as a prosperous nursery to supply the insatiable demand for trees resulting from the mania for landscaping and planting prevalent amongst the aristocracy and gentry at the time. It was here that Dovaston took up the life of a bachelor country gentleman of modest, though comfortable means, devoting his life to literary pursuits. His poetic efforts met with considerable success and, whilst he did not attain major national recognition, he can certainly be classed among the minor poets of the first half of the nineteenth century.

His interests were wide, including not only poetry and music but also natural history and ornithology. Birds were protected at West Felton by Dovaston's prohibition of shooting or any other form of molestation on the estate. He appears to have been one of the unsung pioneers of field ornithology and published some of the results of his observations in Loudon's *Magazine of Natural History* in the 1830s. In 1823 he first met Thomas Bewick, the engraver and author of the popular *History of British Birds*. A firm friendship was formed and the pair corresponded at frequent intervals, Dovaston helping Bewick with the preparation of the fifth edition of the *History*, as well as preparing a preface for the sixth edition, published in 1826. Bewick reciprocated with a profile silhouette of Dovaston (*c.* 1825).

On 2 April 1821 Bowman recorded his first meeting with Dovaston in his diary: 'Spent day with Mr. Dovaston of West Felton the great classical scholar, poet, naturalist, planter, etc., etc., and was very much gratified in

---

4. See footnote 1.

his company. Jones (a surgeon) took me for the purpose of introducing me to him and he gave me a very friendly invitation to West Felton . . . Dovaston . . . is well skilled in botany as well as most other departments of natural history, of which he is passionately fond. He seems to be of a turn of mind and thinking more congenial with mine than I generally meet with; my pursuits are similar to his, but his are infinitely more extensive and numerous and he is better grounded in them.' He added, with a touch of envy, that Dovaston 'devotes his whole time to science and has the great advantage . . . his father was of a similar turn and gave him a university education.'

The acquaintance obviously flourished, because in the autumn of 1823 the two men made a *Tour to the Lakes and Scenery of Westmoreland and Cumberland*, for which a short journal by Dovaston survives, constructed from the notes taken on the spot by both men. In the first page we read of them meeting on the summit of Breidden, between their two homes, to arrange details of the tour; Dovaston continues: '. . . being from long personal acquaintance aware of our uniformity of opinion on some of the most important considerations of Life, as well as a great similarity of taste as to Natural History and romantic scenery, we anticipated and subsequently enjoyed many hours of high gratification.' Later, he paid tribute to Bowman's 'ever-ready and always accurate scientific conversation', and disparaged his own contribtion as 'filmy vapours of flimsy tints of aerial fancy.' Nonetheless, the journey was 'all our hearts had ever wished, and perhaps something more.' (Dovaston, Lake Tour Journal).

By the time they embarked on the Scottish tour, the two men were evidently closely in contact, and quite confident of the success of their partnership as travellers. They went on a Welsh tour in 1824 and no doubt laid plans for their Scottish one then. On March 17 1825, Bowman wrote: 'From Ellesmere I went on to West Felton and spent yesterday with Dovaston . . . we spoke of our Scottish journey this coming summer and are determined to undertake it together. It will remain with me to fix the route and time.' (Diary). The relationship throughout the tour seems to have been relaxed and genial: there was never the shadow of a quarrel and the formality of the Lake Tour journal, in which Dovaston calls his friend Mr. Bowman throughout, is replaced by a certain playfulness, almost a teasing approach towards the staider Bowman. Bowman in turn relished the recording, on August 2, of Dovaston's conduct after a convivial evening with the Scottish chieftains (at which Bowman as usual abstained): 'It was a late hour and I had been asleep, when Dovaston entered, a little unsteadily, our double bedroom – "Bowman", said he, "where's the inkpot?"' He wanted it for 'posting the Log', and to record having been, for once, outdone in conversation. 'So spit in my face and call me horse', he said and, 'mumbling a mixture of Shakespeare, Burns and Sir Walter,' sat down and wrote his journal.

On many occasions, Bowman refers in the journal to Dovaston's brilliancy of conversation, his wit and animation. On the steamer trip to the Western Isles he describes him as 'in continual display' (a suitable epithet for an ornithologist!) and says 'In whatever part of the packet he chose to be, a crowd of attentive and enraptured audience collected round him', so that the captain had to ask them to spread out,' to preserve the equilibrium of the vessel'.

Several times, too, Bowman notes: 'Dovaston became facetious' – with the guide, the coachman etc. and it is clear that he was the more volatile, frivolous and possibly amusing of the two. Dovaston in turn admired Bowman's weightier judgement and superior knowledge on most practical matters; he left the planning of the tour and the management of the money to Bowman and, finally, opted out of the writing up in full of the journal.

The actual construction of the present text is quite complex: following a pattern already established on previous tours, both travellers carried their notebooks in their hands, taking copious notes whenever the situation allowed and then writing them up each evening. Bowman makes constant reference to the laboriousness of this task, which he nevertheless saw as indispensable. Both men frequently stayed up extremely late, battling with fatigue, to finish their writing. On July 24 Bowman says: 'I continued writing until 2 o'clock, when falling asleep in the chair I was roused by Dovaston, who was still plying at his task, and bent upon completing it. Nature was quite exhausted and I found it necessary to recruit her by a few hours repose.' The next day he rose at 5 a.m. to complete the log, whereas Dovaston had continued until 4 a.m. without a break. On another occasion, 'Being occupied till 2 a.m. embodying my notes, I was in a sound sleep when the bagpiper of the steamship gave the signal at 5 o'clock.'

During the day they wrote on board ship, while waiting for meals, sitting by the wayside, or on the stony shore. Occasionally Dovaston rebelled and asked, as on July 20, 'who in the height of such enjoyment could pause to make dull and pedantic observations about lights and shadows and "setting pallettes" as my friend Warren calls it'. But Bowman on his French tour even tried to get down on paper all that he saw from the stagecoach to Southampton and was disappointed that 'the jolting generally rendered the hand illegible even to myself'.

I have been very fortunate in being able to read Dovaston's original (unpublished) account of the tour, entitled *A few short, hasty and discursive notes, each taken on the spot in a Tour to the Hebrides, Highlands and Scotland*, because it has an immediacy and vividness of presentation which is somewhat lost in Bowman's later re-writing of his own notes, combined in places with Dovaston's. Through it we are really present at every stage of the tour, delighted by what is almost a running commentary on scenes and events:

Introduction xv

> *July 21* We are now sitting drinking whisky just before those dismal rocks, seen across the head of Loch Long and the sun has just set behind.
> *July 23* We are sitting at breakfst (in a neat little parlour) on delicious trout, seeing through the window southwards the points of Benlede and Benvolich blue.

On July 27 he noted down his happy encounter on board the steamer with the young Scottish laird, Donald McLean: 'He this morning wore a sprig of red heather, and is now looking over my shoulder and with his sweet voice telling me the names of the islands we are passing . . .'; and, most dramatic of all, on Sunday 31 July: 'I am now on the extreme point of Ben Nevis, writing these notes'.

A detailed comparison of the two journals is impossible here, and probably invidious, but these extracts illustrate the difference between them as regards immediacy and detail of the hour. Dovaston's is by far the shorter (50,000 words approximately) and was not revised, apart from the addition of some lengthy notes at the end of the text – some expanding on incidents such as the Blubberchops encounters, or the hiring of the lime cart, or the parallel lines at Glen Roy, and his own late arrival to bed, copied from Bowman.

The Bowman text, however, is a more composite and elaborate construction. It was not actually written in full until the second winter following the tour, starting in October 1826. The diary reads: 'I make here a memo that I have this day begun to re-write my Scotch Tour. If I can get to the end of it by the next equinox I shall be v. well satisfied.' Evidently there had been some discussion between the two friends prior to this as to who should carry out the task, and because of this it had been delayed. On October 2 1826 Bowman recorded: 'Dovaston wrote me word last wek that, though he was very much interested in our late Scotch Tour, and was anxious to see it well and copiously written, he could not prevail upon himself to ujndertake the job from indolence and occasional ill-health, but that he would assist me by furnishing some articles which he is more competent to handle than I am. These relate principally to the poetry and songs of the Scotch, with which he is well acquainted. . . . He said he should wish to have some conversation with me before I begin, so I went on the 29th ulto and returned home last night. I have with some difficulty prevailed on him to do rather more than the above, and he has given me some general hints. I am going to set about it almost immediately, which I do with diffidence, as I am aware it will be a long and wearisome task to do it well.'

Bowman carried out the task with just the thoroughness and determination we would expect of him. A letter from him to Dovaston dated 18 January 1827 reported his progress:

> '*I am on the road* down from Inverness to Dunkeld and am just out of the

great fir forest of Rothiemurchus; this day's journey was often dreary and wearisome but I flatter myself I shall make the recital of it interesting; indeed if I must tell you what I think, what is added since you were here, maintains the character of what you then saw. I have worked hard since Eddowes (his eldest son) left, and I make a vague calculation that if no unforeseen interruptions arise, I shall see the end of the job in about 2 months – perhaps less.'

He went on to say that his daughter Eliza and Eddowes had each made drawings to be included in the volume, a fact which he felt added to its value as a family heirloom. On 3 March 1827 Bowman wrote: 'I have at length completed the labour of my Scottish Journal'.

It is necessary here to comment on Dovaston's contribution to the completed journal. On reading his briefer account side by side with Bowman's, I soon realised a great identity of phrase and description; it is clear that, admiring Dovaston's literary talent as he did, Bowman often substituted some of the more artistic passages by Dovaston for his own, incorporating them with further comments on the same subjects. Some of the passages are quite long, for instance, those describing the scenery on Ben Nevis and the effect of throwing stones down the slopes; at Staffa, too, he used Dovaston's description of the cave, likening it to a Gothic minster; similarly, at the Foyer Falls – there are many examples to be found. Sometimes he used a brief and particularly felicitous phrase, such as the 'indefatigible piper', 'a delicious breezy morning', or a breakfast of fresh herrings 'white as snow'. All in all the debt is quite considerable, although owing more to respect and anxiety to give as full a picture as possible than to any form of plagiarism.

It has not been possible to establish how the friendship fared in later years, but it would be strange if it had not continued. In June 1827 Bowman visited Dovaston at West Felton and saw 'for the first time since it was bound, my Scotch Tour, which is done to my satisfaction, only it appears very thick'. He added, 'I have made a kind of half promise to Dovaston to draw up a short memoir of his father for the new edition of Phillip's History of Shrewsbury, announced for publication; he has an insuperable objection to do it himself . . .', he wished Bowman to write it rather than the editor, whose abilities he doubted.

A further tour was made in the summer of 1827 by the two friends, together with part of Bowman's family – his parents and sister Catherine meeting him at an hotel near the Menai Bridge, his wife, eldest son and daughter accompanying him and 'taking sketches' of the various scenes. Beyond that, no further information is, so far, forthcoming.

That the Bowman/Dovaston partnership was a fruitful one is evident in the pages of Bowman's journal of their Scottish tour. They were perfect foils each for the other, compatible in every way and ideal travelling

Introduction xvii

companions. Their friendship, although it must have been tested by some of their experiences in Scotland, was clearly as close at the end of the journey as it had been at the beginning. The story of 'the Banker and the Barrister' and their journey through 'bonny Scotland's rocks and lakes' is a living testimony of the long-dead friendship of these two eminently likeable men.

ELAINE BARRY

2. THE HISTORICAL SETTING

This journal of the tour undertaken by Bowman and Dovaston between July and August 1825 presents a fascinating picture of Scotland and northern England on the eve of the Railway Age and the second phase of the Industrial Revolution. It is a record of landscape, places and people frozen in time, as fresh and vivid to our eyes now as they were to Bowman and Dovaston in the hot and dusty summer of 1825. The journal can be read and enjoyed on many levels: as a graphic narrative of the travels of two wealthy and educated men of their time, complete with the trials and tribulations as well as the sheer enjoyment that a holiday can bring; as a faithful record of topography, geology, flora and fauna; and as a mirror of everyday life: the cities, the towns and villages, roads and means of transport, inns and hotels, tourism and tourists, dress, behaviour and social attitudes. It is these myriad facets of life at the end of the first quarter of the nineteenth century reflected in the pages of Bowman's journal which make it such a remarkable and enjoyable record.

Their journey took place at the time when Britain was entering the transitional period which would transform her from a semi-industrial nation into the workshop of the world. Already, the face of the landscape in England and Scotland had undergone the radical changes brought about by the enclosure of open field, common and waste and much of the countryside they travelled through would be familiar to us today. Much more remained on the ground of the monuments left by our more distant forefathers: stone circles, henge monuments, tumuli and standing stones seem to have been both more abundant and more complete than they are today. Although even then, man's destructive urges were evident, for Bowman noted that the avenue associated with a stone circle at Shap in Cumbria had been 'shamefully mutilated; for as the road passes through it, the greater part of the blocks have been blasted and broken up for materials, or used in the stone walls which line it'. He commented: 'It has been left for the taste and science of the nineteenth century wantonly to destroy what our rude and less cultivated ancestors through a period of two thousand years have thought worthy of preservation!' Further change in the landscape since

1825 has had more to do with the industrial development associated with the growth of towns, cities, manufacturing and extractive industries and the infrastructure necessary to them – roads, railways, and the provision of power in the form of gas and electricity. In 1825, most of this lay in the future.

But many aspects of change were already visibly active. The population of England, Scotland and Wales was rising rapidly, leaping from 12 million in 1811 to over 14 million in 1821 and 16½ million in 1831. This growing population was also relatively mobile and there was an increasing migration of people, especially from the south of England to the north, during the late eighteenth and early nineteenth centuries. Although well over half of this population still lived in rural areas of the country in 1831, working either in agriculture or in rural trades and industries, more and more people were moving from the countryside to work in mechanised, factory-based industries in towns. Many towns were growing fast in the 1820s: for instance, between 1801 and 1831 the population of Liverpool rose from 82,000 to 202,000, that of Leeds from 53,000 to 123,000, and Glasgow from 77,000 to 193,000. The Industrial Revolution had yet to enter its more intensive phase, but already urban and industrial sprawl was beginning to engulf the countryside immediately surrounding the towns. The speed with which they were growing is illustrated by Bowman's reaction to Leeds, which he had obviously visited some years before. To his amazement, he found that Kirkstall Abbey, 'which, when I last saw it, was in a quiet well-wooded valley more than two miles from the town. So rapidly has Leeds increased that the streets and factories now extend to within a stone's cast of this magnificent and stately ruin.' Their industrial aspect was unmistakable. The approach to Newcastle-on-Tyne was heralded 'by the great fires on the hills of slack or small coal, which is separated by screens from the large pieces at the mouth of the pits and thrown aside as refuse. The mass soon takes fire from the heat of the decomposing pyrites and continues to burn for years.' The town itself appears to have been no more attractive: 'From the bridge a bustling scene presented itself both on the quays and the river; the numerous steam packets, coasting vessels, keels, and craft of all descriptions moving in every direction, with the immense timber machines elevated high above, and projecting over the water for the purpose of shipping the coal from the tram-waggons that bring it from the pits; the dense and swarthy population on both shores; the noises and the eternally smoky atmosphere from the numerous glass and lead works; – formed a scene, interesting in a commercial point of view, but repulsive and disgusting as a residence.'

The Scottish experience of industrialisation was rather different. There, with the exception of woollens and linen, the development of industry and urbanisation was essentially confined to the Lowlands, where iron-founding, and coal and salt production all developed notably. Glasgow,

Introduction

built on the great trade in the import and re-export of tobacco in the eighteenth century (a trade which collapsed after the American Revolution), received fresh impetus from the boom in water-powered cotton spinning in the late eighteenth century and the exploitation of the surrounding coalfield in the early nineteenth century and grew apace. Bowman was surprised to find that Glasgow was 'so fine a city', which 'on account of its extent and the beauty and uniformity of its streets and buildings is not inferior to the finest provincial cities in Britain.'

The lowlands of Scotland were prosperous in 1825, both industrially and agriculturally, but the Highlands presented a different picture. The clearances of the Highlands and Islands for sheep farms were well under way and the crofters and cottars were suffering from their consequences. Their holdings were small, usually too small to sustain a full livelihood, and natural conditions (so well described by Bowman) rendered the gaining of that livelihood almost impossible. In addition, the collapse of kelp prices after 1815 slowly destroyed kelp manufacture, a small-scale industry which had provided valuable additional income for the Highland peasantry. Large scale migration and the break-up of the traditional Highland way of life still lay in the future, but the harshness of life in the Highlands is vividly reflected in Bowman's observations. After his first investigation of the interior of a Highland croft, 'a solitary turf hut at a short distance from the road', and its inhabitant, he concluded: 'Good God! said I, could those who sleep on down, and revel in the luxuries of life, but see this picture, what a powerful antidote would it prove, to correct those imaginary evils which prey upon them, and destroy their real comforts!' This aspect of the Highlands undoubtedly came as something of a shock to both men, imbued as they were with the romantic image of Scotland current in the early nineteenth century and largely fostered, if not created, by the novels of Sir Walter Scott.

Yet Bowman was impressed with many aspects of Highland life and Highland people. Highland dress, the kilt (fillibeg or philibeg) and tartan stockings, he thought 'peculiarly elegant and pleasing'. He could not, however, adjust to the practice of 'the middle and lower classes of women being always without stockings and generally without shoes, and their feet very dirty' and he commented upon it many times. The Highlanders themselves he found to be generally 'very intelligent and civil' and 'much superior to the lower classes in England'. At Perth he was compelled to say: 'there is a decency of behaviour and a feeling of propriety and subordination in a Scotch crowd that gives a stranger a very pleasing impression of their moral respectability . . . we witnessed nothing of that vacant and brutal gaze, that sauciness and insolence in the men, nor heard those savage yells and disgusting blasphemies amongst the boys, which are characteristic of the rabble in our English towns, and so lamentably indicative of their demoralized habits and gross feelings.'

Bowman and Dovaston journeyed through northern England and Scotland prior to the growth of the railway network, that great watershed in the history of transport, and the narrative gives us a marvellously clear picture of travel and the facilities available to travellers before the advent of mass passenger transit. The canal system was all but complete and Bowman duly recorded and acknowledged the contribution of canals to the economic life of Britain. But it is roads and the various means of travelling on them which are the really dominant theme. Main roads in England, Wales and Scotland were being re-made by Telford and MacAdam, although the process still had far to go in 1825 – Bowman recorded that the roads above Liverpool were only partially macadamized and that 'there is a new line of road forming from Preston to Lancaster, not yet finished.' The 'flying' coaches which travelled on these new and improved roads were the predecessors of express trains. The Highlands were served by a major network of roads built after the Jacobite rebellions of 1715–16 and 1745–6. Although these were essentially military roads, built under the supervision of General Wade, and whilst neither their line nor construction was particularly suitable for civilian travel, they had certainly opened up the Highlands to tourism and were well-maintained in 1825. Bowman described his encounter with a road repair party and their travelling home ('Highland Roads and Bridges No. 27') in Glen Croe, marvelling at the nature of the system and the distance the men travelled from their homes, as well as the hardiness of the Highland race.

The conveyances used by Bowman and Dovaston on these roads varied from the 'flyers', the fast coaches which ran between major towns, through to a hired gig, and a very basic country cart. The fast coaches could be very fast indeed – the coach which took them from Edinburgh to Newcastle-on-Tyne did the 121 mile journey in fourteen hours. These journeys were usually uncomfortable and Bowman complained that the stops consisted of only two minutes, long enough to change horses, but little else. He complained, too, of the treatment meted out to the horses: 'the most objectionable part of the present system is the cruelty exercised to that noble animal, the horse, to whose wonderful powers we are so much indebted; and as coach proprietors and drivers are so devoid of every spark of feeling and humanity, it is to be regretted that the legislation does not fix the maximum rate at which they shall travel.'

Coaches did not run through the Highlands proper, so the short tours they undertook there were made by hired gig and horse, very much as we might hire a car today. The problem was the hired horses, whose quality was doubtful. During their tour from Glasgow to the Trossachs their horse was in such a poor state that they were twice pitched from the gig into the road on a steep stretch and Bowman was eventually forced to walk in order to lighten the load, leaving the invalid Dovaston alone in the gig. They eventually changed the horse twice, but the 'fresh' ones were little better

Introduction xxi

than the first and the unfortunate Bowman was again obliged to walk. To add insult to injury the owner of the last horse accused them of overworking the beast and not feeding it adequately, threatening to prosecute them if they did not pay the full sum demanded. When unable to hire a gig they were obliged to travel in the local carts and this seems to have been even more painful. At Fort William they hired a cart with a seat suspended across the middle by chains, but yet again they had to walk when the road became too hilly for horse and vehicle. *En route* to Inverness, they travelled from Fort William to Fort Augustus in the same sort of cart, but at Fort Augustus 'no such *luxury* could be obtained, and to mend the matter, that now offered to us, had just returned from the lime kiln! For this vile and heavy concern we were modestly asked the sum of thirty shillings.' In this contraption they completed their journey to Inverness. Taking advantage of stranded tourists is no modern phenomenon it seems!

Water transport appears to have been mainly (though not always) more congenial. Travel by steamship in Scotland was well organised by 1825 and the two men made use of it for some of their sightseeing trips. At Glasgow they boarded a steam packet which took them to Dumbarton Castle, thence to Dumbarton via a small boat and by coach to Loch Lomond, where they boarded another steamer to Tarbet. After walking across the isthmus at Tarbet to Arrochar they caught another steamer, the *St Catherine*, which took them back to Glasgow. The comfort of this method of travel provided quite a contrast to road travel. Of the *St Catherine* Bowman said: 'We had felt the heat very oppressive when we first went on board; but a cool fanning breeze soon set up, and we enjoyed, in its highest extent, the ease and pleasure attendant on this mode of travelling. Our packet was fitted up with extreme elegance and provided with every accommodation; the day was delightful, and the company, consisting of many parties of ladies and gentlemen, dined on deck under the open canopy of heaven.' Their excursion to Staffa was also by steamship from Glasgow – the *Highlander* steam packet. Again, this was a well organised journey and, for the most part, extremely comfortable. At the end of the four day tour Bowman commented: 'Before we take leave of the Highlander, I cannot help expressing the satisfaction and pleasure we uniformly received, both from her excellent accommodations, and from the civility and intelligence of the captain and the steward, during the whole of the voyage, a distance of 284 miles. The passage money amounted to £2.8.0 for each of us, including the boats which were provided at Staffa and Iona. Breakfast and dinner are regularly served up in the cabin; but these, of course, formed a separate charge. These steam vessels have opened so frequent, so expeditious, and so easy a communication between Glasgow and the whole of the Hebrides and the western coast of Scotland, that they are effecting considerable changes in those remote places. But. we understood the facilities they afford are confined to the transport of passengers, and that they are not allowed to carry merchandise, on account of interfering with the established coasting trade.'

But their experience of travel by steamship was not always so happy. When the *Highlander* left them at Oban, their plan was to catch one of two other steamers, either the *Ben Nevis* or the *Comet*, which would take them to Fort William. But when the *Ben Nevis* arrived at Oban, five hours late, 'her deck presented such a scene of tumult and disorder that we were at a loss to assign the cause. She was altogether so unsteady, that her wheels were lifted alternately out of the water'. It transpired that the *Comet* was under repair at Glasgow and so the *Ben Nevis* had taken on a double complement of passengers, 280 in all, and that the captain was drunk! Consequently, Bowman and Dovaston decided to find alternative means of transport and, together with five other men, chartered an open wherry to take them to Fort William. Perhaps they should have chanced their luck on the *Ben Nevis*, for the ensuing journey of thirteen hours in an open boat, in unpleasant company and with only flea-ridden straw to sleep on, does not seem to have been one of the highlights of their holiday. They landed at Fort William after dawn, only to find that the *Ben Nevis* had docked safely at 11 o'clock the previous night, although 'the voyage had been attended with the most disagreeable circumstances, and not without many painful apprehensions of danger.'

Travel, be it by road or water, was obviously not something to be undertaken lightly in 1825. Not only could the actual journey be long, often uncomfortable and sometimes hazardous, the accommodation and facilities offered to travellers were also somewhat variable. This becomes evident at the very beginning of the journey, when our intrepid duo booked in to the Star in Dale Street, Liverpool, prior to boarding the Carlisle coach the next day. Bowman remarked: 'They who live much at inns, probably become accustomed to the many repulsive and disgusting circumstances inseparable from them, particularly coach inns in larger towns, but I always enter them with reluctance and quit them as I would a prison.' They boarded the coach at 5 a.m., 'glad to exchange the effluvia and fleas of our confined attic chamber for the invigorating freshness of the morning breeze.' In Scotland, the quality of the accommodation varied considerably. In Glasgow they were fortunate enough to stay at the Prince of Wales Hotel in Brunswick Street, where they found comfort and a caring landlord in the person of Mr John Neilson. At Arrochar on Loch Long they were again lucky, although the rooms were described as 'very indifferent'. At Cairndow 'both the house and the inhabitants were civil and cleanly; we made a sumptuous breakfast upon salmon, herring and eggs, in addition to coffee and toast.' At the other end of the scale lay the only inn at Tobermory: 'It resembled an inferior village alehouse in England; but both the house and its inhabitants were filthy in the extreme, and the combination of effluvia from the peat smoke and other things of no delicate recital, aggravated by the heat of the

Introduction

weather, rendered it intolerable under any other circumstances but necessity. The utensils, the linen, and the victuals, were tainted to loathsomeness, the only beds we could secure by entreaty, were in a room belowstairs, having an earthen floor, and a door without even a latch. Everything was in great confusion; for in addition to our own party from the Highlander, that of another packet on its return from Staffa, was in the house, and it was a long time before we could get anything to eat.' Similarly, at Latter Findlay, 'a solitary and wretched changehouse about fifteen miles from Fort William', where they breakfasted on the way to Inverness, 'everything was so disgustingly dirty, that notwithstanding the pure air of the mountains had sharpened our appetites, we found some difficulty in satisfying them.'

Bowman also found some of his fellow tourists to be rather disagreeable. At Arrochar he noted 'the strange insensibility of several gentlemen of the party' to the beauty of the scenery around them – they preferred, it seems, to joke about the nickname conferred upon Ben Arthur: 'The Cobbler'. He commented disapprovingly: 'Such, I blush to say, from what I have seen, are the generality of fashionable tourists. They travel *because it is the fashion*, perhaps to kill time, or to drive away ennui. Their journeys are little more than a succession of petty vexations and disappointments from the impositions and accidents they meet with, from delays, bad roads and bad weather, or of pleasures equally unimportant arising from occurences of an opposite character. When they meet with superior accommodations and agreeable company, they are in high good humour, and if they keep a journal, these things constitute a red letter day. If dinner has been ordered at a certain hour, the most interesting scenery must be passed by or glanced at with indifference, lest the stomach should crave, or the dishes be overdone.' The tedious journey by wherry from Oban to Fort William was made even more odious to Bowman and Dovaston by a 'big and vulgar English gentleman, who had long been setting in for the sulks', a fellow traveller subsequently christened 'Blubber-chops' by Dovaston. They encountered him again at Inverness, 'buttoning his gaiters and quarrelling violently with the civil and intelligent waiter.' At dinner that evening he invaded the table at which Sir James Grant was dining with his friends and, after dinner, 'having abused the viands he had gorged, fell asleep, breathing hard and heavy, like a sow in the sunshine.'

It is this descriptive detail which is one of the most notable features of Bowman's journal. Its pages are full of minute observation and the social nuances which tell us so much about the behaviour and attitudes of the time. The modern reader will not always be sympathetic either to the opinions expressed by Bowman, or to his social attitudes and those of his fellow travellers, particularly where the 'lower classes' were concerned. The attitude of the upper classes to those they considered to be their inferiors, particularly the vast masses of working people, was changing in the 1820s, but there was still a certain indifference to the lifestyle and hardships endured by the poor. It must be remembered that the French Revolution was still a fairly recent event, an event which had produced in wealthy Englishmen a fear of the lower classes in general and mob violence in particular which was to survive for many years. Undoubtedly it had slowed down the progress of more humanitarian ideas, as well as political change in Britain, but on the whole more enlightened views were gaining ground by 1825.

This is probably the widest historical gulf for the twentieth-century mind to bridge, for the social and political philosophies of today are so far removed from those of the early nineteenth century that it is well-nigh impossible to read a personal document of the 1820s without forming some kind of value judgement of the 1980s. But to do so not only distorts the historical perspective, it also detracts from the integrity of the document. For here, a wealthy, educated banker has, through his words and his view of the country as he saw it, preserved the Britain of 1825 for us to see and to enjoy today. So we must try to read his journal with an understanding of his philosophies and attitudes – only then will the past spring to life.

CELIA MILLER

Volume I

BEFORE I COMMENCE the detail of the journey which occupies the following pages, I wish to say a few words to explain the motives for undertaking it, and the plan which it is my present intention to adopt in drawing it up.

I had for many years felt a strong desire to visit Scotland: – its wild and romantic scenery; its many monuments of rude and barbarous ages; the marvellous events of its ancient and modern history; and the spirit of liberty which still lingers among its mountains, and breathes in its native poetry, had long operated, as so many talismans, to allure me to its soil. When I set out upon the journey, I intended only to take on the spot, such brief notes of the scenery, and incidents that might occur, as would assist my memory to draw out a narrative of them on my return. But I soon found that the objects which demanded my attention were so numerous, that the memory could not retain a sufficient recollection of them to enable me to do so from mere insulated notes; and so interesting, that it would require a larger portion of leisure than I could probably command, to complete the detail hereafter. I therefore soon changed my plan, and decided upon writing out, at the conclusion of every day, as ample an account of the occurrences of it, as the circumstances in which I was placed would allow; though I confess, if I could have foreseen the additional fatigue and labour which it cost me, I should have shrunk from the attempt. I persevered however, and accomplished it; and it was not till within the last month, that I entertained any thoughts of doing more. The reperusal of this rapid sketch brought to my recollection many interesting particulars, which I had either entirely omitted, or but slightly touched upon, from want of time, the pressure of so many things crowding together upon the memory, or from the lassitude of body and mind which followed the ceaseless exertions of the day, and rendered the evening labour of the Journal excessively wearisome. This excited a wish to attempt a more perfect record of it for future reference: for, as in Youth, our pleasures are enhanced by anticipation, so in advanced life, they are often derived from retrospection; and we then often fondly look back, like the traveller in the desert, to the Oases we have left behind us on our pilgrimage.

> And, lingering, love to haunt the greenest spot
>   On memory's waste.

The wish was strengthened by the idea that it might be interesting to my children, and amusing to my friends, to accompany me through the many pleasing scenes of this journey. For the benefit of the former, I propose to insert those moral reflections which occurred to me at the time; had they accompanied me, I should have communicated them for their improvement; and my motive in recording them, is, that they may derive instruction as well as pleasure from the perusal of this volume. I am aware that they will not suit the taste of many readers; but it is enough for me, that they are in unison with my own feelings, and likely to be of service to those in whose future welfare I am most interested.

I enter upon my task quite sensible of the time and labour it will require of me; but I know not how I can employ a portion of the ensuing winter evenings more agreeably, than in travelling again, by my own fireside, a journey so fraught with interesting recollections, and in endeavouring to render permanent those impressions which the events and cares of future years will necessarily weaken.

I have preferred to adhere to my original plan of a Journal, as being best calculated to recall to my own mind, a faithful picture of the events of each successive day, as they actually occurred. I shall also retain as much as possible of the descriptions, as well as the remarks and observations I made upon the spot, from a belief that impressions made and recorded while the mind is warmed by the subject, are more likely to possess the spirit and freshness of nature, than any subsequent effort, however studied and polished: as the first rough sketch of a master is often more correct and striking than a laboured copy. I intend rather to enlarge, than to alter, my former plan; and shall not be scrupulous in confining myself to what I may conceive to be new matter; for most of what fell under my observation, has been both seen and described by others. What I saw, I shall describe as accurately as I can; if I should occasionally fail I must plead in excuse the inauspicious circumstances already alluded to, in taking down the notes. Notwithstanding these disadvantages, arising from the rapidity with which we travelled, my own and my Friend Dovaston's notes soon swelled to a bulk I had no idea of at setting out. Though we lost no opportunity of procuring information, we could not have gleaned so rich a harvest, but for the superior intelligence and liberal communicativeness of the Scotch; who seeing us with our Note Books in our hands, not only politely answered our questions, but pointed out the various objects as we passed along; and took pleasure in imparting many interesting particulars respecting them. We were of course cautious in receiving it indiscriminately, and some things were necessarily rejected. It must be judged by others, how I have discriminated, by what I have retained; but strict justice compels me to say, that we generally found intelligence and civility in that class of society which in England is characterized by ignorance and brutality. The historical references, and the mention of scenes and places, now rendered familiar and doubly interesting by the justly celebrated romances of Sir Walter Scott, I shall insert from books. It would be unpardonable to omit them altogether; though, as I do not profess to write a history of Scotland, the notices will be but short.

I have already alluded to my esteemed friend and fellow traveller; but I must not forget to acknowledge that I owe much of what is valuable in the following pages, to his abilities and friendship. It would be difficult to speak in too high terms of his superior talents, his profound knowledge of Nature, his literary and scientific attainments, and his extraordinary powers of memory and fancy; but they are too well known to those who are likely to read these pages, to need any encomium from me. When I named to him my intention of re-writing our tour, he liberally allowed me the full use of his own notes; and has moreover, kindly promised to furnish me with the state of Poetry and Music in Scotland, which he is so competent to give from his long and intimate acquaintance with those subjects, and which I could not have undertaken myself. Anything else he may favour me with, will be acknowledged in its proper place.*

He left it entirely to my choice to draw out the line of our route which I did before we set out; and to this sketch we adhered with scarcely any deviation. Circumstances over which we had no control, prevented us from visiting Glencoe, the romantic scenery about Loch Tay, and the far famed Melrose; excepting these, I am not aware that we omitted anything of peculiar interest.

I shall only add, that as I cannot afford the additional time which would be required to draw out a rough draft of this Journal, I shall compose it at once from our united notes and from my own recollections, interweaving with these sources, any illustrations or corrections I may meet with elsewhere. I state this, to extenuate any errors in grammar or style which I may probably fall into, and to account for any defects or incongruities in digesting or arranging the materials

Court, 6 Oct. 1826

---

* He subsequently requested me to insert them silently.

Friday, 15 July 1825 My Friend Dovaston and myself having previously fixed upon this day for the commencement of our tour, he left his own lovely groves at West Felton very early; and after breaking fast with me at the Court, we left Wrexham at 10 o'clock, passing through Chester and over the Mersey at Birkenhead, to Liverpool, where we spent the evening. Places so near home, and so well known to everyone, need no description in a private journal; I shall therefore pass over them in silence. On our arrival in Liverpool, we secured places on the coach to Carlisle for the following morning, and slept at the Star in Dale St. from whence we were to set out, as a matter of convenience rather than of choice. They who live much at inns, probably become accustomed to the many repulsive and disgusting circumstances inseparable from them, particularly coach inns in larger towns, but I always enter them with reluctance and quit them as I would a prison. Yet here much of life and character are to be seen, and much may be learnt to make us thankful for the quiet and comfort of domestic life.

Saturday, 16 July At 5 o'clock this morning, we mounted the roof of the Carlisle coach, and were glad to exchange the effluvia and fleas of our confined attic chamber for the invigorating freshness of the morning breeze. The morning was delightful, and the picturesque appearance of the houses and cottages with their tasty gardens and shrubberies, and the long lines of carts filled with garden stuff which we passed for the first six or seven miles of the road would have impressed a stranger who had never seen Liverpool, with some idea of its population and commercial importance. Large fields were covered, not only with potatoes, carrots, &c, but with onions, celery, asparagus, and other culinary vegetables, the individual consumption of which is but trifling. The soil, though originally poor, is light and suitable for potatoes, and the immense population of the eastern parts of Lancashire causes them to be grown in amazing quantities. This county is indeed the point from which the invaluable root was first disseminated over England. It was first introduced into Ireland from America in 1565; and in consequence of an Irish vessel being cast away on the western coast near North Meols on the estuary of the Ribble, some of the roots were planted near that place; but it was not till many years after, that they were adopted as an article of food in London.

The surface of the country on our left, towards the coast, seems low and flat, and generally speaking, is uninteresting. The substratum I noticed in several places, is the new Red sandstone, bearing sandy loam or claymarle, which by proper management forms a very productive soil. In the neighbourhood of Ormskirk it has a black appearance, probably from having been originally covered by peat moss. The only object that struck me in Ormskirk, worthy of a remark, was the church, apparently of some antiquity and having a very broad and low square tower, and close adjoining it, but entirely detached, a light taper spire, a singular feature, and, as we were told, the result of the whim or obstinacy of two maiden sisters, who erected the church, and were determined to gratify their peculiar tastes. It was market day here, and the town bore the appearance of a manufacturing place. Many fields of onions are seen in the immediate neighbourhood; and in marshy spots and pools near the road, I observed the Rumex sanquineus, the elegant Butomus, and the magnificent Nymphaea alba and Nuphar lutea. About two miles beyond Ormskirk, near Latherhall on the right, are the ruins of Burscough Priory, which appeared rather extensive and not devoid of interest, but we travelled with so much expedition, that we had but a glance of it. We were only allowed two minutes to change horses; and at the end of several of the stages, the ostlers were standing in readiness 40 or 50 yards from the place where the coach was to stop, and ran along side the horses, disengaging the harness, while the coachman was pulling up. The road was generally the old pitched pavement being as yet but partially macadamised; and my feelings were often hurt at the inhumanity of the drivers and the distress of the poor horses. The transition from one extreme to the other is often short. But a few years ago a coachman could scarcely pass a pothouse but he must stop to drink his dram and waste the time of his passengers; and now in the course of a day's journey, the latter are scarcely allowed time to swallow a meal. But the most objectionable part of the present system is the cruelty exercised to that noble animal, the horse, to whose wonderful powers we are so much indebted; and as coach proprietors and drivers are so devoid of every spark of feeling and humanity, it is to be regretted that the legislation does not fix the maximum rate at which they shall travel. We had occasional glimpses of the Irish sea, but nothing peculiar caught my attention till we approached Preston, which stands on an eminence of the river Ribble where it first forms itself into an estuary. The landscape is very fine where the road takes a sudden direction to the eastward to cross the river over a long bridge. Here the banks are bold, and well clothed with hanging woods, from among which peep out several gentlemen's seats. The town itself is handsome and well built, with broad regular streets; many of the houses vying with the best in first rate towns; and the gay groups who were promenading about, not spoiling the comparison. Its commanding situation, and the air of cleanliness and elegance which seemed to pervade the whole, when added to the above traits of superiority , may have procured for it, its general appellation of Proud Preston. The river was formerly navigable as high up as Ribchester, a Roman station of considerable importance, if we may judge from even the present state of the remains. This is inferred, because anchors have been dug up there, and the hull of a vessel larger than would now float as low as Preston.

We breakfasted at Preston, and took up there, a young Irish gentleman, a student of Dublin College, and his two sisters, travelling, like ourselves, for amusement; also a Mr. Fergusson, a quaker from Kendal, fond of ornithology, and otherwise a sensible man: conversation soon became general, and occasionally animated, turning chiefly on literature and poetry with the former, on natural history and philanthropy with the latter, and liberally seasoned with wit and anecdote by my fellow traveller, with whom the quaker was particularly taken. There is a new line of road forming from Preston to Lancaster, not yet finished. The country on our right, hilly and barren; the hills having the character of the mountain grit series, flat, bleak and sterile. Before we reached Preston, we had twice crossed the Leeds and Liverpool canal, a line which completes the water communication between the Irish Channel and the German Ocean, by the assistance of navigable rivers, and has tended much to increase the commercial prosperity of this county. In our way up to Lancaster, we several times crossed the Lancashire canal, by means of which, coals are conveyed from the southern parts of the county, and lime from the northern; thus materially benefiting both. England is indebted to the inhabitants of Lancashire for setting the example of canal cutting, as well as the planting of potatoes; the Sankey Canal, from St. Helens to the Mersey near Warrington, being the first artificial water communication that was planned and formed in the country. The act to authorize this novel though useful undertaking, was obtained in the year 1761.

Lancaster is a seaport, situated on the river Lon, or Lune; formerly called, as it still is by the lower classes, Loncaster; but of late years its trade has much declined, and its port and warehouses are deserted, being eclipsed by the rival and more advantageous situation of Liverpool, which from being little more than a century ago, only a small fishing place, is now the emporium of the western world, and the second port in the Kingdom. The town presents nothing prepossessing to a stranger; but after we had left it, we were much struck with the noble appearance of the Castle and a church, situated on a commanding eminence north, or north-west of it. I have seldom seen anything of the kind so truly magnificent; the former of great extent, and, as we were told, consisting in part of the ancient castle built by John of Gaunt, Duke of Lancaster; the latter in the gothic style, with an elegant & lofty tower, and the whole of white freestone. On the same eminence was a Roman station, of which some vestiges are said to be still visible. We crossed a fine bridge of five arches over the Lune; a little farther on the right, the Lancaster canal is carried over it by a substantial and elegant aqueduct, by Rennie. The peculiar difficulties which he had to encounter in the bed of the river, made it necessary to have for a foundation, a flooring of timber, which alone cost £15,000. We witnessed immediately a manifest improvement in the quality of the land; its great fertility and the luxuriance of the vegetation reminded me of the Derbyshire valleys, and indicated the presence of the mountain limestone, which here prevails. The whole of the hundred or Barony of Lonsdale (valley of the Lon, or Lune) was, long after the Norman Conquest, included in the county of Lancaster;

but the Lake District is not mentioned in Doomsday, either because it was uninhabited, or because the land was not considered of any value at the time of that survey. We had several views of those dangerous sands which lie between Lancaster and Ulverstone, and which annually occasion so many accidents to unwary travellers. They are alternately covered and left dry by every tide; and the distance across them to Ulverstone being but eleven miles, and the circuit by Kendal nearly forty, they offer a great temptation, and we are informed there is now a daily coach over them to the former place, the time for which, is of course governed by the tide. Many dreadful accidents have happened; for independent of the quick sands and the insulated pools which the inequality of the surface causes, thick fogs often suddenly arise and envelop the traveller, who, having lost sight of the landmarks, becomes bewildered, and falls a prey to the devouring element. The rapidity with which the tide rolls over these level sands, is so great, that a man on horseback at full speed, cannot always escape. Formerly guides were stationed on the shores, called carters, to conduct passengers across. They were originally established and maintained by the religious houses in the neighbourhood, and obliged to be in attendance from sunrise to sunset; but at the dissolution, the king charged himself and his successors with the payment; since that time it is held by patent of the Duchy of Lancaster, and the salary is paid out of the revenues of it.

We proceeded to Burton, a small market town on the southern confines of Westmoreland, (or the Moorland to the west) and about a mile beyond it, passed on the right, Farlton Knot, a very protuberant limestone hill, said to bear a resemblance to the Rock of Gibraltar. Our road to Kendal was through a fertile valley, principally in meadow and pasture land, prettily interspersed with coppices and watered by rapid clear streams, here called 'becks'; but it was evident from the character of the vegetation that it is a region of rains and fogs. We entered the neat busy town of Kendal, leaving the ruins of the old castle on our right; now a shapeless ruin, but worthy of note from having been the birthplace of Catherine Parr, the last queen of the tyrant, Henry the Eighth. It belonged to her family. Kendal is pleasantly situated on the river Ken, or Kent; the verdant hills which rise in gentle swells around it, thickly sprinkled with clean cottages and tenter-grounds, give it the appearance of retirement as well as of industry. The houses are clean and respectable, the older ones of plaster; the more modern, of the mountain limestone which abounds in the neighbourhood. The church has a shabby exterior, but is remarkable as the scene of the strange exploit of one Major Phillipson, commonly called Robin the Devil, in the time of Cromwell, so singularly characteristic of the animosity and fanaticism of that turbulent period. The particulars are fully related in a note to the sixth canto of Rokeby.

We dined at Kendal, and left here our new friend Fergusson, who took his leave of Dovaston with very evident feelings of affection and respect.

Thus far we had only retraced the ground we travelled on our former tour in 1823; from this point all may be said to be new, the stage from Penrith to Carlisle having been performed in the dark. We soon ascended out of the valley, and on rising the hill, had a beautiful view of the town and surrounding highgrounds, spread round it like an amphitheatre, a pleasing and lovely landscape. On my former journey I had found several rare plants near Kendal; today I only recognized the elegant Geranium pratense, and a large white variety of the Campanula latifolia growing in the copses on each side of Kendal. The land for sometime continued rich and fertile; but this gradually gave way to a short and starved vegetation as we approached Shap Fells. The trees became low and stunted, then totally disappeared; and the only plants that seemed to exist at all, were heath and peatmoss, with the common species of Juncus, Carex (sic), and Scirpus. We had now passed the mountain limestone and entered upon the primitive clay slate; but I looked in vain for the Chiastolite which abounds in this formation on the top of Skiddaw. It is a long and steep ascent to Shap Fell; we walked to ease the horses, and though my eyes were fishing for new plants, I observed nothing uncommon but the Polypodium Phegopteris. Dovaston who walked behind, was more fortunate, for he found the Cnicus heterophillus (sic), or gentle thistle, which I do not yet know. Shap Fell is bleak, barren and inhospitable; incapable from its great elevation & continual moist atmosphere, of beneficial cultivation; yet certainly not so repulsive and horrid as Blackstone Edge. It would appear that the proprietor of it does not think it worth while to plant on it the hardy larch and pine of the north; at least I saw no attempt at the experiment. We saw it under the most favourable circumstances of a July day, hot and bright, and the refreshing coolness of the breeze counteracted the gloom which such scenery casts over the mind; for here Spring never puts on her robe of green, and no broken crags relieve the wearisome uniformity of the black and level moors. Tall guide posts, white below and blackened at the top, are placed at regular intervals along the road, to guide the weary traveller through the snow; for her fleecy mantle may be said to be their natural covering. I could not see any of the granite of this district *in situ*; but observed many detached rounded blocks, brought for the purpose of the road, and secured a specimen. The felspar it contains is of two kinds; the one lamellar and flesh-coloured, the other compact & of a dull pale green; the former more plentifully diffused, & frequently in large masses. The mica is quite black, uniformly disseminated in small grains, and scarcely translucent at the edge, even in the thinnest laminae, giving to the whole specimen the character of sienite rather than of granite. Seen from the coach, the blocks might easily be mistaken for a coarse breccia or pudding stone, so large were some of the pieces of imbedded felspar.

 The road is excellent, and, except in passing over such elevated ground, is planned to wind gradually round the sides of the hills and along the vales, so

A Nineteenth-Century Tour

as to avoid the declivities of the former. Previous to the Rebelion in 1715, the public roads of this county were almost impassable; in that year several new ones were projected, but little was done to them till the more serious insurrection in 1745. This event impelled the Government to direct some effectual repairs to be made; but it was not till 1774 that the first Stagecoach from London to Glasgow was established to run on this line, nor till 1786 that a mail passed along it.

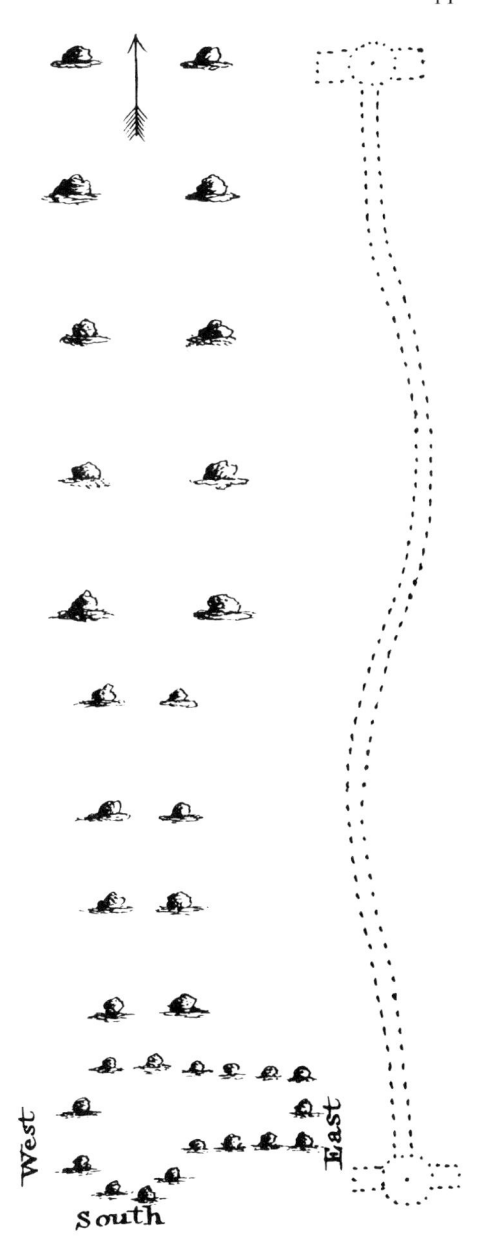

Nearly a mile before we reached Shap, we saw on our right and within twenty yards of the road, the southern termination of a great Druidical Relique, which excited our interest in a very high degree. Dovaston's enthusiasm rose to a greater height, from having frequently in early life heard his excellent father speak of it. That most extraordinary man applied his powerful mind to the study of this and other similar remains of antiquity, and collected a vast mass of information respecting them with drawings, plans &c, &c, which are now in the possession of my friend. The annexed ground plan is copied from one of these, which was done for Mr. Dovaston by his friend Nelson of Shrewsbury about thirty years ago; and is now valuable, as shewing the Remain in a more perfect state than it is at present. It is probable however, that a double line originally extended towards the west, to correspond with that in the plan on the east side.

The stones of which it is formed, are the granite of Shap Fell, and are rolled boulders of different shapes and sizes, varying in weight, perhaps from four to twenty tons each. The whole length was originally above a mile, running due north in a serpentine direction, and extending beyond the village of Shap, where it terminated with another circle, and somewhat resembling the dotted figure I have added on the last page. The great Druidical remain at Avebury in Wiltshire is of the serpentine form. The southern end of this great avenue is much narrower than the middle; but it soon widens considerably to about eighty feet, which is also the distance between the blocks. It does not preserve the same parallelism through out, but gradually narrows towards the north, for near Shap the width does not reach sixty feet. I recognized the circle at the north end when we had passed the village; but the stones had been deranged, which diminished the interest. Indeed the whole of it has been shamefully mutilated; for as the road passes through it, the greater part of the blocks have been blasted and broken up for materials, or used in the stone walls which line it. One of them, more circular than the rest, has been divided and placed as an *ormanental finish*, upon the pillars of a gate leading to a gentleman's house! He could not have selected a more decisive proof of intellectual sterility and contempt of those feelings of veneration, which even the multitude are prompted to indulge, when viewing monuments which have survived the waste and accidents of so many centuries. It has been left for the taste and science of the nineteenth century wantonly to destroy what our rude and less cultivated ancestors through a period of two thousand years, have thought worthy of preservation!

Shap is a pretty straggling village, having few houses that do not adjoin the road; they are mostly built near or under groups of very fine sycamores & ash, though no trees appear in the vast plain of the surrounding fells. The sycamore is well adapted for such bleak situations, for it never bends its sturdy trunk from the storm, though from the compactness of its top, this peuliarity would not have been expected. Here we changed horses, and I noticed with pleasure, the clean healthy and intelligent countenances of the children who collected round us, though they had probably seen little more of the world, than was contained within the horizon of their native village. We took up an amorous pair on their way to Gretna Green; the groom a boy of 17, with a very long wooden leg, and the bride a tolerable girl of about 30; we brought them with us to Carlisle; but were not curious to enquire into their history. There is, near Shap, a fine ruin of an abbey; but it was not within sight. They also find here an inferior kind of coal, called crow-coal. A few miles farther, we passed Lowther Hall, the seat of the Earl of Lonsdale, enveloped in trees; and beyond, on crossing the river Lowther, saw on its eastern bank, peeping above the trees, Brougham Hall, the seat of the enlightened Henry Brougham, the intrepid champion of Liberty and Education. The bank of the Lowther on which it stands, rises so perpendicularly and regularly from the river, that it has the appearance of a vast artificial amphitheatre. Near this interesting spot is Mayburgh, a vast circular dyke of loose stones; also in Whinfield park, near Brougham Hall, the pillar erected by the Countess dowager of Pembroke in 1656 for a memorial of her last parting on that spot, with her good and pious mother forty years before. It is pleasing to record such amiable feelings, which must have been strong indeed to show themselves so substantially after so long an interval.

Just before we crossed the river Eamont, and still very near Brougham Hall, we passed the famous circular entrenchment called Arthur's Round Table, close to the road on our left. It is an area of 30 or 40 yards in diameter, surrounded with a vallum & fosse, through which, two openings lead into the central area from the opposite sides. The area has a still smaller circle raised in the centre. The whole of it is covered with a fine green sward, and is close to the small village of Eamont, through which we passed; and on crossing the stream of that name, (pronounced Yemmot) entered Cumberland; and very shortly after, reached Penrith.

We stopped only to change horses; from the hill we ascended soon after leaving it, we had a noble view of the mountains of the Lake district, from Place Fell over Ullswater, to the south, to Skiddaw in the western horizon, fronted by the fine hanging woods around Lowther Hall, and the town of 'Red Penrith' at our feet. We did not indeed see Ullswater, but traced its zig-zag form by the fine misty haze which hung over it and concealed the bases of its barrier mountains. We kept the whole group in view for many miles; and had leisure to retrace our wanderings among them. Beginning from the East, amid the mighty mass of almost innumerable summits, we saw Place Fell, St. Sunday Fell, Stibra Craggs, Helvellyn, Langdale Pikes, Bow Fell, Scaw Fell, Mell Fell, very near, the White Pike at the end of the Vale of St. John, the long ridge of Saddleback, which as we proceeded, became gradually foreshortened, and over it, Skiddaw, which from hence appears long and flat, and not with the two elegant but unequal points which mark its outline from Keswick. The two latter were occasionally capped with clouds, and a heavy mass hung over the Pikes of Langdale; while many of the Lakes might be traced from the exhalations which the increasing coolness of the evening rendered visible. These soon formed themselves into light cumulous clouds, realizing the beautiful imagery of our favourite poet;

> As when the setting sun has given
> Ten thousand hues to summer even,
> And from their tissue, fancy frames
> Aerial knights and fairy dames.

The country through which we passed after leaving Penrith not being so interesting as before, allowed us to seek delight in these more distant objects; yet were we more acquainted with its former history, we should doubtless recognize every spot, as the scene of bloody conflicts and midnight pillage. Cumberland also contains a greater number of British and Roman antiquities than any other English county, owing to its contiguity to the Border, and to their having suffered fewer spoliations than those of more agricultural districts. From the rate at which we travelled, these, whatever they were, escaped our notice, and we reached High Hesketh, a village in Inglewood forest, where we caught the first glimpse of the Solway Firth, and the distant hills of Scotland. Here I gathered the first new plant I have seen on the journey, which I plucked hastily out of the hedge as we changed horses. I have just found from Galpine's Synoptical Compend, which I carry with me, that it is the Galium mollugo. Its light elegant flowers tufted the hedges to the height of 4 or 5 feet, and had a very ornamental appearance. It was half past nine when we arrived at Carlisle, where I wrote the notes of this long day's journey of 122 miles.

We were occupied till near 12 o'clock this evening in seeking out a conveyance to Dumfries tomorrow. It seems that by the law of Scotland, no public coach is allowed to travel on the Sabbath, except the mail, and the fare is so high, that we have been endeavouring to get on some other way, but hitherto without success. Our landlord has despatched his scouts over Carlisle to hire a gig, but every wheel is engaged by the cits to enable them to enjoy their weekly holiday in the country. At length he has informed us that we may be *accommodated* with two saddle horses as far as Annan for half a guinea each, with an additional sum to send them back! and we find, on calculating, that this with attendant expenses, and the probability of meeting with the same imposition at Annan, will throw the balance of expense in favour of the mail. The contrast in manners and customs between neighbouring kingdoms, is apparent to a traveller on passing through a frontier town, where the lines of definition approximate. On the Continent this contrast is frequently very striking; but we have seldom an opportunity of witnessing it in our own island. No coach except the mail leaves Carlisle on Sunday for the North, while they go southwards in all directions. Such is the difference produced by the same event, the Reformation, in England and Scotland; and such the fidelity with which one generation after another, throughout a whole country, receives and transmits established customs and forms of faith, whether right or wrong; for in fact, the multitude take little trouble to satisfy themselves on this head. We feel that we are entering a country whose established religion has been moulded upon a Calvinistic basis, by Knox and other frenzied zealots, after a struggle in which some of the worst passions that demonize the human heart, formed the leading features of both parties. The harsher points are now softened down by time, and we shall doubtless have frequent opportunities of observing its general influence on manners. I mean not to speak with the slightest disrespect, of this or any other creed, however different from my own; for when we consider the variety of religions in the world, and the many sects into which each is divided and subdivided, and also find that wise and good men have enlisted under the banners of each, he must be either very bold or very ignorant, who can confidently say that he himself is right, and that all others are wrong; or can restrict the terms of salvation within the narrow pale of his own church. If we venture to judge at all, Deeds, and not Creeds, ought to be the criterion of our judgment –

> For modes of faith let graceless zealots fight;
> His can't be wrong, whose Life is in the right.

Sunday 17 July We rose early; and with our minds full of the events of past ages, paced the streets of this venerable city, not unmindful that every part of them had been stained with blood during the continual border feuds of seventeen centuries. The three principal streets of Carlisle are disposed nearly in the form of a Roman Y, the lower portion of which, looking to the south, is called English Street, the right hand branch of the fork, to the north, Scotch Street, and that on the left, to the north west, Castle Street. The city was surrounded by a wall, built during the Saxon Heptarchy – now in a dilapidated state – and had three Gates, one at the end of each of the principal streets, and called respectively, the English, Scotch, and Irish Gates. The English Gate was originally built by Henry the eighth, and has recently been modernized. It is called the Citadel, and is flanked by two round, low, and very broad towers of soft red sandstone, in which the Courts of Assize are held. The Cathedral is not remarkable either for its size or structure, being an incongruous group of different styles and periods, the greater part comparatively modern, while the circular arches and zigzag mouldings of other portions bespeak the Saxon era, and exhibit beautiful detached specimens. It was sadly mutilated during the Civil wars of the seventeenth century. The Castle, to a merely modern eye, possesses little interest, *that* must be sought in the historical events connected with it. It stands near the Irish Gate, and consists of an outer and inner ward; it is square and lofty, and its walls are immensely thick. Over one of the gateways we observed an ancient portcullis, which 'had oft rolled back the tide of war', and now remains as a memento of a state of warfare superseded by more destructive engines. Some repairs are now in progress, dictated, I trust, rather by policy than necessity. We ascended the tower, 'where the sun shines fair on Carlisle Wall', and had a pleasing view of the surrounding country, clothed with fertile meadows watered by the Eden, the Caldew and the Petteril, backed on the south by the fine group of the Cumberland Alps and on the north, by the faint and distant hills of Scotland. The castle at Carlisle was the first English residence of the beautiful and unfortunate

Mary Stuart, after she was compelled to quit Scotland in consequence of events resulting partly from her own imprudence and inexperience, partly from the ill-timed acts and counsels of her advisers, and partly from the temper and circumstances of the times. The apartments she occupied in the castle are still shewn. She escaped across the Solway Firth in a fishing boat from Dundrennan in Galloway, and after landing at Workington, came to Carlisle, where she was for a while treated by her jealous and haughty rival with the respect due to her station, but soon found herself the inmate of a prison;

> Shipwreck'd upon a kingdom, where no pity,
> No friends, no Hope, no kindred wept for her,
> Almost, no grave allow'd her.

The castle of Carlisle has been the theatre of so many tragical events connected with the bloody and barbarous warfare which so long devastated the Borders, that the author of Waverley has very appropriately fixed upon it for the death scene of the noble-hearted Chief of Glennaquoich, Fergus McIvor, after the last struggle of the Stuart family, and the final retreat of their partizans from England. Sir Walter Scott has admirably portrayed in his character, the bold and undaunted spirit of Liberty which glowed in the breasts of the Highland Chieftains, and their unconquerable ardour to support a hopeless cause. In his last interview with Waverley on the morning of his execution, and in allusion to the barbarous custom of fixing the lifeless heads of the victims on the city gates, Fergus is made to say, 'I hope they will set mine on the *Scotch* Gate, that I may look, even after death, to the blue hills of my own country, which I love so dearly.'

Harribee Lee, near Carlisle, is also made the scene of a frightful incident in the 'Heart of Midlothian', where they *hangit* the mother of the screeling imaginative Madge Wildfire; whom doubtless Sir Walter (as he is incessantly copying Shakespeare) meant for a coarse copy of Ophelia: as Catherine Seyton is a water-colour one of Beatrice.

After breakfast we ascertained that we could have inside seats in the mail to Dumfries, and left Carlisle at half past ten o'clock, crossing the Eden over a fine bridge, and soon got upon a new line of road stretching for several miles in a straigh line over a flat, planted rather extensively with young pines, commonly, though erroneously, called Scotch firs. The old road went north through Longtown, (pronounced Langtoon) the new takes a northwest direction to Gretna Green, more commonly Graitney, and saves from three to four miles. We crossed the Esk over a handsome light iron bridge of three arches, just above its entrance into the Solway. This river is here broad and brisk; but from the dark brown colour of its waters discovers its sources to be among extensive peat morasses. The country through which it runs appeared for the most part a flat moorish tract having a character of wildness and desolation, without inclosures or tillage, except near the few mean and solitary huts which here and there caught the eye. We crossed several black, sluggish, half stagnant streams, which soaked, rather than flowed, through the spongy peat which choked up their beds as they moved towards the Esk, and whose half fluid surfaces quivered as the coach rattled along, indicating that the road itself was formed upon the morass. This is the 'Land Debateable', formerly claimed by both kingdoms and inhabited by moss-troopers, who made predatory incursions into both, and neither submitted to the laws, nor were entitled to the protection of either. Similar tracts occurred along the whole Border; and at the Union of the two crowns, were finally divided by Commissioners appointed for that purpose. Sir Walter Scott in his serious works has thrown much light upon the manners and customs of the freebooters who inhabited them. We saw Longtown a few miles to our right, and just beyond it, on a rising ground, Netherby, which was formerly a Roman station of considerable importance. Part of the intermediate tract was Solway Moss, which in the year 1771, after heavy rains, burst its barriers and covered upwards of 500 acres of cultivated land, burying it in some places thirty or forty feet deep, with twenty eight houses and cottages. The inhabitants were surprized in the night, and fled before the destroying torrent of liquid moss in a state of nudity, losing all their cattle, furniture and moveables.

We shortly came to the Sark, an insignificant stream which divided the two kingdoms, and crossing a stone bridge of a single arch, entered Scotland about noon. Just beyond it is a tollgate, where Southron fugitives when closely pursued, are sometimes married; but they generally go on to the village of Graitney, about half a mile farther, and are married at the inn, a large house a little distance from the road on the right, called Graitney Hall. The Scottish law does not require any prescribed form of words, nor is it necessary that the rite should be performed by a minister, though in regular marriages it usually is so. Advantage is taken of this facility, and the officiator is generally an illiterate person. When any service is read, it is that of the Church of England; but the marriage is valid if the parties simply declare their mutual consent before witnesses, who give a certificate to that effect. It has more than once been decided in our courts of law, that a marriage of English subjects celebrated in Scotland is good, and entitles a woman to dower in England. It is not more than 60 or 70 years since these clandestine marriages began to be celebrated, and it seems probable that they will not be permitted to disgrace the country much longer.

Graitney is a very small village; its church (we must call them kirks *noo*) a very modern structure, close to the roadside on the left, more like a coach house than a place of worship, with large tawdry windows, and a little narrow belfry in the centre and a solitary bell wagging in the open air, like those in Anglesea. Behind it is the manse, synonymous with our rectory or vicarage house. The scenery around is very flat and barren; the few trees we saw were pine, ash and sycamore, and rows of bushy birches, but all unhealthy and stunted, except some very large Scots or Scotch laburnums in the hedges. Looking back towards England, the whole group of the Cumberland mountains rose majestically beyond the broad mirror of the Solway Firth, which powerfully reflected the beams of the midday sun. Among them we recognized Skiddaw by her superior height and bifurcated summit. She, individually, appears more graceful than from the hill above Penrith, though the whole group, taken collectively, is displayed to greater advantage from the latter spot. On our right were the hills of Dumfriesshire, and before us, the mighty Cruefell or Skriefell,* the highest mountain in the south of Scotland, on the summit of which was formerly one of the beacons for alarming the country during the frequent incursions of the English Borderers. Cruefell on the north and Skiddaw on the south of the Solway Firth are conspicuous objects along a great extent of country; and Camden quotes a common proverb in Cumberland,

'– If Skiddaw wears a cap
Scruefell wots full well o'that –'

meaning that the same meteorological appearances are seen on both, and that from the rising or falling of the clouds on their sides, the inhabitants below can foretell the changes of the weather. This is a very general circumstance.

We had now entered Scotland, and considered ourselves on poetic ground: Netherby lay behind us, Cannobie Lee was on our right, and Lochinvar before us, and Dovaston repeated with great animation the beautiful song of Lady Heron in Marmion, relating the bold exploit of the young Laird of Lochinvar, 'who swam the Eske river where ford there was none', and carried off the fair bride of Netherby from the party assembled to witness her espousal to a 'laggard in love, and a dastard in war'.

In the kirkyard at Dornoch, many hundred persons were assembled, and the minister was addresssing them from a green coloured moveable pulpit having a sounding board which bent forwards like the cover of a gig. Many of the audience were sitting on the stone walls, and the men all wore their hats, though a fine warm day. As the congregation seemed to exceed the population of the whole parish, we made inquiry, and found it was the Sacrament, which was only administered in country places once a year, and was attended by the inhabitants many miles around. As this rite is a peculiar feature in Scottish manners, and we shall have other opportunities of witnessing it, I shall defer any observations upon it, till a more advanced period of our tour. We now soon arrived at Annan, a pleasant, healthy-looking town with a wide street; a pretty kirk with a light spire on entering

* This word is very variously spelt.

it, and at the western end, a tolbooth, or prison, also with a spire resembling that of a church, from the grated windows of which, a few prisoners gazed at the coach. The buildings are principally of new red sandstone which is the stratum of the district. On leaving the town, we crossed the river Annan where the scenery is pretty, compared with the general cast of it; but Skiddaw even here loses but little of her elegant height and gracefulness.

We passed the small villages of Ruthwell and Caerlaverock on our left, and through the scrubby plantations of Glen Stewart. About 50 years ago, an old road was discovered near Ruthwell, six feet below the surface, leading through a deep morass, towards the Solway. It was formed of strong split planks of oak, fastened down by stakes, driven through the boards into the earth. We passed over several broad tracks of turbary land, and formed no prepossessing opinion of the peasantry, either from their personal appearance or their cottages. Though it was Sunday, they were for the most part ragged and dirty, and the young women generally barefoot. The cottages are of two sorts, the older of mud and covered with peat, having low wide chimneys formed of stakes of birch wood bound round with ropes of twisted straw. From the empyreumatic odour of the smoke, turf seems to be the ordinary fuel; and hence they are but little exposed to accident from fire, as the ignited particles which ascend, speedily become oxidized. A small stripe only round the doors and broken windows is whitewashed, as in the remote parts of North Wales. The modern cottages form a striking contrast to the old ones, being built of hewn new red sandstone, and covered with quarries of the same, or baked square tiles, the corners pointing downwards. For the last 30 or 40 years the great proprietors of the Border lands have paid much laudable attention to the improvement of their estates, and to the comforts of their tenantry. Among these, the Duke of Buccleuch and Sir James Graham of Netherby may be particularized: the former appropriated 5 per cent out of the whole rent of the parish of Cannobie to the formation of new roads, and gave other encouragement to his tenants. The author of Guy Mannering says, 'The present store farmers of the south of Scotland are a much more refined race than their fathers. Without losing the rural simplicity of manners, they now cultivate arts unknown to the former generation, not only in progressive improvement of their possessions, but in all the comforts of life. Their houses are more commodious, their habits of life regulated so as better to keep pace with those of the civilized world; and the best of luxuries, the luxury of Knowledge, has gained much ground among their hills during the last thirty years.'

We had hitherto enjoyed an uninterrupted view of the Cumberland mountains since we left Carlisle; and although they now began to recede behind us and to grow faint from distance, they still appeared magnificent from a small elevation in the road about half way between Annan and

Dumfries. They formed the left screen of a picture, of which the estuary of the Solway occupied the centre, and the convex Cruefell, robed in muffled clouds, and occasionally shewing his giant top or bulky sides through misty curtains, the extreme right. Dumfries appeared across a vast black flat of turbary, amid a few groups of trees, but in a vale very superior to anything we had yet seen in Scotland, backed by a varied group of hills, bearing a good resemblance to those which form the western boundary of the Vale of Clwyd. They were the mountains of Kirkudbrightshire; the valley at their feet was Nithsdale, not less celebrated for its fertility, than for the extreme beauty and tenderness of its pastoral poetry. We soon descended in to it, and in losing sight of Skiddaw, bade adieu for a time to 'merry England.' The land, tho' fertile, is wet and spongy with occasional patches of bog; the hedges have a good deal of privet; and the sweet, or bay-leaved willow (Salix penandra) and rows of Tachamahac (Populus balsamifera) and Scotch Laburnum, frequently line the road.

We reached Dumfries about 3 o'clock; and were agreeably surprized at its very neat appearance; the houses very large, light and clean, mostly built of red sandstone, the streets spacious and the town, what may be called large, but not overgrown. After ordering dinner, we repaired to the old church, or St Michaels, in the cemetery of which is the superb mausoleum lately erected over the high master-poet, Burns, which was one chief object of our visit to Dumfries. On entering the church-yard, our curiosity was strongly excited by the very numerous and superb monuments erected against the walled inclosure and over the area, many of them tall and elaborate, in the forms of obelisks, altars, pillars, tombs, and pedestals, some Gothic, and others very chaste Grecian of various orders. They give to the churchyard a very different appearance to any I have seen in England, and appeared to me very inconsistent with that simplicity so characteristic of the church worship of Scotland. They differed also from English tombs in what would be considered by many a more essential point. With us, the bodies are universally laid with the feet towards the east;[*] but so violent was the hostility of the Scotch reformers against everything that savoured of popery, that they abolished this custom along with many others of a less ambiguous tendency and character.

In the south-east corner of the church-yard, stands the splendid mausoleum erected to the memory of that great poet of nature, Robert Burns; which, though it may survive a few centuries, will be blended with other dust, while his more enduring monument, his inimitable poetry, will

---

[*] From the earliest ages of Christianity, the East has been the point of adoration, altars have been placed, and bodies have been interred in that direction, that on rising again, they might face the Saviour, who was supposed to have ascended from, and at his second coming, would appear again in that quarter. The custom was probably derived from Heathenism and ingrafted upon Christianity with many others, at its first introduction, to reconcile converts to the change.

be coeval with the language in which it is written. The Edifice is altogether of fine white marble, secured from the weather by an hemispherical dome, supported by rich and chaste pillars, having the sides open, but secured with an ornamented iron railing. The group consists of the Poet, dressed in a close coat and short gaiters buttoned over his ankles and shoes, with the shirt neck open, looking up to the Muse Coila (sic), who is flinging a mantle over him. The figures are in alto-relievo, the size of life; that of Burns is holding the plough, whose point seems buried in the barren gravelly soil of the north, and the sward is strewed with daisies and other flowers. A mouse was sculptured upon it, but since has been removed. The features do not much resemble the common prints, but are very finely expressive of rapture and enthusasim; and when it is considered that there never was a portrait taken of him during his life, the discrepancy will not be wondered at. Dovaston remarked to the sexton that the face resembled Sir W. Scott, he said in reply that Sir Walter himself had very strongly made the same remark. Several on our tour with whom my friend has been conversing about Burns, have, at different times, told him he was a good deal like him. The only inscription is on the panel of the pedestal; it consists only of the word 'BURNS', and more would have been superfluous. The sculpture is by Turnerelli; it is fair, but by no means first rate, though the whole cost £1,500. The flowers, which are no doubt intended for the mountain daisy, in allusion to his delightful little poem, are botanically incorrect, and seem to be copied altogether from the ragwort. The remains of the poet were originally laid in another part of the church-yard, but they now repose in a vault beneath the mausoleum, which is intended to contain those of his widow and family. Around the vault, and within the iron railing are planted holly, portugal laurel, philarea (sic), rhododendrons and other evergreens, with a few fine plants of the Onopordum acanthium, or woolly leaved thistle. A book stands on a desk on one side, in which we inscribed our names. But I cannot pass by the tomb of this inspired poet, without paying a passing tribute to his amazing powers of fancy, nor without a sigh that his brilliant career should be so clouded and so short, and withal so stained by depravity and folly, aggravated by the consciousness he felt of the errors which he had not sufficient resolution to reform. As a proof of this, I need only cite the following lines, written for his own epitaph by himself.

> Is there a man, whose judgement clear
> Can others teach the course to steer,
> Yet runs, himself, life's mad career,
>   Wild as the wave;
> Here pause — and, thro' the starting tear,
>   Survey this grave.

The poor inhabitant below
Was quick to learn and wise to know,
And keenly felt the friendly glow,
   And softer flame;
But thoughtless follies laid him low,
   And stain'd his name!

After we had indulged our feelings at the mausoleum, we turned into the church where plainness and simplicity prevail as much as ornament does in the monuments without. Service was over, but in many of the pews, were from four to six boys or girls, and to each separate group, a lady or gentleman was allotted, teaching them to read.

While we were at dinner, a gentleman arrived in the mail from Port Patrick, and was very indignant on finding that he was too late for public worship. He had been told, he said, that he should reach Dumfries in time, which was his only motive for travelling on the sabbath, though on urgent business. Conversation, soon turned on Mr. Owen and his establishment at Lanark, and on his plans for the education and maintenance of the poor in colonies. He censured, in no measured terms, that gentleman's general principles and patriotic zeal; but when he adverted to the part of his system connected with the education of the children, his eyes flashed fire, and he vented forth such a torrent of vituperation against him, that it required little insight into human nature to perceive, that he would have condemned him, without reluctance, to the scaffold or the faggot, if his power and the spirit of the times would have allowed him. We so far ventured to defend Mr. Owen, as to say that his efforts to promote morality and general happiness might be presumed to be sincere from the unimpeached purity of his own character. This he was compelled to admit, but he qualified the admission, by adding, that morality, not founded upon faith, would be found of no avail, and Mr. Owen wanted to get rid of the 'drag-chain of religion' altogether! There are occasions, when argument is folly and silence, wisdom; and thinking this was one of them, when we had finished our dinner, we left this spiritual Quixote, thankful that the laws of our country sanction that diversity of sentiment which ever has and ever must exist; and which bigots in vain endeavour to suppress.

We strolled about, and turned in to another church; the preacher was not without ability, though his arguments appeared weak and hackneyed; and being close to the door, we quietly withdrew when we saw the deacons preparing to make a subscription (previously announced by the preacher) for missionary purposes. When will the public see through the errors and abuses of this system of extortion? It has long appeared to me, that our missionaries to heathen countries, begin where they ought to end; for who, that reflects at all, can imagine any permanent benefit is likely to arise from forcing the mysteries of Christianity, which those who have studied them

A Nineteenth-Century Tour

from childhood cannot understand, upon savages whose common sense revolts at them, before they have prepared their minds by teaching them the pure morality of the gospel, and the common arts and charities of civilized life? If the well meaning contributors knew that not one tithe of the sums collected, is applied to the legitimate object of their intention, they would withhold their benevolence, and defeat the designs of those who only encourage, to abuse it.

We strolled over the fine new bridge across the Nith, and along a very inviting walk upon its bank, shaded by rows of lofty lime-trees, under which numerous groups of gay dressed burghers were enjoying the refreshing coolness of a delightful summer evening, and listening to a military band. From the numbers assembled, we concluded that the Scotch are more cheerful than the dissenters of their persuasion in England, though they will not allow any coach to travel on Sunday except the mail. The setting sun tinged the light spires and elegant buildings of Dumfries with a rich glow, and threw a mellow purple hue over the vast bulk of Cruefell and the more distant mountains; while the meanders of the Nith, the fine bridge, and the luxuriant limes, forcibly reminded me of a scene, familiar from early life, where stands

> 'Admir'd Salopia, that with venial pride,
> Eyes her bright form in Severn's ambient wave.'

We had in the course of the afternoon, made several calls at the house of Mrs. Burns, the widow of the poet, who was from home; and as Dovaston was very anxious to see her, we made a fourth attempt which proved successful. She lives in a small street, called *Burns'* street (so spelt at both ends) as another near it is called Shakespeare's. She received us very kindly; and on Dovaston's apologizing for the intrusion (as he understood so many called), she said they did, but she knew not how to refuse them. He told her he hoped his great enthusiasm from infancy for her husband's genius would obtain her pardon; cited a few passages; told her he was an old and intimate friend of Roscoe; and had seen her son and John Murdock in London; and that, ere the poet's fame had become so universal, he had defended many of his poems in Oxford, where the merely learned, thought them vulgar. She said she had never seen Roscoe, and Dr. Currie only once, and that John Murdock had left Scotland before she was married. Her house was very neat, and she appeared genteelly dressed, inclined now to plumpness, of very pleasing manners, and her voice mild and melodious. She seemed but slightly affected by the conversation; but it must be considered that time and the many circumstances connected with her husband's fame, have so long familiarized her mind to his death, that the idea must now be softened into a pleasing melancholy. She told us that Burns died in the house where we then sat, and such was the reason they gave the street his name.

I was desirous to have seen Lochmaben, situated about five miles from Dumfries, interesting from being the paternal estate of Robert the Bruce, who by his valour and exploits, fought his way to the throne of Scotland: but our time would not permit us. We are told there are still some remains of his castle, built on a promontory which juts out into the lake. The vicinity of Lochmaben also derives no small degree of celebrity as the scene of some of the heroic actions of the renowned Sir W. Wallace.

A terrible instance of the savage brutality of ancient times is recorded of the murder of the regent John, called the Red Comyn, or Cummin, committed in the Grey Friar's church at Dumfries by Robert Bruce and two of his adherents. They met at the High Altar; and after some insulting language, Bruce drew his dagger, and stabbed Comyn. Rushing to the door, the former met his two powerful barons, Kirkpatrick and Lindsay, who eagerly asked him "What tidings?" "Bad tidings" answered Bruce, "I doubt I have slain Comyn." "Doubtest thou?" said Kirkpatrick, "I make sicker" i.e. *sure*. With these words, he and Lindsay rushed into the church and despatched the wounded Comyn. The Kirkpatricks of Closeburn, (which is about nine miles from Dumfries) assumed, in memory of this bloody deed, a hand holding a dagger; and for a motto, the memorable words, "I make sicker." This event hastened Bruce's elevation to the Scottish throne.

Monday 18th July As we took places last night to Glasgow in the 'Robert Burns' coach which was to leave Dumfries at 8 o'clock this morning, we rose at 5, and walked to the ruins of Lincluden Abbey, called here the 'Old College,' which stands on a secluded spot at the junction of the Cluden and the Nith, about a mile north of the town. The morning was delightfully serene and cool,

> —in all her spangled beauty bright;
> For, hung on every spray, on every blade
> Of grass, the myriad dewdrops twinkled round.

The ruin is so shaded by fine trees, principally ash, that we had some difficulty in finding it; the land about it very fertile, and being situate on the banks of the two rivers above-named, both famous for salmon and trout, it proved, if any proof were wanting, that the monks loved the good things of this life as well as the solitude which they considered necessary to fit them for the next. It is built of the soft red sandstone of the district, and has suffered much, both in the entire destruction of much of the original building, and of the rich ornaments with which it has been very profusely decorated. The choir or chancel, and some of the south walls are in the best preservation, and shew some beautiful pointed gothic arches, with remnants of small statues in niches, shields &c. Against the north wall of the chancel, is a very superb tomb of Margaret daughter of Robert the 3rd, and wife of Archibald Earl of Douglas, in the form of an arch richly studded with sculpture, tracery and escutcheons. Pennant says there was an effigy on the stone within the arch, the head resting on two cushions, in his time much mutilated, but now entirely gone. The inscription also is much defaced, though most of it is legible, it is as follows: 'Hic jacet Dña Margareta Regis Scotia filia quōdam Comitissa de Douglas Dña Gollovidix et vallis Annandiæ.' Some of the cornices are double and broad, with a profusion of flowery sculpture; having numerous figures, groups, and devices between. Opposite the tomb are niches or stalls, with a piscina; the corbels of the windows are shields and busts. The nave is entirely destroyed and over the doorway, leading into it from the choir, a very highly ornamented frieze, consisting of a double row of figures; the upper row being half lengths of angels and mitred abbots, and the lower, crowded groups in various shapes and spirited attitudes, either representing events connected with the history of the building, or, as Pennant conjectures, designed to express the preparations for the interment of the Saviour. It is to be regretted that the soft and perishable nature of the stone, and long exposure to the elements, has destroyed all the finer touches of the sculptor, and rendered the subjects so obscure, that in a few years more, they will be totally destroyed. Without the building, and before the east window, is a large quadrangular sunk area, which may have been a garden; and near it, towards the south, a high tumulus or artificial mount, whose connection with the abbey we could not conjecture.

By eight o'clock we had breakfasted, and were seated on the coach which soon after set out for Glasgow, crossing the Nith over a fine bridge, keeping the river on our right. Passed near the site of Lincluden abbey, and crossed the Cluden near Holywood. We were told that though these rivers unite, they have each a distinct species of salmon; those of the Cluden being considerably thicker and shorter in the body and much longer in the head than those of the Nith. The valley which takes its name from the latter river, is wide, and where cultivated, rather fertile, principally pasture land, with some oats and a few potatoes; but a large proportion of it is wet and boggy, and from lying too near the level of the stream, cannot be drained. In the sheltered spots, there is a good deal of wood, principally larch and pine; but they are stunted and unhealthy.

We again crossed the Nith at Aldgeth, to the north of which it meanders very boldly and gracefully amid sheltering and finely wooded banks. Just beyond this spot, a remarkable oak, or probably three oaks, originally planted quite close together, was pointed out to us, called the three brothers. Its size would not be thought great in England; but here it is considered extraordinary. At the next village, the name of which I do not recollect, the two roads to Glasgow unite. We took that to the right which is said to be the more picturesque; but if this be the case, it speaks but little in favour of the other. We kept ascending the stream of the Nith, which was frequently in sight, and still wandered through meadows or between swelling banks fringed with copse wood; but the hills, as yet, had no pretensions to loftiness of height, or to picturesqueness of outline, nor were their smooth and swelling slopes either broken by crags or variegated with wood. From Thornhill, a village with a very wide street and a tall cross, surmounted with a griffin and sundials, we saw on the left, surrounded by extensive plantations, the large modern square castle of Drumlanrig, the residence of the Duke of Queensberry. Till within these few years, the park contained some of the original breed of wild cattle; perfectly white, (except the tip of the nose, which is black) and without horns. I believe the only places where they are now to be seen in Britain are Chillingham Castle in Northumberland, Gisburne Park near Skipton in Craven, and Lyme in Cheshire. Some years ago our friend Bewick made a very large and beautiful wood engraving of the bull of this species, by desire of the Duke of Northumberland, but after four impressions had been worked off, the block (which was composed of many parts, screwed together) cracked in different directions, and was thrown aside as useless. The execution was considered to be so fine, that one of the four impressions was sold for twenty guineas. It has since been repaired by the ingenuity of this highly-gifted man, who has kindly presented each of us with a fine impression.

When we had ascended out of Nithsdale we skirted the bank of the river Carron, on which is the site of an old castle, near Yornock, with a very deep dell or ravine on the right. The new road takes a N.E. direction, winding thro' the desolate and dreary passes between the Lead Hills, which separate the Counties of Dumfries and Lanark. The hills on each side are lofty, smooth, and bold, covered with a short and sickly verdure, but not a single tree or crag of rock on which the eye can rest and refresh itself. There is no grandeur or mountain wildness in the scenery; it only gives an idea of vastness and solitude. The pass along the summit level is called Dalveen glen; and the hills on each side rise so high, that the inhabitants of a solitary hut which was pointed out to us, do not see the sun for two months before and two months after the winter solstice. Though so diminutive as to be scarcely visible amidst the vast and sweepy hills which shut it out from the world, – a speck only in the ocean of desolation, as if to mark more forcibly the surrounding solitude – we were told it was a mountain farm, and that the occupier of it was supposed to be worth £30,000! It would be difficult to select a more striking instance of the utter uselessness and vanity of wealth; for to what earthly purpose could it be applied in such a place? Near to this, and at the division of the counties, is a neat stone obelisk with inscriptions, on a small mound close to the road, to mark the site where a Mr. Menzies, Laird of a neighbouring district called Troloss, on Crawford muir, his wife and sister, are buried by their own particular desire. It is useless to speculate on the diversity of tastes and feelings; but to ordinary minds it seems singular that a wealthy farmer should select such a spot to live in, and that a laird should fix upon it for his last earthly resting place. In every region and condition of life, man is the creature of habit and of circumstances, 'formed and moulded,' (as Dr. Blair beautifully expresses it) 'by the incidents of his life;' and of the two characters just mentioned, the farmer probably would not have enjoyed his wealth, if removed from the scenes and habits of his early life, nor the laird have endured the idea of being laid in any other soil but his own.

We entered Lanarkshire by a new road, formed upon the line of a Roman Way, which seems to have branched off to the Lead Hills in opposite directions, from the great military communication between Carlisle and Sterling. This deviation proves that the Romans worked these mines; for besides the many encampments in the neighbourhood, other antiquities, such as tools, utensils, and coins of Marcus Aurelius and Marcus Antoninus, have been found here. We saw the Roman road in several places; and, on the eastern bank of the infant Clyde near Crawford, a very perfect and regular oblong raised terrace at the foot of a high hill, which was evidently a Roman camp. Not far from it, but on the western bank is the unpicturesque ruin of Crawford castle.

We passed between the villages of Duresdon and Lead Hills, each a congregation of wretched hovels, the abodes of the miners; and though lying at the foot of the hills, they have an elevation of nearly 1,600 feet above the level of the sea. The district under which the ore has hitherto been found, is of very limited extent; the veins principally lie north and south, at various depths from the surface, and are sometimes very productive. Besides the different varieties of the sulphuret, they find the crystalized carbonate of Lead: formerly a considerable quantity of Gold was procured from the bed of the Elvan, a rivulet that runs into the Clyde, and among the neighbouring gravel that lies under the peat; but I could not learn whether it is all exhausted. It is among these hills that the Clyde has its source; and it was pointed out to us while yet a tiny rivulet. Hitherto we had travelled against the streams, and been continually ascending towards a high level; we now observed with pleasure that we were running with them, and were about to exchange a wide, naked and dreary tract, for the verdant meadows and sheltered woods of Clydesdale. But we were aware that the transition must be gradual; for around and before us, were still many formidable hills which must be skirted. Among these, Lowther Law, the highest mountain in the south of Scotland, towered high above the nearer hills on our left, and Tinto Top, the second in elevation raised his bulky and obtuse cone more immediately before us. Lowther Law is upwards of 3,000 feet high, and was pointed out to us by a person on the coach, as the ancient burial place of suicides. Hogg, in his Winter Evening Tales, relates that one of those unhappy victims of despair had a similarly situated grave on a height called Cranemoor, near Lochmaben. We should thence infer, that in Scotland it was customary to bury them in these silent and unfrequented spots; but from the little we heard, of rare occurrence.

We dined at old Lanark, which stands pleasantly on a rising ground above the river. It is one of the oldest towns in Scotland, having been occupied by the Romans, soon after they gained possession of the southern provinces; and is subsequently connected with some of the most interesting events of Scottish history. Here the great Wallace made his first effort to relieve his country from the yoke of tyranny, by slaying Mowbray the English governor; the house erected on the site of the edifice in which it is said to have taken place, is still standing and shewn to strangers; and over the principal gate of the tolbooth we saw a very bold statue of this intrepid warrior. We observed for the first time, several houses thatched with heather.

The principal dish at dinner was Hotch Potch. It consisted of mutton chops boiled and served up in thin, very thin, broth, with peas, turnips, and chopped cabbage, the eternal vegetable of the Scotch. Dr. Johnson says somewhere that hotch potch is only fit for hogs; but we begged leave to dissent from this dictum, and pronounced it very good after our mountain journey. Here we felt the heat excessively oppressive; when on the top of the coach, passing rapidly over the high ground near the Lead Hills, we could scarcely catch a breath of air, though in elevated valleys, the reflection of the sun's rays generally rarifies the air so much, that a current is caused by the rushing down of the colder air to restore the equilibrium. At eight o'clock in the evening at Glasgow, the thermometer stood at 75 deg. and I have since found that its maximum height this day, in the neighbourhood of London, in the shade, was 90 degrees.

It was with much regret that we passed the celebrated Falls of the Clyde and Mr. Owen's establishment at New Lanark, as seen. In the former there was so little water that we determined to proceed direct to Glasgow, and return to them, if circumstances should permit. Our subsequent plans however prevented this; and all we saw of Corra Linn and Bonniton was the tops of the fine trees which overshadow them, at some distance below us, a little before we reached Lanark. For beyond them towered the lofty Loudon, near to which, at Drumclog, the first battle between the Covenanters and the royalists took place, as finely related in 'Old Mortality', where Claverhouse was routed; and Bothwell killed by the fictitious zealot Burley of Balfour. We looked in vain for the imaginary castle of Tillietudlem, and for the house where the most violent of the Cameronians retired after their defeat at Bothwell Bridge, and from which Norton was rescued by the timely arrival of Claverhouse and Cuddie. The deliberations of the fanatics here, and the religious scruples which deferred the execution of their vengeance upon Morton till the hand of the clock had reached the hour of twelve on Sunday night, are drawn with a masterly hand, and are highly illustrative of the temper of those dreadful times.

About a mile beyond Lanark, we crossed the dismal, deep, and horrible glen of Cartland Crags by a handsome new bridge, having two tiers of arches, one below and three above, the road being 118 feet above the bed of the linn, which is called the Mouse. The sides of the glen are well covered with ash and birch, but so precipitous, that it is horrible to look down into it from the top of the coach, and so narrow, that the projecting crags seemed scarcely to allow a passage to the foaming torrent. It is celebrated among botanists for many rare plants. We afterwards passed over several other glens of similar character, but less terrific, all teeming their tributary streams into the Clyde. This is entirely a new road and has been formed at a vast expense; the scripture prophecy is literally fulfilled, for every valley is exalted and every hill made low; the crooked places are made strait, and the rough places smooth. We had scarcely passed Cartland Crags, when, at a sudden turn of the road, the mountains of Argyleshire (sic); lying west of Ben Lomond, and forming the southern boundary of the Highlands in the west of Scotland, appeared before us in very full and fine display, with their wavy and pointed outlines piercing the bluer sky among the floating and fleecy clouds of summer. They extended from the high ground above the Clyde on the west, to the nearer and long level ridge of the Campsie hills on the east; and their noble and majestic forms, broad bases, and conical summits, somtimes bifurcated, excited a high degree of mental emotion and pleasure. The spires of Glasgow were faintly seen below them. The distance of Ben Lomond, one of the nearest of this range, was little less than fifty miles in a right line, that of the Argyleshire mountains, much more; yet such was the serenity of the sky, that their outlines were clear and well defined; and I could now comprehend and believe that the Alps and Pyrenees may sometimes be seen at a hundred miles distance! As we skirted along the top of the eastern bank of the Clyde, the fertile and wide expanded valley through which it winds its mazy course, was spread out as a map below us; the course of the river might generally be traced by the sinuous line of lofty woods which form a thick umbrageous canopy over it, and which occasionally leave its banks and occupy portions of the higher grounds. The interest which such delightful scenery itself excites, was much enhanced by a recollection of the historical events connected with the stately ruins which here and there rise above the luxuriant woods in which they stand. Of these, the Castles of Craignethan, of Cadzow, and of Bothwell, were pointed out to us; nor could we forbear taking a rapid glance at the pomp and grandeur displayed in them in their days of glory, and contrasting them with the mournful silence of their now deserted halls and mouldering turrets. Of the modern buildings which help to fill up this varied and extended landscape, the splendid mansions of the Duke of Hamilton, and the castle of Bothwell may be named, and of other objects, the towns of Hamilton, Bothwell, with its memorable ancient bridge, and Rutherglen, the woods of Chatelherault, and villas, almost without end.

 We passed through Carluke, Wishawtown, and several other long villages with very wide streets composed solely of cottages where the inhabitants and everything about them appeared excessively dirty, and the women and children altogether without shoes and stockings. On the hills indeed this morning, we met with a Scotch lassie or two extremely neat in plaid dresses, but barefooted. I had no opportunity of observing the stratification of the country till we got near to Glasgow, where it is the soft sandstone of the coal measures. Coal is got here in amazing quantities; which indeed might be inferred from the numerous manufactories around, which sent forth dense columns of smoke and obscured the view of this fine city, which we reached about half past 7 o'clock after a ride of very varied interest, through ninety miles of country. Of Glasgow I shall say nothing till tomorrow; save an expression of surprise at finding it so fine a city. We were weary, exhausted with the extreme heat of the day, and covered with dust. On alighting from the roof of the coach, as it stopped at a very large and noisy hotel, and as we were likely to make Glasgow our temporary residence, as well as the point from which to take several excursions, we enquired for one more suitable to our ideas of comfort, and were recommended to the 'Prince of Wales' hotel in Brunswick Street. We were courteously but far from officiously received by the landlord in person, Mr. John Neilson, a bluff, open featured man, upwards of sixty. On showing us into a room, and finding we were strangers travelling for pleasure, he honestly and familiarly entered into conversation with us. His figure, though somewhat grotesque, was very prepossessing: long smooth black hair, on which the healthy winter of age had just sprinkled its earliest snow; a large protuberant nose fringed with a few black hairs, between two long black eyes sparkling beneath bushy raven eyebrows. His large irregular yellow teeth might reconcile every schoolboy to Homer's eternally repeated metaphor of a fence or hedge; and his upper lip was well begrimmed with scotch snuff, and harmonized in colour with the stakes below: yet his smile at once assured us of confidence and benevolence. His clothes were quite of the old fashioned cut, but perfectly good and clean; and his broad splay feet set off his polished shoes to vast advantage. Dovaston being unwell with a bilious complaint, instantly became the object of his kind and tender care. Niceties were named for supper, and every allurement put in requisition to console a disturbed constitution and excite a capricious appetite. The good man was a widower, but at his bidding, his niece, a fine bonnie lassie, and Colin his waiter, a mild gentle youth, united cheerfully and obligingly in every care of the table and chamber. When returning from several long excursions which we made from this house, we always felt as though we were returning to a home and to friends and should we visit Glasgow again, shall endeavour to seek out the hospitable roof of good Mr. John Neilson.

Tuesday, 19th July Before breakfast I purchased a map and itinerary of Scotland, having hitherto travelled without either, in hope of procuring more accurate ones here than I could have done at home. I soon found that excellent editions of standard works might be purchased here very cheap, and that my prejudice against Scotch books was unfounded. Formerly they were very inferior; even those printed by Foulis far from accurate, though neat. Dovaston was still so unwell that I feared we should be detained here on that account; the heat of the weather being so great that I thought it imprudent in him to travel. I also wished him to call in medical advice, but he declined it, and anticipated that he should be able to travel tomorrow. We therefore devoted this day to Glasgow, which, both on account of its extent and the beauty and uniformity of its streets and buildings is not inferior to the finest provincial cities in Britain. The principal streets are wide, and either at right angles or parallel to each other; the houses lofty, all built of freestone, and very handsome, (particularly in Argyle Street, which is the principal thoroughfare) most of them being finished with fluted or plain pilasters, cornices, &c. Stone is so plentiful in the immediate neighbourhood, and so easily worked, that a brick building is quite a novelty; yet the quantity of oxide of iron which appears in large irregular blotches upon it, frequently disfigures the fronts of very fine edifices. In the principal streets the shops make an elegant and rich display, and the pavements are almost as thronged as those of London; the English eye is long before it becomes reconciled to the middle and lower classes of women being always without stockings and generally without shoes, and their feet very dirty. Even the ladies do not dress neat, their legs are thick, and their gait ungraceful. Yet even the lower classes, and the tradesmen, waiters, etc, are very intelligent and civil, and shew no contempt for the English, as so many of us do for the Scotch.

Glasgow contains about 80,000 inhabitants,* a large proportion of whom are one way or other employed in commerce and manufactures. It is by far the first commercial city and seaport of North Britain, the Liverpool of Scotland; while Edinburgh, as the metropolis, is the resort of the nobility and gentry not connected with trade. It stands principally on the north bank of the Clyde, and on a declivity facing the south. Two handsome stone bridges and a neat light wooden foot bridge connect it with the opposite bank of the Clyde, the upper or higher stone bridge has large circular perforations over each abutment to lighten the weight. Its public buildings are elegant and spacious; particularly the Exchange in Argyle Street, in front of which is a fine equestrian statue of William the 3rd; the Tolbooth with its light and lofty spire, Nelson's Monument, a stately plain Obelisk; and the Courts of Justice with the Jail behind them. The last is altogether a magnificent pile of buildings, with a façade of singular beauty and classic elegance, facing the Clyde. As we only saw the exterior of these in the course of our ramble through the city, the above is all that I can say of them

---

* This I find was the census of 1801. That of 1821, gives the population as 147,000!

from actual observation; and as this Journal is not designed to contain the descriptions or remarks of others, I shall pass on to the Cathedral and the University, which we made the particular objects of our attention.

The Cathedral, now called the High Kirk, stands on an eminence at the extremity of the High Street, and is really a very fine specimen of the middle style of Gothic, though neither so large nor so rich as many of our English Cathedrals. Perhaps it bears the nearest resemblance to that of Lichfield, though rather in the details than in the design or appearance of the whole. It is said however, to be the largest and most perfect gothic building in Scotland, and very narrowly escaped destruction about the time of the Reformation. It has two towers; on one of which has been subsequently placed a lofty spire, somewhat similar to that of Salisbury. All comparison however between it and any other cathedral vanishes on entering it. As the simplicity of worship adopted by the church of Scotland does not require or admit the space or decorations indispensable to the performance of British ceremonies, the great aisle or nave has been divided into two parts, by a wall built entirely across it. The western half is a kind of vestibule, that towards the choir is pewed and appropriated to public worship. This again is separated from the choir by another wall, and the arch over the rood loft usually occupied by the organ, is filled up by a crimson curtain. The choir is also fitted up as a distinct place of worship, the monuments and decorations being removed from both. About twenty two years ago, a third congregation assembled in the crypt or vault under the nave, but they have since erected a new edifice contiguous to the church yard. We saw the steps which descended into these crypts from the floor of the western portion of the nave; and were told they are now used as a cemetery. The readers of Rob Roy will recollect that it was in these vaults that Francis Osbaldistone sought for MacVittie on his arrival in Glasgow; and where he was seen by Rob Roy, who appointed to meet him at midnight on the bridge, and accompanied him to the tolbooth to search out Owen. The stalls are removed from the choir, which is lined with galleries; the central seat over the rood loft and facing the east window, has the royal arms carved in front, those of Scotland being in the first and fourth quarters, those of England in the second, Ireland in the third, with those of Hanover, Lunenburgh & Saxony, on an escutcheon of pretence; with 'Nemo me impune lacessit' below: The altar has been removed, and its place supplied by a screen of plain glass, the square panes having crosses, flowers, and other devices opaquely cut thereon with a diamond, having altogether a very chaste effect. The Lady Chapel is not used; and in common with the pillars and walls in every part of the structure, seems much neglected for want of a little whitewash. The great eastern window is composed of four long lancet shaped compartments extending from the top to the bottom, filled with modern stained glass, in which are figures of the four evangelists. The pillars and mullions of the windows throughout, are profusely clustered. In the groinings of the roof of the nave and side aisles are arms, devices, names, and Latin sentences, rudely and obscurely traced, which is a feature I have not observed elsewhere.

We now ascended one of the towers, for the purpose of getting a correct view of the city and surrounding country. The steps towards the top were very dangerous, being only a slender rotten ladder, after which we climbed over great beams, the floor much broken, and making the head giddy from seeing through into the murky depths below. On getting into the open air, we had a noble view of this fine city and the surrounding country. The day was hazy; yet Ben Lomond raised his high and nodding head through the mist. In the *yird* below were many numerous tombs and singular raised monuments, but not so rich as those at Dumfries. The north yard was divided into four compartments by low parallel walls, and these again subdivided. Many of the tombs were surrounded with iron palisades and secured by iron bars across their tops, to prevent the bodies being stolen for the numerous students in anatomy; and for better protection, a guard house is built in one corner of the yard. While ascending Dovaston became facetious with the sexton, who was a merry, but very self-important personage; amid other objects, he pointed to an elegant and extensive building at the border of the city, and with a shrewd and good humoured smile, said, 'It was a hoose for the daft.' (Lunatic asylum.) The Scotch are no admirers of steeple melody, for very few of their churches have bells; even this vast cathedral has only one very small one, not larger than is commonly seen on gentlemen's houses, on which the clock strikes. The hand of the dial being now on the hour of noon, the sexton, on our descent through the difficult and even dangerous rafters of the old tower, made us pause, as the ponderous rusty clock gave warning, 'to ken what a muckle sound the bell would gar in our lugs;' and when it had tinked its dozen strokes, he stared with astonishment at our indifference, and enquired with very evident disappointment, 'Gin we had ever heerd sae muckle a soond?' Had it been Great Tom of Oxford, he could not have been prouder of his bell. The cathedral altogether is a very interesting building, independent of the reminiscences it calls forth, both in history, and in the matchless Scotch Romances.

We now proceeded to the University, or College, a very massive, large, and incongruous edifice in High Street, with three gateways and four square flagged courts or quadrangles. At the back was a sort of close or garden, sloping towards the Clyde, of about ten acres, with a few stunted trees. We saw no students, for I believe it was the vacation, and Dovaston said it would be difficult for an Oxonian, at first sight, to believe it to be an University. In an open area between the College and the garden, is a very handsome modern building with a bold Grecian façade of the Doric order, created to contain the Museum of Dr. Wm. Hunter, which he bequeathed to this institution; for admission to which, tickets are obtained at the porter's lodge. This splendid, though not very large, collection, deserves our highest admiration, and demands a minute description; but who can praise the flowers of the field, or count them on an hour's inspection? The edifice is large, and has four wings standing at right angles to each other, with a circular room, or dome, in the centre – yet all open together, both below and above. On the floors stood stuffed specimens of the larger animals, lions, leopards, elephants, &c, &c, prodigious albatrosses, and other subjects. Round the sides, were cases filled with British and foreign birds, the former not numerous, and though neatly preserved, the attitudes bad. The walls were hung with many fine original painings, both of the old and modern masters. There was an excellent collection of geological and mineralogical specimens; among these was a very fine fossil Encrinite, or stone lily, about ten inches high, the head of which a good deal resembles the fructification of an Equisetum, but having its stalk composed of innumerable knotted joints, the transverse sections of which are beautifully radiated. The stems of the Encrinite are rather common in the carboniferous or mountain limestone, but the heads are extremely rare. I have seen one in the small museum at Chatsworth, and it is said, I know not with what truth, that only three exist. The department of ancient coins appeared to me the most complete, they are considered of inestimable value, and we heard that the British Museum had offered £25,000 for them alone, besides defraying the expense of an Act of Parliament to empower the trustees to sell them. They are in the highest preservation and beauty. The library also is considered to be of uncommon value, consisting of about 6,000 vols, besides many rare and splendid manuscripts and missals. There is a perfectly astonishing quantity of preparations of every part of the human body, and other subjects preserved in spirits; of the human foetus in all its stages, from conception to parturition, anatomical preparations of all descriptions, lusus naturae, skeletons &c, insects, reptiles, shells, fossil organic remains, Egyptian mummies, Grecian, Roman, and British antiquities, implements of war, dresses and other curiosities from almost every part of the globe, which days and weeks would not be sufficient to examine with the attention they deserve. My visit to and rapid survey of this splendid and multifarious collection, was attended with regret that circumstances would not allow a more deliberate and minute examination of it, as nothing is so delightful and instructive as the exhaustless variety of Nature.

We learned that the number of students averages about 600, and that the funds of the Institution are very ample. Lectures in the different branches of science and philosophy are given, to which may be attributed the excellent education and taste for literature and scientific pursuits which is so general, not only among the merchants and manufacturers of Glasgow, but throughout the whole country. There is an observatory here; but the situation not being a good one, another has been erected in the suburb, which contains a choice assortment of superior instruments.

There is a large suburb to Glasgow on the opposite bank of the Clyde, and the whole of the environs are thickly sprinkled with manufactories, bleaching grounds, villas and gentlemen's houses, giving assurance of its wealth and commercial importance. Its commerce with the Eastern parts of the kingdom, and the continent of Europe, is carried on by means of the Forth and Clyde canal, the cutting of which has been of incalculable advantage to the whole country.

After dinner we took another stroll, and engaged a gig to visit some of the interior parts of the Highlands, through which no coaches run. In the old parts of the town, the buildings are very much crowded, and the streets and alleys very narrow. Indeed, in all the streets, the air is far from being pure, and the effluvia, of no delicate description, which assailed us on passing the alleys which communicate with the main streets, gave no very favourable impression of the general cleanliness of the Scotch, and must be very prejudicial to the health of the inhabitants. The thermometer this day in Glasgow stood at 91 in the shade!

Wednesday, 20th July. We rose early; and at six o'clock got aboard the Marion Steam Packet at the Broomielaw, a long modern quay, at the west end of Glasgow, where all the vessels belonging to the port, have their station. Fifteen years ago, vessels of 50 tons could not approach Glasgow, on account of the shallowness of the water; but so much attention has since been paid to the deepening and embanking of the river, that vessels of 250 tons burden can now lie at the quay. The plan adopted for this purpose was so simple and economical, that it is worth while to mention it. Projecting dykes or jetties were constructed on either bank, pointing in to the stream at right angles to its course, and placed at small distances from each other along the whole line of the navigation. These jetties intercepted much of the earth and gravel washed down by the floods, by lessening the force of the current; and thus supplied the materials for ultimate contraction without the expense of carriage. The bed of the river many years ago was also deepened by means of machines, called ploughs, which were large sharp pointed boxes, dragged along the bottom by means of capstans; by which process 1,200 tons a day were cleared away. This process is still continued at intervals, and the sand and gravel is drawn up between the projecting jetties. By the constant repetition of this simple process, a considerable part of the river is now contracted to less than one half of its original breadth, and has gained above four feet of additional depth. We also observed large quantities of quickset thorns &c, in the shallow sides of the water, which are found to increase the deposition of the mud and sand. These operations have been crowned with the greatest success, though they have diminished the beauty and effect of the river, which for six or eight miles below Glasgow, appears but little wider than the Severn at Shewsbury. Its banks however are very fertile, and soon become prettily undulated, and enlivened with the seats and villas of the more opulent merchants. The towns of Renfrew and Paisley are seen on its southern shore, and a small island called New Shot, so named from its recent appearance, being formed of mud, deposited it is said, on a raft of heavy timber. Approaching the village of Kilpatrick on the northern bank, the river widens and gently inclines towards the south, suddenly revealing a scene of extraordinary grandeur, and assuming at once the character of a broad estuary. On the left are the beautiful, cultivated, and gently swelling shores of Renfrewshire, occasionally wooded; on the right, the steep and rugged hills of Kilpatrick, at the foot of which the castles of Dunglass and Dumbarton project into the water, while the towering mountains of Argyleshire, seen at a distance of about thirty miles, stretch across the estuary in front, and seem to transform it into a bay. Dunglass is an insignificant and melancholy looking ruin, standing on a low rock which projects into the Clyde, and is believed to be either the western termination of that line of forts which Agricola constructed from the Clyde to the Forth, or an outpost connected with it. All that now remains of it, is a single low and small circular tower with a conical stone roof, and two sides of a square building or wall, partially covered with ivy; with a solitary inhabited cottage within the fort. The line of forts just mentioned, was afterwards connected by a Wall, called Antonine's Wall, because it was built by that Emperor to prevent the incursions of the unconquered Caledonians; and is sometimes also called Graham's Dyke. About two miles farther down, on the same side, the singularly bold conical rock of Dumbarton rises out of the water, apparently designed by nature for the protection and defence of the Clyde. This, in fact, it has been for ages, as it is supposed to have been the site of the Roman Station, Theodosia; and if it be true that there is on its summit the remains of a Vitrified Fort, it was probably a place of defence in the time of the original Celtic inhabitants. Dumbarton Castle has occupied a conspicuous place in the page of history, from the period of the Roman conquest of Britain to that of the union of the two crowns; and even after this period, it was considered of so much importance, that it was one of the four castles stipulated in the Act of Union in 1707 to be kept always in repair and garrisoned. The Castle and outer walls occupy one of its summits, and the Governor's house, a white modern building, is placed in the cleft between the points, and spoils the effect of the whole. It is a basaltic rock about 500 feet high, and is nearly perpendicular on every side, and is ascended by different flights of steps and fancy passages, apparently cut with much labour and difficulty. Here we left the Steamer, and tugged up the Leven towards Dumbarton in a small boat, close under the rock. The side towards the town is absolutely perpendicular, and its base is strewed with a confused heap of enormous blocks and fragments, which time and the elements have hurled down its sides. At this point it exhibits something of the columnar structure. From the very low isthmus which connects it with the shore, it has no doubt been an island; and a writer in the fourteenth century says, that the tide flowed round it twice in twenty-four hours. Of a single object, it is by far the most conspicuous and picturesque feature in the Clyde, its double top assuming a different outline as it is seen from different points of view.

We breakfasted at Dumbarton, an ancient, though small and dull town, and went in a coach by the side of Leven Water to Balloch, at the foot of Loch Lomond. Crossed the classic stream of the Leven, on whose banks the poet & historian, Smollett, was born, and where he first 'tun'd his rural pipe to love.' About two miles from Dumbarton, on the left of the road, stands a tall Tuscan obelisk erected to his memory; but it is shamefully mutilated, and seems fast hastening to decay. Many gentlemen's seats and elegant houses, with plantations, &c, enliven this cultivated and pleasant vale. The face of the country reminded me a good deal of the tamer valleys of North Wales, though it is less interesting. The nearer mountains had hitherto prevented us from seeing Ben Lomond; and the haze in the atmosphere made us apprehend we should not see it to advantage, but as we approached the foot of the lake, it grew clearer, and our hopes brightened with it. At a small ferry over the Leven, about half a mile before we reached Loch Lomond, we took boat, which the sailors pushed against the rapid though shallow stream, by fixing the points of long poles into the gravelly bottom, and walking along the broad sides. We got on board a magnificent steam vessel which was in readiness, and from her deck, had the first view of this expanded and enchanting lake, surrounded by a noble amphitheatre of lofty mountains, and studded with numerous islands, varied with trees, naked crags, and patches of corn and verdure. Its whole breadth however is not seen at first, for besides being very narrow towards its southern extremity, the island of Inch Murrain, which is two miles long, stretches across it, and intercepts the view. This is the largest island in the lake, and contains two hundred head of deer and a house inhabited by the keeper. It belongs to the Duke of Montrose. At its west end it is studded with very picturesque groups of trees; and over it we had the first good view of Ben Lomond, towering in very rough majesty, and partly muffled in clouds. The mountains at the foot of the lake are gracefully bold, the wood brushy, but fine.

We sailed to the right of Inch Murrain, and while we were passing it, the full extent of the lake was stretched before us; the day cleared apace, and the sun partially peeped forth, displaying a scene of perfect enchantment. I was so completely absorbed in wonder, that for a while my mind seemed to have lost all her powers of observation and description: I was mute and motionless, and could not express my feelings. The mountains which surround the lake, rise to an astonishing height, in every variety of character, tint, and outline; and where they are seen in perspective towards the upper end, their tops seem to rise in undulations one above another like the waves of the ocean, and to dip down towards the water on either hand.

The immense scale of the landscape afforded every gradation of distance and atmospheric effect; and the fine blue lights, filmy mists, and softened shades of the farther and mingling mountains, contrasted with the glowing colours thrown by the partial sunbeams upon the trees, the golden furze, the purple heather, and the green herbage of the nearer islands, and upon the smooth blue mirror of the transparent water, excelled everything that fancy can conceive or that language can hope to express. It was

> The negligence of Nature, wide and wild,
> Where, undisguis'd by mimic art, she spreads
> Unbounded beauty to the roving eye.

The shifting clouds acted the part of a mighty magician in the scene, alternately throwing each island into shade or rolling off, and giving a passage to the brilliant sunlight to light it up in unimaginable splendour. Of the encircled islands, some lay flat upon the surface of the lake, clothed with smooth herbage, and cattle, or with patches of oats and barley; while others rose to different heights above it, their craggy rocks and clefty fissures interspersed with tufts of heather, furze, and bracken, crowned with trees and copsewood of every foliage and shades of green.

We inclined towards the eastern shore, sailing through the narrow strait which separates the island of Inch Cailleach from the mainland, and where we saw high above us, over a ridgy hill, the pass of Bualmaha. This pass forms one of the southern boundaries of the Highlands, and divides them from the district of Lennox, which is now comprized in the county of Dumbarton. This tract was formerly held by the formidable Clan of the MacGregors, which under the celebrated Rob Roy was the terror of the whole country. We fancied that this must be the spot to which Osbaldistone and the wily Baillie Jarvie were conducted by one of Rob Roy's gillies, when they crossed the lake on their return to Glasgow after their adventurous journey to Aberfoil, as the latter place lies over the mountains in this direction. The bagpiper on board our vessel was playing some Jacobite tunes and Gathering pibrochs; and we could not help peopling the neighbouring glens and mountains in our imaginations, with hundreds of kilted highlanders, whose common practice it was, within the memory of old persons still living, at such a summons from their chief, to rush down from their retired dwellings to the appointed place of rendezvous, to pillage and slaughter any hostile clan: presented some singular effects. Here the views are most sublime, affording every gradation of form and colour necessary for a grand picture; and as the vessel alters her course, which she constantly and most judiciously does, the grouping of the scenery is perpetually changing giving the idea of enchantment.

We touched at Luss to take a lady on board. It consists only of a few mean and scattered cottages round the Kirk and manse, interspersed with some fine oaks, firs and limes. Ben Lomond was still struggling with the cloudy curtains which floated round him, and only occasionally shewed us his rugged and warty sides and his lofty peak; in front was Ben Arthur, ruggedly grand. We sailed under a small ridgy island not far from the shore, called the Jail of Luss, because criminals are left here till they can be sent to the tolbooth at Dumbarton. From the scanty population, and the moral habits of the people, this can very rarely happen. Above Luss there are very few islands, and they cease to give that peculiar character to the scenery which distinguishes the lower portion of the lake. A vast lofty wall or screen of mountains, grey and faint from distance, were now seen high above those which closed in the head of the lake; they were the range near Glenurchy; and even beyond them, and of a still fainter hue, Ben Cruachan showed his double coned summit. This mountain is on the north of Loch Awe, and is 3,400 feet high. These remoter mountains were finely contrasted by the bulky mass of Ben Lomond, towards which we were gradually advancing. The ridge of it rises like a hog's back and ends in a cone, near which we saw some enormous blocks and veins of quartz, a common character in the mica slate rocks, and Ben Lomond is of this series. The lower half rises precipitously from the deep bosom of the lake, portions of it are thickly clothed with fine oaks, reaching down to the very water's edge, interspersed with patches of furze and heather covered with flowers, and in the sun, gleaming with gold and purple. In this part of the sail also, the scenery before us was awefully sublime, with a greater proportion of shadow than hitherto. From Inveruglas, Ben Lomond appears more conical, from the foreshortening of his sides. Here is a ferry across the lake to Rowardennan, where a small inn was pointed out to us as the place from which the ascent up the mountain is commenced.

The clouds were now entirely cleared away, and as the vessel majestically glided under the frowning precipices and hanging woods of Ben Lomond, we saw again the detached and very distant cones of Ben Cruachan and others of the Grampian range, piercing the azure sky of an uniform and pale grey shade. Looking northwards, the loch has the appearance of a very large broad river, hemmed in between almost perpendicular rocks, and black from the breadth of their shadows; but this circumstance brings the rich and varied features of the side-screens more immediately before the eyes. At the Point of Firkin we were in the narrowest part of it; and this is said to command the finest view of this delightful lake and its numerous islands. Nearly opposite to it, and under the very summit of Ben Lomond, we saw a mass of rock hanging over the water, with a level top and perpendicular side walls both above and below, which tradition points out as the place to which Rob Roy let down his prisoners by a rope, and where he confined them till they acceded to his demands! There was evidently no escaping from this perilous situation but by being drawn up again, or by leaping down into the lake, which is deeper here than in any other part, and has

The Cobler, Loch Lomond

been ascertained to be 120 fathoms. The deeper and upper reach is never frozen, but on the southern part, which is the shallowest, the ice is sometimes so thick that horses pass to and from the different islands. In wet seasons the water rises as much as six feet above its usual level. Some wild fowl, sea gulls, and swallows were hovering about as if to break the awful stillness which reigned around. When we had passed Ben Lomond, a very intelligent gentleman on board, and to whose kindness we are indebted for many of our notes on this voyage, pointed out to us the summits of Ben More, Ben Vane, and Ben Vorlich, faintly pencilled on the lofty horizon to the extreme right, but they were soon lost behind other intervening hills.

We were now about to bid farewell to this lovely scenery; and passing the pretty villa of Mr. MacMurrich, called New Oak Cottage, we came to the small village of Tarbet. Loch Lomond extends still farther towards the north several miles, filling up the bottom of Glen Falloch, which we were told, abounds in rich and striking landscapes; but the Steam boat returns from this point to Balloch. We had been informed in the course of the voyage, that another steamer was waiting at the head of Loch Long, and would reach Glasgow in the evening; we therefore disembarked at Tarbet, and walked across the isthmus, thereby embracing the opportunity of seeing a greater variety of Scottish scenery. The pebbles on the shore are principally micaceous schist, quartz, and coarse red jasper.

The situation of Tarbet is eminently fine and commanding. When we had ascended to the road which leads from Luss to Arrochar, the view was stupendous indeed. Loch Lomond with her thirty islands lay far beneath, in quiet repose, at the bottom of the immense basin scooped out of the surrounding mountains, hiding her dark and gloomy head among the impending forests which skirt the gulfy Glen Falloch. Ben Lomond wore a very majestic appearance; the sun just caught the wavy tops of the sombre woods which covered his enormous base, and threw out into high relief, the heaving precipices which swelled his sides; while the mossy channels of the ever flowing rills between them, appeared like belts of golden green, and the blocks of snow-white quartz which crowned his summit, glittered like an encircling diadem. The ridge of the Grampians, a few only of whose tops we had seen from the surface of the water, now rose to a great height, and shewed a lengthened chain from Ben Cruachan on the west to Ben Lawers on the east. Sublimity sat enthroned on every cloud cap'd summit on which the eye could rest. Ben Arthur was now very near us, frowning in terrific grandeur. His top is dreadfully rended, as if by the explosion of some mighty subterranean power, and is composed of huge pointed and shattered blocks, piled on end like a vast and complicated Druidical remain, which absolutely curl and overhang the frightful crater within. The sight of it made us absolutely shudder. At the top of one of the 'thunder-splinter'd pinnacles,' and apparently raised there by giant force, is a vast fragment, the outline of which very much resembles the sitting figure of a *Cobbler* at his last, with his elbows extended; which fanciful circumstance has given this vulgar name to the dreadfully magnificent rocks of Ben Arthur. Tradition says that in ancient times, the Chiefs of the House of Argyle (sic) were required to ascend the highest point of these desperate crags, to prove themselves true descendants of their illustrious progenitors, and to entitle them to the privileges of their clanship! The eye recoils at the thought of climbing; the soul shrinks with horror at the attempt. Frequently glancing at these frightful heights, and at the grand panorama of mountains which rose around us, we walked on, under a burning sun, to the inn of Arrochar, where we found a fine steam vessel, the St. Catherine, waiting for passengers at the very head of Loch Long, a distance of not quite two miles from Tarbet.

The word Tarbet is of frequent occurrence along the western shores of Scotland, and is given to villages or houses situated on an isthmus. It is derived from words in the Gaelic, signifying 'dragging a boat,' because it was formerly the custom to draw boats, and even vessels across these narrow necks of land, both to avoid the tedious circumnavigation of the promontories and headlands, and to escape the dreadful currents which are so fatal to small craft in these stormy seas. An inspection of the map will shew the extent of the sea track from East to West Tarbert, round the peninsula of the Mull of Kintyre, which I just name to illustrate the remark; but I intend to touch upon it more at large when I come to that place.

As we were walking to Arrochar, I could not help being struck by the strange insensibility of several gentlemen of the party, to the grandeur and sublimity which was scattered so profusely around us. The only part of the scenery which seemed to attract their notice, was *the Cobbler*, not the mighty mass of perpendicular crags which compose the summit of Ben Arthur, but the Cobbler alone, that insignificant and insulated fragment, which by its ridiculous resemblance, would diminish the interest of the whole group, if it was more conspicuous. This, among other trifling conversation, was a fertile subject for several jokes. Such, I blush to say, from what I have seen, are the generality of fashionable tourists. They travel *because it is the fashion*, perhaps to kill time, or drive away ennui. Their journeys are little more than a succession of petty vexations and disappointments from the imposititious and accidents they meet with, from delays, bad roads and bad weather, or of pleasures equally unimportant arising from occurrences of an opposite character. When they meet with superior accommodations and agreable company, they are in high good humour, and if they keep a journal, these things constitute a red letter day. If dinner has been ordered at a certain hour, the most interesting scenery must be passed by or glanced at with indifference, lest the stomach should crave, or the dishes be overdone. The great volume of Nature is to such travellers as a sealed book, or rather, though it is spread open before them, it is written in a language of which they know only the letters; just as a mere English reader cannot understand a Latin or Italian book. Hence it is, that they who have never studied her exhaustless beauties, can see nothing in the grandest and most luxuriant landscapes, but a confused mixture of trees, rocks, and water, which are scarcely worth the trouble of a peep out of the carriage window, at the expense of losing the thread of a tale, which they acknowledge to be more interesting than the scenery, by reading it as they roll rapidly along the road. And in fact, how can it be otherwise? Nature is not so lavish of her charms as to reveal them alike to all; she must be wooed like any other mistress, and courted long, before she can be fully understood.

We found the St. Catherine moored to the shore under the bank on which the large inn at Arrochar stands, and went immediately on board. Loch Long is a sea loch or arm of the sea, which runs up among the mountains from the estuary of the Clyde, about twenty miles in a northern direction. Its general depth is from 50 to 80 fathoms, the water is perfectly clear, and in the bright sunshine was as transparent as an emerald, shewing the pebbles and various sea weeds at the bottom, as through a green crystal medium. This loch is narrow and quite clear of islands; and lies between two parallel ranges of smooth grassy mountains, which are bold and pleasing in their general character, though destitute of those striking views with which those round Loch Lomond abound. They are sufficiently lofty to exclude every other object except Ben Arthur and the peaks round the northern end of the loch; and the soil upon them is so scanty that the bare rock frequently appears, without either trees or broken crags to relieve the eye, or remove the impression of sterility. There are however some tolerable landscapes on its western shore and near the head of the loch, particularly about the entrance into Glen Croe, where the low and sheltered spots are interspersed with fine timber, corn and pasture lands. But our imaginations were full of Loch Lomond; and rich indeed must that scenery be, which could interest us under such circumstances.

We had felt the heat very oppressive when we first went on board; but a cool fanning breeze soon sprang up, and we enjoyed, in its highest extent, the ease and pleasure attendant on this mode of travelling. Our packet was fitted up with extreme elegance and provided with every accommodation; the day was delightful, and the company, consisting of many parties of ladies and gentlemen, dined on deck under the open canopy of heaven. The novelty of the scene, the refreshing breeze, and the wit and anecdotes with which my excellent fellow traveller amused the company, raised my spirits to an unusual height. The uniformity of the scenery also gave the mind a degree of relaxation which the overwhelming grandeur of Loch Lomond would not allow, and I resigned myself to the full enjoyment of it. Secluded from the rest of the world by the mountains on either hand, our little company seemed as one family in the midst of a solitude - one individual only was wanting to complete my happiness; and the void was greater, because from the perfect unison of our minds, I *felt* how much she would have enjoyed the whole.

   About halfway down Loch Long on its western side, we saw the entrance into Loch Goyle, which fills a glen about six miles long. The lower sides of it are well clothed with ancient oaks, and on the water's edge is the Castle of Carrick, of which the Duke of Argyle is keeper, with a salary of £500 per annum, though one of the gentlemen said he had never seen it. Here the Loch widens very much, and makes a graceful bend to the south east; and shortly the noble and serrated rocks of Arran and Bute, with the low green island of Great Cumbray and the coast of Renfrewshire, burst into view. On our right was the little bay and mansion of Ardentinny, the residence of the Earl of Dunmore, backed by rough mountains. It stands in the peninsular district of Cowell, ironically called the Duke of Argyle's Bowling Green, from the extreme irregularity of the surface. The water was as smooth as glass; and the broad and lengthened ridge which the prow of the steamer traced on its bright surface as she glided rapidly along, reflected a clear and inverted image of the mountains by which we were surrounded. As we approached the estuary of the Clyde, the continual alteration of our course produced the effect, so well known to sailors, of changing the relative position of the various islands and headlands which surrounded us. It was difficult for a landsman to believe it real, and might be compared to vast and unwieldy ships moving to and fro, or to the masses of clouds which partial currents in the atmosphere sometimes carry in opposite directions. The sea views here are both very extensive and very grand; the wide expanse of water was studded by the picturesque islands already enumerated, backed on one side by the blue and wavy peaks of the Argyleshire mountains, and on the other by the undulating and fertile tracts of Renfrewshire with towns, country seats, and cottages, scattered along its winding shores; the lighthouse of Cloch on its extreme north-western point, and the remains of the castle of Dunoon a royal residence, on the opposite side the channel, while between them, on the extreme southern horizon, was faintly discerned the magnificent basaltic crag of Ailsa, rising perpendicularly out of the ocean. When to such fine natural objects, are added the numerous snow-white sails that moved in all directions across the smooth mirror of the estuary, a lively idea may be conceived of this enchanting view. As we passed the gently sloping and wooded headland which the Gair Loch separates from the eastern part of Dumbartonshire, we saw peeping over the trees, and illuminated by the western sun, the chaste and beautiful mansion of the Duke of Argyle at Roseneath.

   Opposite to Roseneath is Gourock, a neat long village, and a little higher up the Clyde, the flourishing and important seaport town of Greenock. Hence, from the quay, looking northwest, is seen to great advantage, the sublime and grand group of the curled topped mountains of Argyleshire, with Ben Lomond, and many others. On the quay facing the Clyde, is a very handsome Custom-house, with a fine fluted Doric portico. Here we both took in, and left, many passengers. On the opposite shore is the neat village of Helensburgh, with many beautiful villas scattered round it; and a few miles higher, on the Renfrew coast, Port-Glasgow, being in reality, what its name implies, the Port of Glasgow. The new town house and spire have a pleasing appearance, contrasted with the green hills that rise behind the town. Very close to Port-Glasgow, is Newark Castle, a large old castellated mansion with round towers, with a low ruin in front, very similar to that of Dunglass on the opposite bank. Dumbarton rock is not so picturesque an object sailing up the Clyde, as it appeared in the morning.

The remainder of the voyage has been already described in the sail from Glasgow to Dumbarton, and will not require to be repeated. We reached the former place about 9 o'clock, after a day of 15 hours and a voyage of about 96 miles, full of interest and of high mental gratification, resulting from the contemplation of nature in her sublimest forms, and inspiring the most exalted ideas of the Almighty Architect of such stupendous scenery. The thermometer had stood this day in Glasgow, at about 80° in the shade.

Thursday 21st July The weather having been uniformly fine since the day we left home, and appearing to be quite settled, and the packet for Staffa and Iona which best suited our plans, not being to sail till Tuesday the 26th, we determined to lose no time in commencing the short inland tour we had traced out. It was to embrace Inveraray, Glenurchy, Killin and the scenery round Loch Tay, Loch Earn Head, Callendar, and the Trossachs; and I expected we should comfortably accomplish the whole in five days; as we stipulated for a good horse. As we had few preparations to make, we left our good friend Neilson's immediately after breakfast, taking the road to Dumbarton. The fine and extensive suburbs of Glasgow impress a stranger with an idea of its great wealth and commercial importance, but beyond this general remark, and the mere mention of the Botanic Garden, and the ruin of the Palace of the Bishops of Glasgow, between which we passed, it is not my intention to enlarge. As the road runs along the north bank of the Clyde to Dumbarton, the leading features of the scenery have been already described. The river with its numerous sails, and the opposite coast of Renfrewshire were seldom out of sight, but we saw the latter to much greater advantage than from the packet, from the greater elevation of the road we now travelled. We were particularly charmed with the magnificent view from Dalnotter hill, just before we reached Kilpatrick, embracing Dumbarton Castle-rock, the opposite shore, the estuary of the Clyde, and the towering mountains of Argyleshire and of the alpine isle of Arran. As we were not previously apprized of it, it struck us with double force, and was the more enchanting from being seen between the trunks of some fine trees which overshadowed the road.

We descended the hill to the little village of Kilpatrick, said to be the birth place of the tutelar saint of Ireland; which however might be doubted, were it a subject worth the trouble of enquiry. The range of low naked hills to the north, called the Kilpatrick hills are of the trap family, and contain some rare varieties of zeolite &c; they are a portion of an interrupted chain commencing at Dumbarton and extending to Sterling. Antonine's Wall, already mentioned, commenced near Kilpatrick, and may still be traced in the neighbourhood. There is also a Roman bridge very near.

While our horse was feeding at Dumbarton, we strolled about the town, which possesses little interest, save what is derived from historical associations; many of the houses shew it to have been formerly a place of some importance; but it now wears a gloomy and desolate appearance. We fell into conversation with the landlady, a red, round, and smooth buxom widow, who readily guessed we were tourists, and asked our route. When we named Loch Katrine and the Trossachs, we found she had been there but a few months before; and she favoured us with some particulars of her journey, and of the descent to Aberfoil, which I believe cooled the ardour we felt to see the celebrated clachan."I gaed there ance,'" she said, "wi' Jock Blinkabune, and whene'er I mind it, I feel gin I were a' ae sark fu' a' sair banes, for ae muckle stane whombled th'cart the tae side, and ae heather brae jour'd it o'tother, that feart me o 'my life, and pat hunches o' my skin as black an saft as a peat bog. Then the rain drizz'd ith' lift, and the snell gust pipe'd i' the howe. Wow, Sirs, 'tis ae awsome pass in murky weather. But ye may see it i' sunshine, wi' the purple heather fringing the warm neukes o' ilka crag; and ae fine day gars a' things blink bonnie." With a good deal of such chat as this, she waved kindly and courteously her plump arms after us, as we departed for Luss. As we left the town, we crossed the stream of the Leven, and just beyond, saw the castle rock over the bridge, having here a much more picturesque appearance than from the Clyde; the western peak being more conical, and that on the east more rugged and broken. The town seemed to be almost surrounded by water, particularly to the north and west, where it covers a broad flat, confirming the opinion already expressed, that the castle rock was once an island. There are some very extensive glassworks in the neighbourhood, whose great black cones emitting volumes of smouldering smoke, (however necessary and important in a commercial light), are a great eyesore to the lover of natural scenery. For the first four miles, we went along the same road as yesterday, through the pretty vale of the Leven, and then turned to the left, skirting the western shore of Loch Lomond. The road is sometimes sheltered by the natural woods and plantations that clothe the hills, and sometimes emerges from them and winds round the indented borders of the lake, affording a variety of magnificent views of the islands, Ben Lomond, and the other hills on the east. Crossed the opening into Glen Fruin, whose well-wooded sides rose above us on the left. This 'glen of sorrow,' for such is the meaning of Glen Fruin, was so named on account of a dreadful conflict which took place in it between the Colquhouns and the Mac Gregors in the time of James the sixth, 'who let loose his vengeance upon the cruel victors, the Mac Gregors, without either bounds or moderation. The very name of the clan was proscribed; and those by whom it had been borne, were given up to sword and fire, and absolutely hunted down by bloodhounds like wild beasts.' The dreadful detail may be seen in a note to the second canto of the Lady of the Lake.

A little beyond Glen Fruin, is Rossdhu, delightfully situated on a low promontory among large groups of spruce and silver firs, ash, sycamore and holly, several of the latter being of very large size. Between this and Luss, the banks are very finely wooded, and though the timber is not large, except in sheltered situations, it looks very healthy. After frequently stopping, to imprint more strongly on our memories, the rich scenes that lay before us, we came to Luss, or rather to a good inn a little beyond the few miserable cottages which form the village. We had leisure while the horse was feeding, to walk into the churchyard, where we saw the tomb of Dr. Stewart, who translated the Bible into Gaelic, and died here in May 1821. The church is small and mean, but its situation most romantic, standing on a promontory which projects considerably into the lake, and amidst fine oaks, spruce and silver firs, and some very large limes and sycamores. Over the tops of the trees which fringed the margin of the lake, we had a most lovely view of detached portions of it, of its various wooded islands, and of the mountains beyond, rising above each other very sublimely.

Luss is one of the southern boundaries of the Highlands, though here is no striking pass to mark the line of definition so decidedly as in many other places. The country is mountainous enough, but the transition is gradual, and not distinguished by one of those bold and romantic defiles which frequently mark the natural, as well as the geographical limits between the Highlands and the Lowlands. Before the commencement of the last century, little or no communication subsisted between them, as they were not connected by regular roads and bridges, and the entries from the one to the other, were, for the greater part of the year, impassable. In order to facilitate an intercourse between these different parts of the country, and to keep in check the wild habits of the Highlanders, Genl. Wade, under a commission from George the first, travelled in 1724, to the most difficult and dangerous passes of the mountains, and projected the bold undertaking of forming spacious roads in these rugged districts. In 1726 he began the work, and by means of 500 soldiers employed under proper officers, in the summer season, he completed it in 1737. Many of these roads are cut through rocks which it was thought impossible to penetrate; and pass through districts which formerly afforded no other thoroughfare to the natives, than the paths of sheep and goats, along which even the hardy Highlander crawled with difficulty, and kept himself from slipping down the precipices, by clinging to the shrubs and brushwood which 'took anchor in the rifted rocks'. Some of the rocks would not yield to the ordinary methods of excavation, and the miners were obliged to blast them with gunpowder; and he was frequently compelled to commence his labours, where nature denied him a footing, suspended from above by ropes on the face of the horrible precipice. The bogs and moors likewise presented innumerable difficulties, but all were at length overcome by the skill of the officers and the perseverance of the troops. In certain situations, they imitated the plan of the Roman soldiers, of engraving on the face of the rocks, or on stones placed by the road, the names of the regiment or detachment which the party belonged to. Though these military roads were of incalculable advantage in many respects, they were not always judiciously laid out, frequently running in straight lines over every change of surface, instead of winding round the hills according to the modern system.

Leaving Luss, we continued for some time to skirt the margin of the lake, and were highly delighted to find one of our rarest and most beautiful plants growing in the greatest profusion. It was the Saxifraga aizoides (sic), which we had neither of us seen more than once before, in one of our pedestrian excursious near Ambleside, covering the face of a wet rock with its golden blossoms. We also saw here, Pinguicula vulgaris, my favourite Parnassia palustris, Drosera rotundifolia, &c &c. The military road was narrower than that on the other side Luss and frequently the surface was washed away by the streams which passed over it in their descent to the lake. The original road strikes off to the left near Inveruglas, and ascends the promontory called the Point of Firkin by a very steep, rugged and arduous path, to Arrochar; this is now abandoned; and a new line has very recently been formed, which winds round the Point of Firkin, ascending very gradually from the shore of Loch Lomond to Tarbet. Here we stood as it were, on an island in the lake, and had on either side, a most magnificent view of it. In the projecting masses of micaceous schist which had so lately been blasted to form the road, we saw, during the course of many miles, sections of it, in which the wavy veins of quartz had a most beautiful and curious appearance, imbedded in the solid green substance of the stone. They were of a snowy whiteness, and of every thickness, from the 1/16th part of an inch to nearly a foot, uniformly preserving their respective thickness and parallelism, though constantly twisted and contorted into the most fanciful figures imaginable; as though the curled tops of the waves of a stormy sea had been suddenly arrested and turned to stone. It was very evident that this effect must have been produced by some violent agitation of the mass while in a half fluid state; no other idea will account for the freaky gyrations of the veins. The sinuous and wavy streaks of different colours seen in some kinds of marbled paper, may assist the imagination to form a correct idea of it.

The new road winds *very circuitously* round the bases of the promontories and headlands till it reaches Tarbet, where we arrived, not without making many pauses to reimbibe the beauties of the enchanting Loch Lomond, particularly the very crusty and cloud-curl'd ridges of the mountains round the upper part of it. I must not however, give all the merit to our enthusiasm for scenery; let humanity have its due; for the day was hot, and we sometimes stopped when we should not otherwise have done so, to relieve our horse, as we had found, even before we reached Dumbarton, that he was jaded, and that our progress would be very slow. At length about 8 o'clock, we reached the inn at Arrochar, where we embarked yesterday at the head of Loch Long, and immediately ordered dinner and insured beds. While dinner was preparing, we walked down to the beach, but saw nothing new, either in botany or geology. The scenery I have already described, it presents nothing striking, except the dreadfully rended rocks of Ben Arthur, which now looked black & horrid, as the sun set behind them. We find the 'Cobbler' is a modern as well as a vulgar name; till lately it was called in English, Arthur's Seat. From the window where we dined we had a constant view of it, above the smooth hills which rise immediately from Loch Long. It seemed to rear its head like the gigantic strong-hold or citadel of the 'Children of the Mist', far above the reach of the nether world, and in the region where they could enjoy their native freedom and security.

The inn is spacious and well furnished, and stands pleasantly among some fine groups of trees; but the accommodations were very indifferent. We dined upon herrings, with which all these sea lochs abound, and furnish occupation during the season for the bulk of the scanty population. By extending the influence of the sea breezes farther inland, the lochs also render the climate more temperate. Snow seldom lies long in situations not much elevated above the level of the sea; though it often falls in considerable quantities, and long continued frosts are not common. The first Gaelic we have hard spoken was on the road, near Inveruglas; where we met a man driving a quantity of sheep. He was speaking to his dog, and we were not aware that he could speak English, till he thanked us for drawing to the side of the road, in very good language, and without the broad accent of the Lowland Scotch. We found at Arrochar that Gaelic, or Erse, is the language usually spoken, but that most of the people can talk English, which they learn grammatically at school, as we do Latin or French.

Friday, 22nd July This was the brightest morning we had had since the commencement of our tour, not a cloud, or even exhalation from the loch was to be seen, and the sun shone so bright on Ben Arthur, that at Dovaston's request, I attempted to sketch it for him; but the size of his note book was too small to do it justice. When I had finished it, the gig not being quite ready, I set out on foot, for the fineness of the morning seemed to invigorate every sense, and to invite exertion. Passing round the head of

Loch Long, I saw a good many Highlanders, who mostly wore the Kilt or fillibeg, not of chequered particoloured stuff, but of coarse blue woollen cloth; the children wore the same. I spoke to several of the men, who answered me very civilly in excellent English, their cottages were on the bank to the right, and they said they were the owners of herring boats; but had caught very few fish this season.

Dovaston now overtook me with the gig, and it appeared that he had been ruffled in a smart dispute with the waiter. Being *banker* to the *expedition*, I had paid the bill while he was gone to take a last view of his admired Cobbler, and before I set out, had told him *all* was settled, without recollecting that a broken strap had been repaired the evening before. After I had left, the waiter also recollected it, and asked Dovaston for 1/6 for it; he told him his friend had settled all; each contended he was right, and as my friend is no little akin to the irritable race, he called the waiter a 'Scotch rascal.' "Sir," said the calm Caledonian, "I am indeed a Scotchman, but no rascal." Dovaston paid the 1/6; and on my recollecting that I had not paid it, he expressed a strong wish to go back and apologise; for, said he, a wagging tongue should have a warm heart.

We had now travelled four miles round the head of the lake, though not much more than one in a direct line from Arrochar, when we turned up to the right and began the ascent through Glen Croe, which is considered the second wild pass in the Highlands. Its length is about five miles, and the road has a continued ascent, the pitches occasionally very steep; and the naked rocks rise up from the bottom of the glen like immense perpendicular walls, particularly on the western side. After we left the side of Loch Long, not a tree, nor a cottage appeared for miles, and only here and there a little scanty vegetation: we were inclosed by wild and desolate precipices, rude without grandeur, with nothing to relieve the eye from the uniformity of barreness, except the enormous blocks which had been hurled from the heights and strewed the bottom of the glen, personifying a second chaos. Dovaston being still weak and unwell, I walked through its whole length, and found the rocks mostly of micaceous schist, with veins and patches of quartz. About the middle of the defile, I passed ten or twelve Highlanders repairing the road, and another seated on a tuft of heather, at a little distance from the road, reading. Just beyond them, a large and very broad green caravan, like those which contain wild beasts, was standing in the road without horses, on which was painted, 'Highland Roads and Bridges, No. 27.' A stout and rather short Highlander with swarthy complexion and black hair, and having more of the Celtic character than I had yet seen, was fetching water to boil his oatmeal and seeing me look at the caravan with some attention, set down his iron pot, and asked if I had any wish to see the interior. It appeared from my informant, that the great military roads are kept in repair at the expense of government, and the caravans furnished by it for the temporary lodging and accommodation of the workmen, the

Glen Croe

country being so thinly inhabited, that much time would be lost, in going to and from the widely dispersed huts. The respective parishes however, are not wholly relieved from the charge, as every male in each house pays six shillings per annum, or gives three day's labour. There is not a single turnpike gate upon any of the military roads throughout the Highlands. It is probable that the man who was reading, was an overseer or farmer of road, though I forgot to ascertain this. At each end of the caravan, were six oblong open boxes, which were the beds or berths of the workmen; they were placed one above another at right angles, the ends for the feet all meeting together, and only half the depth of the opposite ends, or head of the bed. In the middle of the caravan was a stove, so contrived that it would boil a pot; furniture of any kind there was none, not even a bench; I saw nothing but a bag of oatmeal and a few bed clothes. I expressed some surprize, and his civil and open demeanour emboldened me to ask if they had no animal food, bread, or potatoes? nor was it lessened when he said that their sole food was 'porridge', or oatmeal and water, seasoned with a little salt. Upon such simple food do these hardy people labour hard and brave the rigours of a Scotch winter! A powerful lesson to the pampered inhabitants of England, more than one half of whose diseases are the offspring of luxury and indolence.

When these labourers have repaired one part of the road they remove the caravan to another; some of them were 40 or 50 miles from their own huts. A little farther on, I saw some black cattle cropping the partial and scanty herbage, and near them a group of children, bare legged and in kilts, who were probably set to tend them; these could not speak English. I was now getting near the head of the glen; and looking about for a break in the tiers of rocks to afford a passage for the road, saw high before me, a very steep zig-zag staircase, and in the middle of it, Dovaston in the gig; but so reduced in size from the height and distance, that had I not known he was before me, I could not have recognized the shape of the gig and horse. I give the following extract from his Notes. 'The road now becomes extremely steep and zigzag. Bowman had got out at the bottom of the glen to walk and botanise; and as I was creeping up among the crags with the gig, we seemed often to be going different ways, and meeting each other. As I looked down on my friend, he seemed strangely diminished, and scarcely distinguishable, but by his motion, from the rocky stones; he reminded me of poor Piraneisi, in his own wonderful engraving, toiling up the eternal staircases. When I got at last to the summit of the road, having still amazing rocks towering above me, I saw him so near, apparently meeting me on the road below, that I called to him to climb up the cliffs, and save himself half a mile's walk, which he did.' I did indeed; but it was a road fit only for the chamois or the ibex; and it required all my agility and address to skip from crag to crag, and over the spongy spots that intervened, without broken limbs and soaked feet. When I at length reached my friend, he told me he had passed the spot called 'Rest and be thankful,' which was placed in the angle of the road I had avoided by climbing the precipice, and which I had therefore missed seeing. He waited while I turned back to see it. It is a semicircular seat formed of turf beside a trickling thread of water, with a good hewn stone bearing this inscription: 'Rest and be thankful 1748. Repaired by the XXIII Regiment, 1767.' The seat was placed to afford weary travellers a little rest when they have finished the long and laborious ascent; and truly thankful must everyone be when it is accomplished. It faces the original road of 1748, and is on the summit level. We experienced a strong current of air passing down the glen, as the day was becoming very warm. At the top of it, are some views which took our attention, from the contrast and relief they afforded, after the imprisoned desolation of Glen Croe. We passed a small mountain lake, called Loch Restal, in which I saw the Lobelia Dortmanna, and soon began to descend into the long valley of Glen Kinglas, of a totally different character from Glen Croe. Its length is about four miles, the mountains very high on each side, but smooth and covered with verdure, more simple and gentle, but not so wild and striking as the one we have left behind. The descent also is more easy; but the mountains still very vast, particularly the Stroan of Glen Kinglas at the bottom, standing at the head of Loch Fyne. The day was lovely and sunny, and light filmy vapours played round it, enwreathing, like breezy crepe, the brows of the highest crags; and we felt the force of the pleasing expression of good Mrs McFarlane, the Dumbarton landlady, that 'a fine day gars a'things blink bonnie.' For a considerable way up this glen, the stream which runs down it from Loch Restal, is skirted with flourishing larch plantations; and at the bottom, are some very extensive ones surrounding a fine mansion called Ardkinglas, delightfully situated on a promontory jutting into Loch Fyne, the residence of Sir A. Campbell. Over these, we had a lovely view of this beautiful lake, when about halfway down the glen, stretching its broad and level waters across the opening between the sidescreen with a distant glimpse of the pretty white town of Inveraray on its opposite shore. Loch Fyne, like Loch Long, is a vast arm of the sea, running up the country between parallel ranges of mountains in a fine sweeping curve, for about forty miles. On emerging from Glen Kinglas and passing Ardkinglas on the left, we came down at once upon the upper end of it; and after a short drive along its green banks, reached the pretty village of Cairndow, to breakfast.

  The road on this stage, though hilly and narrow, has a hard and smooth surface, being coated with small gravel and sand. After entering Glen Croe, we did not see a single cottage or hut till we came near to Cairndow, a distance of at least ten miles! Where could the soldiers have been lodged and fed, while making this arduous alpine road? In Glenkinglas we saw a few shepherds tending their flocks, and were particularly struck with the fine limbs and open countenances of several young Highlanders. Their costume was peculiarly elegant and pleasing: the fillibeg, or as we call it in England, the kilt, was of tartan plaid, reaching almost to the knee, the upper part (about six yards long when unfolded) gathered round; and flung very gracefully over the left shoulder; their head banded with the plaided blue bonnet, showing below their fine black or brown curled hair. They had not the prominent cheekbones of the Lowlanders; and on the other hand, the only one I have seen who displayed any Celtic blood, was the young man at the caravan. In person and manners, they are much superior to the lower classes in England; and their peculiar dress, in my opinion, sets off their fine faces and limbs to great advantage. We are told the Highland dress has of late years been much disused, particularly in towns and places on the coast, where they have much intercourse with strangers, and is principally confined to the more secluded districts of the interior. The fillibeg and tartan hose have generally given way to the trews, or trousers; but the blue woollen bonnet is still almost universal.

We were much pleased with our temporary accommodations at Cairndow, both the house and the inhabitants were civil and cleanly; we made a sumptuous breakfast upon Salmon, herrings, and eggs, in addition to coffee and toast. The freshness of the morning air and the laborious walk up Glen Croe, helped to make the landlord a hard bargain; he was inclined to be communicative, and gave us much information respecting the dress, manners, and language of the Highlanders and felt gratified at the satisfaction we expressed. In the room where we sat, was a bed of exquisite neatness in a recess, concealed by a fine plaid curtain. While at breakfast, we were much delighted with examining the Festuca vivipara which I had gathered in Glen Croe, and filled with wonder at the exhaustless bounty of the Great Author of Nature, in providing for the preservation of all his productions. In the highly important tribe of the Grasses Nature has in many instances gone out of her usual course, one of which appears in the plant before us. Found only about the cloud capped summits of the highest mountains, where a perpetually moist atmosphere would prevent the farina of the blossom from being developed, and the seed from ripening, she has endowed it with a power of bearing bulbs instead of flowers, which when at maturity, drop off and germinate! The Festuca vivipara is a most valuable grass in such situations, being highly nutritious, and the favourite food of sheep, who fatten upon a very small quantity of it.

From the beach at Cairndow, there is a most enchanting view of Dunderave castle on the opposite bank of the lake, and of the ranges of mountains and hills of different heights and distances sloping down into it, the lower tiers covered with the thick plantations of the Duke of Argyle, the more distant ones, barren, and towering above them. This view we afterwards saw from different points as we drove round the head of the lake to Inveraray, and I thought it of all others the most exquisite scenery I had ever seen. The road doubles here, as round the head of Loch Long, and in three miles returns opposite the inn on the other side, the lake being here only about one mile wide. During the whole stage it winds along the margin of the lake, and is raised on a low terrace out of the reach of the tide, with few and gentle inequalities. It passes close behind Dunderave castle, a square ruin with circular watch towers at the corners, resting on corbels, and having gathered conical tops. The view here over the lake is most lovely; it is impossible for language to convey an adequate idea of it. About two miles farther, as we were skirting round a point of land that encroached upon the lake, the town and castle of Inveraray suddenly and unexpectedly burst upon our sight, backed by rich hanging woods which rose to a great height, and varied by the precipitous and craggy sides of the hill Duniquaich, and so near that every feature was clearly distinguished over a narrow intervening bay of the smooth lake. The effect was like that produced by the magical drawing up of a curtain from before a fairy landscape. In passing round the head of the creek, we again lost sight of this scene of enchantment, but it was only for a moment, and to reappear in a brighter dress. We now found ourselves under the bold and picturesque hill of Duniquaich, whose broken crags were finely interspersed with trees which flung their waving branches in verdant canopies over the rifted fissures. We passed the magnificent chateau of the Duke of Argyle; and after crossing the steam of the Ara by an elegant modern bridge, a short drive along the shore brought us to Inveraray.

Inveraray, or Inverara, though a royal borough, and the capital of the County of Argyle, is not larger than many villages in England, and consists principally of a single row of modern and respectable looking houses, all whitewashed and slated, belonging, with a single exception, to the Duke of Argyle. It stands close to the shore on the western side of Loch Fyne; and between it and the richly wooded hill which rises behind it, is some very fertile land, in corn and pasture. The old town stood between the Castle and the lake, and being burnt down about sixty years ago, the present site was fixed upon; and this accounts for the modern and uniform appearance of the houses. As a good deal of English is spoken here, the kirk has been divided into two compartments, and Gaelic and English services are performed at the same time by different ministers. In a garden near it, is a monument with a long Latin inscription to commemorate the massacre of a minister and nineteen of the Clan of the Campbells (pronounced Caummils) who were basely murdered on this spot in 1685, and lie buried beneath. Not far from it is an elegant Town House, where the assizes are held. Inveraray sends one member to the Imperial Parliament; we observed throughout our tour, that the Scotch are always careful to call it the Imperial Parliament. There is little trade here except the herring fishery for which Loch Fyne is so celebrated; the fish are said to be suprior in quality to any found in the Western seas, and so numerous, that in some seasons the loch is said to contain '*one* part of water and *two* parts of fish.' Five or six hundred boats are sometimes employed, many of them from distant parts, and in a good season, 20,000 barrels have been caught and cured, each containing on an average, 700 fish. They are chiefly caught in the night, and cleaned and cured in the day; and each boat is partially covered with a roof made of sail cloth, to afford shelter to the crew.

Next to its scenery, the Castle of the Duke of Argyle forms the chief attraction of Inveraray. It is situated about half a mile to the north, the road passing through a noble avenue of beech trees; and stands on a gentle swell, surrounded by the noble amphitheatre of mountains which rise round the lake on every side. We repaired thither almost immediately after our arrival, and went through the whole of the apartments; but I should first describe its exterior. Its form is square with a round tower at each angle; in the centre rises another square tower of smaller dimensions, embattled, and having on each side, three large light gothic windows; and this is again surmounted with another and still smaller tower, also square and embattled. It is of a dull grey green colour, and so far, harmonizes well with the surrounding scenery; but its square and compact shape and boxy turrets piled one upon another, looked like a baby house of cards, or like the Borromean Palace on the Isola bella of Lake Maggiore, amid such an amphitheatre of luxuriance. It is said to be built of Lapis ollaris, or pot stone; but from a specimen I brought home, I think it is rather a soft variety of mica slate.

The hall, or vestibule, is very large, and open to the top of the centre towers, from which it is lighted. On the walls on each side, are large oval compartments, in which the muskets and bayonets used in the rebellion of 1745, are arranged in a radiating form, the muzzles pointing inwards, and the bayonets in smaller stars in the centres. It seems scarcely worthwhile to go thro' the detail of the state apartments; yet, as we had now got pretty well into the knack of taking notes, we practised it here, and I will merely transcribe them. 'In the north gallery was a small organ; in the Saloon, many fine family pictures, the later ones by Opie. The Duchess's Drawing room was hung with Italian tapestry; the subjects Harvest home, and a Country Marriage, the figures very spirited; the chimney piece was inlaid with a large slab of Tiree marble, in which I noticed horneblende. Tiree is one of the Hebrides, and belongs to the Duke. The turret rooms are circular and contain many fine paintings. In the Duke's bedroom is some beautiful light Gobelins tapestry, the colours very brilliant. The Duchess's dressing room is hung with painted paper, containing landscapes and figures relating the history of Louis the 15th. Here is a noble full length painting of the good and great John Duke of Argyle and Greenwich, by A. Ramsay, 1740. Dining Room, medallions in compartments, painted well to represent relief, very light and airy. In the Drawing Room, rich and splendid tapestry, the flowers wonderfully flush and bloomy. A grand pianoforte; fine minute tessellated quadrant marbles, standing on eagles; the furniture splendidly flowered and the roof highly ornamented with gold and flowery garlands. In the first Library, a full length of Lady Charlotte Campbell, sister to the present Duke, as Flora, by Sir Thos. Lawrence, lovely, beautiful; books numerous. In the second library, a full length of Lord Frederick Campbell, by Gainsborough; among other works, a copy of Boydell's Shakespeare, very superbly bound. All these rooms were on the ground-floor.' Upstairs, in the gallery, were antique statues, some of which, we could not at first sight recognise, and had not time to study; we went through many rich bedrooms, and were not hurried through, as in England, but civilly permitted to note down the particulars; but towards the last, the honest butler cock'd his eye through a window, and saw some ladies approaching, and somewhat hastened us, in fear of losing an additional fee. We then ascended one of the turrets and had a fine view of the Loch, the town of Inveraray, and a protuberant mountain overhanging Glenkinglas, called the Old Man's Head, from a very striking resemblance thereto. Ben Arthur was in this direction, but was not visible. This was a complete panorama of delightful scenery. We strolled into the park, through which the Duke has a ride under avenues, extending eight miles each way from the Castle. In it are some of the largest limes I ever saw, tall and healthy, branches very pendant and graceful, and in flower; large tulip trees, vast spanish chestnuts; great larches and silver firs, Dovaston and I girthed the largest we saw of the latter, which at five feet from the ground, was eleven feet in circumference. Some of the larches and silver firs had many years ago been broken by storms, and the heads were now crowned with twelve or fourteen large tops, having a singular and grand effect. The whole of the trees have no browsing line, and are feathered down to the grass. We saw but one Cedar of Lebanon, and that neither so large nor so elegant as those at Felton, planted by my friend's excellent and highly talented father.* His comprehensive mind grasped almost every department of science and of Nature; and among his multifarious pursuits, he was indefatigable to enrich his groves with the finest and choicest trees. Could he now look down, and witness the fruits of his labours, and see the veneration with which my friend regards and fosters them, both as memorials of him and for their own beauties, how would he be delighted!

We now, with many a weary step and frequent intervals of rest, ascended to the top of Duniquaich, wooded almost to the point, which is bare, having an old unsightly square tower. The hill is about 700 feet high, and very precipitous on its north and north east sides, as already mentioned. While ascending it, I saw one of the rare and beautiful silver spotted butterflies, Papilio Adippe, but did not attempt to take it, as the day was very hot, and I had no convenience to bring it home. Even on the summit, the heat was very great; and we threw ourselves down, quite exhausted,

---

* The largest of my friend's Cedars of Lebanon, has a circumference of 8 feet 3½ inches at five feet from the ground.

upon the velvet sward, to view in silence the amazing scene around. The blue expanse of waters, in perfect repose, lay stretched before us, studded with many a sunny sail; the nearer hills which rose from the edges of the lake, were completely covered with forests of dark pines, backed by the vast undulating and heaving mountains of Argyleshire, many of them at a great distance. The pale ghosts of Ossian rode on the light-winged gale; 'and each whispers in Fancy's ear as he passes, when noon-day is silent around.'

By the time we had descended and walked back to the large inn, we found dinner waiting. We had for the first time, the national dish of a sheep's head, which we relished more than did poor Owen at the table of Baillie Jarvie. In the evening we walked along a fine avenue of beech trees, which by our stepping we computed at twenty yards wide. We went about three miles, but it appeared to extend much farther. We left it, and strolled through a perfect forest of romantic trees, peeped up the enchanting glen called Essachosen, where we were shown a very large beech, called the marriage tree, which at about twenty feet high, divided its two boles, and twelve feet higher, perfectly united them, by an enormous branch naturally enarched and grown most clearly together. The air was now become delightfully cool and fragrant; and the numerous feathered tribes were singing in full chorus their evening hymn.

We walked back along the shore, where another lovely scene presented itself. The outlines and the features indeed were the same, but the effect was new and altogether different. A brilliant sunset tinged every object with a mellow, harmonious glow, and gave the idea of bewitching softness and repose. The gentle breeze scarcely moved the surface of the placid lake, but the margin, more visibly affected by the swelling tide, kept encroaching upon the sand as each successive wave crisped with a soft murmuring ripple against the silvery beach. Near the edge were some swans tossing lightly on the playful waves; while high overhead, we noticed a very large bird hanging stationary in mid air, its white plumage tinged with a ruby glow from the setting sun; when in a moment it dropped perpendicularly down, made a tremendous splash upon the surface of the water, and instantly disappeared.* After enjoying this delightful scene till the sun had sunk behind the western hills, we retired to the inn, and were occupied till a late hour in writing down the transactions of the day.

Saturday, 23rd July This was a most delicious breezy morning, and the day as yesterday, without a cloud. We left Inveraray about six o'clock, and passing through the noble plantations behind the Castle, entered Glen Aray, whose sides were clothed with fine forest timber, and among them, some very large spruce and silver firs. The sunset intervals darted his slanting

---

* We did not at the time know its name; but when we reached Newcastle, we described the circumstance to our good friend Bewick, who said he had no doubt it was a gannett.

beams through the branches which overhung the road, and lighted up a thousand sparkling glories, far more splendid than the diamonds which glitter in the crown of an eastern monarch;

> – a host
> Innumerable as the stars of night,
> The stars of morning, dewdrops, which the sun
> Impearls on every leaf and every flower.

This glen takes its name from the small river Ara or Aray, which runs through it and empties itself into Loch Fyne. It also gives name to the town; Inver, or Inner, signifying in the Gaelic, a mouth of a river, or estuary, and is synonymous with the Welsh, Aber.* It was however more applicable to the old town, which stood at the confluence of the river and the lake. We observed several fanciful and picturesque cottages in different parts of the roads, built in a taste which corresponded well with their situation among the trees, or amid glens, and under precipitous rocks, grey with lichen, or green with moss. About three miles from Inveraray we passed on the right, a pretty waterfall called Glouton fall, not large, but the rocky bed highly picturesque and overshadowed by the overhanging woods. I got out of the gig to enquire the name of it from

> a wither'd hag, with age grown double,
> Picking dry sticks, and mumbling to herself,

whom I saw near the spot. She was most disgustingly dirty, and fancy might easily have transformed her into one of Macbeth's witches. The plantations extended for about five miles up this glen, and from the very young trees of some of them, appeared to be still increasing. The road is altogether on the ascent, and in some parts very steep; and by this time we were got upon a pretty high level, the country became gradually barren, and the river Aray, which we followed up to its source, reduced to a narrow brook winding among the boggy mountains. We had no back view of Inveraray and Loch Fyne; but saw the mountains which form the rugged and indented shores of Argyleshire. We soon reached the summit level, indicated by the contrary direction of the streams; and observed before us, a very lofty mountain, which I did not recognize without referring to the map. It was our old friend, Ben Cruachan, which we had first seen from Loch Lomond.

What I could observe of the stratification and texture of the rocks, appeared to be schist and talcous slate, and occasional pebbles of granite, probably from Cruachan, the upper part of which is of that formation.

* This word, among many others, shews the affinity between the two languages.

Though the surface of the road is good, it is a succession of inequalities without any intervals of level ground. Some of the pitches were so steep that our Rosinanté had great difficulty in pulling the gig up them. Neither skill nor labour seem to have been employed either to avoid or lower them; Genl. Wade only thought of going in a straight line; and the result is, that this road is one of the worst laid down, and the most irregular we travelled in Scotland. I was therefore obliged to walk a considerable part of the whole stage, from policy as well as from humanity, as the consequences would have been bad, if either my friend or the horse should be rendered unfit to travel.

After toiling up one of these wearisome hills, I saw a solitary turf hut at a short distance from the road; and being desirous to examine its interior, and to form my own opinion of the way in which life is spent in these remote and desolate solitudes, I made towards it. It was of an oblong shape, about six yards long by three wide, and formed wholly of turf, the walls not five feet high, and the roof very steep, particularly at one end, where it rose a little higher in a conical shape, and ended in a smoke hole. A good deal of the smoke, however, was making its escape through the entrance. The interior was dark and gloomy, for there was neither window nor lattice; and the little light that was admitted through the roof and the door place, was barely sufficient to shew the blackened sides and the slender poles which scarcely supported the roof. The floor was of earth and very uneven; and at the farther end, under the aperture, a few peats surrounded by stones, were burning upon it. There was no chimney; and the draft was therefore so imperfect, that its smoke completely filled every cranny of the hut, and so impregnated the atmosphere with the empyreuma of the peat, that with the addition of other nauseous effluvia, it was very difficult to breathe. The only furniture was a bed upon the floor covered with a dirty rug, in a corner near the fire; an iron pot, and an earthenware half pint. I had made my way to the farther end before I perceived a figure sitting on a large smooth stone by the embers; he did not appear to be aware of my approach till I enquired if I was in the right road to Dalmally. He then raised his head, and asked if I had lost my way; and getting upon his legs, I perceived he was a tall elderly man, hale and strong, and wore a jacket the chequers of which were nearly reduced to an uniform shade by smoke and dirt; he had also a fillibeg, and his legs and feet were quite naked. I asked him several questions, the bent of which was to draw him into the open air to survey him more distinctly, and with some address I at length succeeded. His features were anything but Celtic; though his skin was so discoloured by dirt and smoke that his complexion was effectually concealed; and his eyes and eyelids were much inflamed from the same causes. I feigned to have lost my way, as Dovaston and the gig had passed on; he directed me right, though apparently but half awake; and when I turned my head after having left him, he had retired again to breathe the smoky atmosphere of his wretched hovel. Good God!

said I, could those who sleep on down, and revel in the luxuries of life, but see this picture, what a powerful antidote would it prove, to correct those imaginary evils which prey upon them, and destroy their real comforts!

The Highland huts, their exterior at least, are not all so wretched as the one I have just described: many of them are built of rude stones without cement; others have the stones embedded in mud or clay; but in the remote districts they are generally without chimneys and very frequently without any window place. I understood from several persons during the tour; that the Highlanders are so much attached to their ancient dwellings, that they can hardly be persuaded to exchange them for the more comfortable modern cottages. They are certainly much warmer, because the smoke and heated air must fill every cranny before it can escape through the hole in the roof. They may also possess another advantage so long as the want of cleanliness continues to pervade the lower orders; that of preventing diseases; for though the ventilation is slow, it is effectual and extends to every part of the building; whereas in the close modern cottages with grates and chimneys, the ventilation, though quick, is very partial, and the effluvia arising from the causes already named, are accumulated, and when other circumstances are favourable, they generate fevers and various diseases. The empyreuma of the peat smoke may also operate favourably in counteracting contagion; for it is a singular, though well ascertained fact, that bugs are never found, even amidst the greatest filth, where peat fuel is used; whereas they abound in similar cases, where coal is substituted.

Before I overtook the gig, I came in sight of the eastern end of Loch Awe, (pronounced Loch Howe) lying in a fine wooded valley on the left, interspersed with beautiful islands crowned with fine trees, reminding me of Loch Lomond. Its banks are also clothed with forests, among which, towards the western side, was a gentleman's seat. This lake is about thirty miles long, but very narrow, and is singular, in discharging its superfluous water by a small stream into Loch Etive, at its *farthest* point from the western sea, into which it runs. On a nearer view its scenery appeared to be rich and lovely, but it was too far removed from the eye. From the face of the country, I thought the road might have been carried advantageously along its south eastern bank. The lofty range of Ben Cruachan rises immediately from its opposite shore; its lower sides are covered with wood, but above, all is smooth and bulky barrenness. Its height is said to be 3,390 feet, and it ends in three obtuse conical tops, which rise round a crater; the crater becoming more visible as we approached Dalmally. It is composed principally of granite, and is of a pale or whitish red colour. It is said to be the weather guage of the people within view of its lofty top; before the storm, 'the Spirit of the mountain shrieks,' and its head and sides are enveloped in clouds. Some of Ossian's sublime poems relate to Ben Cruachan, and are said to be familiar in their original Gaelic to many of the inhabitants of this district. The last wolf in Britain was killed on this mountain in the year 1680; and eagles are still found here, notwithstanding the premium given for their destruction.

When I overtook Dovaston, I found him ruminating on an idea which had struck me very forcibly as I walked along. We were both surprised, after the respectable dimensions our imaginations had given to Loch Awe, formed from the space it occupies on the map, to see it so insignificant and confined. We even entertained doubts as to its identity till I had again consulted my map. On investigating the cause of this ocular deception, we found it in the immense naked masses of Cruachan, which rose in one smooth heavy pile from its shore, and was only broken into small cones near its summit. Though the superficies of its base, on the side we looked upon, extended to the length of about ten miles, its entire and unbroken surface and vast height, deceived the eye in a very considerable degree. It embraces it at once, and there is nothing else for it to seize upon, whereby to estimate its enormous bulk. Loch Awe therefore, which lies prostrate at its base, and in a valley far below the level of the point of view, necessarily suffers the same ideal diminution. Kilchurn Castle also, which stands nearly insulated on its shore under Cruachan, and is a very picturesque object, both from the magnitude and integrity of its towers, suffers in the same proportion. It seemed to our view only like a fairy palace, or as St. Pauls would do, if placed at the base of the Andes. When we first saw the base of Cruachan, it appeared to extend about two miles; yet we had not passed it when we reached Dalmally, a distance of at least ten miles from the former spot! Thus is the eye deceived in estimating the bulk of such vast objects.

In going down a steep pitch in the road to Cladich, our poor horse came upon his knees, and threw us both out of the gig, but fortunately without injury to himself or either of us. On the brow of this hill, we first saw the blue summits of Ben Lawers and Benyvue (Ben Venue of the Lady of the Lake) towering high above the tops of the nearer Grampians; and here we passed a road on our left which leads to Oban, crossing Loch Awe by a ferry. Cladich is a mean straggling village of huts, tumbled together like turf-stacks, and their gables facing all points of the compass, as if in defiance of regularity. They are chiefly covered with fern (bracken) the brown leaves beneath, and the strong stalks uppermost. Here we crossed a bridge over a small torrent with a very rocky bed. The surface of the country about Cladich is curiously undulated with natural mounds and green hillocks, which would seem to indicate some geologial peculiarity; but it was impossible even to guess at their probable origin from merely passing through it. They appeared to me to deserve attention. They are mostly covered with fine ash and sycamores, the former of very large size and apparently of great age, notwithstanding which they are luxuriant and healthy.

After leaving Cladich, we kept still winding along the shore of Loch Awe, the mighty base of Ben Cruachan still stretching far ahead. On one of the wooded islands called Inishail, is the remain of a monastery, and on another Inish Eraith, a chapel in ruins. Kilchurn Castle is a tall and stately building, in tolerable preservation. It was the original seat of the Earls of Breadalbane, and still forms part of their vast possessions. The view here is grand and interesting. It is to the influence of such sublime features of nature that we are indebted for the luminous glow of fancy, the happy combination of imagery, the sentiment, and the flowing diction of the poetry ascribed to Ossian. I shall record my opinion of the authenticity of this personage in another part of my tour. Without admitting it, I may however say, that the ancient poets of Caledonia, contemplating the magnificent yet gloomy outlines of their country, intuitively acquired that corresponding tinge of wild melancholy, so evident in most of their compositions.

From the hill before we descended into Glenorchy, the view of its pretty white church among groups of noble trees, principally scotch pines, and surrounded by wild and lofty hills, had a very cheering effect at the conclusion of our long and weary stage of sixteen miles. The scenery on each side is of a very different character; barren, wild, and vast on the left; on the opposite side, or rather before us, more picturesque and pleasing. The finest views have constantly lain before us; those behind, except when at the top of Glen Aray, of little interest. Almost close to the church of Glenorchy is Dalmally inn, where we breakfasted.

Glenorchy is a very scattered village romantically situated in the bosom of stupendous mountains which rise around it with horrible grandeur to the clouds. The cottages and huts, as well as the lower parts of the valley are interspersed with pleasing groups of fine timber, among which

> They peep, like moss-grown rocks, half seen
> Half-hidden in the copse so green.

The trees are principally Scotch Pines, and are probably the remains of those great natural forests which not more than a century ago, skirted these mountains nearly to their summits. The lower part of the land is fertile. The inn is called Dalmally, but whether this name applies to any part of the village of Glenorchy, or is a topographical synonym I cannot determine. The church and manse stand pleasantly on an oblong islet in the river Orchy, which is connected with the mainland by a very romantic and picturesque bridge leading from the inn. The channel is narrow, and the stream sunk so low between the perpendicular rocky banks, that it is not easily discovered to be an island. The body of the church is an octagon, the tower is square and lofty; but the most interesting objects are the numerous old gravestones which almost cover the burial ground. A large proportion of them are elaborately though rudely sculptured in relief, with figures of warriors, spears, claymores, animals of the chase, &c &c, and surrounded with knotted and entwined ornamental borders. Many of these have no inscriptions, but are supposed to be the tombs of the formidable clan of the MacGregors, whose residence and principal property lay in the vale of Glen Orchy. When we reflect that the dust beneath them was once animated by ambition or inflamed with revenge, and that the same sublime scenery by which we are surrounded, has witnessed their daring achievements and their acts of cruelty and rapine, the associations which History furnishes of the rude manners of those turbulent and dreadful periods, strike the mind with a peculiar force. We dwell upon them for a while with horror, but turn from them with delight and gratitude that our lot is cast in more secure and peaceful times. Other stones have hammers, pincers, and similar tools carved upon them, with borders like the MacGregors. These are over the burial place of the MacNabs, a family of blacksmiths who have been resident in Glenorchy for nearly four hundred years, each successive generation having followed their herditary trade. Its present representative does not degenerate, and has the reputation of making excellent Highland dirks.

The gravestones at Glenorchy are principally of hornblende slate full of black mica, with a few of talcous schist; many of them in the state they have been got from the quarry, thick and shapeless, and without even initial letters. Of the others, many of the inscriptions are in Gaelic or Erse, and the name of Campbell seems to be most common, being doubtless the clan of the Campbells of Loch Awe, from whom the Earls of Breadalbane are descended. For many centuries they resided at Kilchurn Castle, just below. Thus we see lying together in the peaceful sleep of death the mighty and the mean, the tyrant and the oppressed, the victor and the vanquished! The universal conqueror here, as everywhere else, has levelled all distinctions, and has extinguished the ardour of those restless and turbulent spirits, who spread fear and devastation everywhere around them. It seems to be the singular custom to insert the *maiden* name of the wife on these tombstones, thus, 'John MacAlpine died (date) also Ellen Campbell his spouse died (date)'.

Immediately after leaving Glenorchy, the road to Tyndrum ascends with very undulating windings into a vast elevated valley, the mountains on each side towering to an immense height, smooth and green, but without either a hut, a tree, or even a bush, to relieve the tedious uniformity of the scene, till we reached the latter place, a distance of twelve miles!

> But wilds, immeasurably spread,
> Seem lengthening as we go.

The worst possible line seems to have been selected for the road, which besides its continued ascent, is full of steep pitches. It was my destiny, for the reasons already assigned, to toil up and down them on foot, under the reflected rays of a burning sun, without my coat, and under the friendly shade of my umbrella. I had already walked two thirds of the first stage from Inveraray, and now first saw the impossibility of reaching Killin in the evening. As my weary eye stretched along the winding road in front, anxious to see the termination of the valley and a more level surface, it seemed like a long line of white tape thrown carelessly upon the ground, and gradually reduced by distance to a hair's breadth. When I had proceeded a considerable way up the valley, on looking back, I had a distant and partial glimpse of Loch Awe. Cruachan also, from being seen nearly in profile, appeared wonderfully foreshortened, and its outline quite changed.

The vast alpine valley we were now traversing, is characterized by nothing but barrenness and immensity; the race of man appears to be extinct; there is nothing to remind us of humanity, and no sound is heard but the rushing of the waters or the solemn roar of the winds. It is totally abandoned to the matchless finger of Nature, which Man does not presume to interfere with. It seems to admit of no description, yet has a soul residing in it, which, animated by its gigantic features, furnishes a recompense to counterbalance its silence and its solitude. Though it speaks a language clear and distinct, various and powerful, it is permitted only to pause and to meditate, but not to describe:

> These lonely regions, where, retir'd
> From little scenes of art, Great Nature dwells
> In awful Solitude.

After passing an insignificant lake, we began at length to lose sight of the now tiny rill which accompanied the road and to approach the summit level; the mountains diminished in height; the intermediate space was a flat turbary, and the blue and peaked Grampians rose before us in considerable grandeur. From the few opportunities I had of observing the formation of the mountains since leaving Glenorchy, they appeared still to consist of mica schist. We saw a few scattered and wretched huts and a single house, sprinkling the wide and desolate waste before us; and though we had strained our eyes in looking for Tyndrum till they were weary, we feared to trust ourselves with the idea that we were so near it, lest we should be disappointed. It was so prominently laid down on the map, that we mistrusted these hovels; – yet they were Tyndrum; a fit counterpart to the village of Lead Hills. The sight of a human habitation, (the first we had seen since leaving Glenorchy) the prospect of a temporary respite from our toilsome journey, and a bright day, divested it of a portion of its horrors, and we alighted at the solitary change-house with considerable satisfaction.

Tyndrum is situated among the mountains which separate Argyleshire and Perthshire, and is said to be the most elevated village in Britain. The celebrated Tay takes its rise at a very short distance from it, running towards the east. It has long been celebrated for its lead mines; yet notwithstanding we were told that there was plenty of ore of good quality, we understood they had not been worked for the last twenty years, when the company which held them, failed. They are the property of the Earl of Breadalbane, to whom also belong immense districts in the north part of Perthshire. I have been told they were never very productive; all the levels we saw appeared to be forsaken.

The noble proprietor with a laudable attention to the wants of travellers and to his own interest, has erected suitable inns at the different stages between Kenmore and Inveraray, a distance of sixty three miles. Without these it would have been impossible to cross Scotland in this direction. The inns at Glenorchy, Tyndrum, Luib, and Killin are of this description. We had already travelled today twenty eight miles; and finding it impossible from the worn down state of our horse and the heat of the weather, to reach Killin, we determined to make an effort to go as far as Luib Inn, twelve miles from Tyndrum. With very great reluctance, and after in vain discussing every plan we could suggest, we were compelled to give up the thought of seeing the beautiful scenery round Loch Tay, as we were obliged to be in Glasgow on Monday evening, to sail with the Steam packet for Staffa on the following morning. Had it been possible, we would gladly have hired another horse for the purpose, but we might as easily have procured one in the deserts of Arabia.

From the inn at Tyndrum we had a magnificent view of the high peaked Grampians under which we were to pass; particularly the group around Ben More. Each separate mountain has a peculiar name indicative of its height, its shape, its situation, or some other feature by which it is distinguished. These names are generally, if not always Celtic, and in this respect, as well as in their sound, bear a very strong resemblance to the Welsh; the two languages are indeed but dialects of the same original tongue. After leaving Tyndrum, we passed through a wide, uneven, moorish country, from which many lofty mountains rise on all sides: it is consequently intersected by many small streams, which ultimately run through Strath Fillan, and are so many souces of the Tay. We crossed the principal of these, called the Fillan, now, from the dryness of the season, almost lost among the crags of its rocky bed, but it would be a respectable fall after rain. We were now in Perthshire, and found to our great joy, a most marked improvement in the road. It has lately been much widened and levelled, the projecting bases of the hills being cut down and carried to fill up the hollows, and good bridges built across the streams. We soon entered Strath Fillan, a wide sweeping valley running parallel with the Grampian chain on its northern side, the lower parts principally in meadow land, and the pastures running pretty high up the sides of the mountains. Sheep and small cattle were grazing far above us, apparently no larger than emmets; and here and there was a solitary farm or hut, with scanty patches of oats or potatoes. The climate is too moist for wheat. About four miles from Tyndrum we passed on our left

A Nineteenth-Century Tour

the kirk and clachan of St. Fillans, near which is a spring, famous in these regions for the cure of maniacs! Oh superstition! when will the mists which thou hast thrown over the human mind be dispersed? The Scotch peasantry are probably the best educated of any in Europe, yet few are more superstitious. We asked each other, was this the spring over which the Minstrel Harp of the North had so long hung mouldering, when the incomparable Sir W. Scott took it down, and has since touched with such sweet and varied melody?

The kirk of St. Fillans is in the parish of Killin, which extends westward as far as Tyndrum, a distance of twenty miles in a straight line; it was built by the Earl of Breadalbane for the convenience of these remote parishioners. We found from a printed handbill, nailed on the porch of the little inn at Dalmally, that the Games of the Highland Society are to be celebrated this year at St Fillans. As the subject of this paper was new to us, my friend Dovaston, with some compunctious visitings of nature, contrived to get possession of it; and as it gives a copious account of the efforts of the Highlanders to preserve and perpetuate their ancient language and customs, I will give a condensed compendium of it, as it is very diffuse.

'*St Fillan's Highland Society Games, 1825.* The seventh annual general meeting will be held at the village of St Fillans, Perthshire, on the 30th August next. The office bearers and Committee to meet early, to make arrangement for the Games. The other members to be fully attired in the Highland Garb, and march to the arena of Games. Boys in Highland costume, will be allowed to walk in the rear of the procession, and have superintendants and two Pipers appointed to them. Among the Prizes offered for competition are the following; 1st To the best player of Pibrochs on the Great Highland Bagpipe, – A handsome full-mounted Pipe. 2nd. To the second best Do. A silver mounted Dirk. 3rd. To the third best, Ossian's Poems in Gaelic. 4th. To the best player of old Highland Reels on Do. a handsome brass mounted Dirk. 5th. To the best Dancer of the ancient Scottish Sword dance, a set of patent leather sword belts. 6th. To the best Dancer of Highland Reels, a Silver Brooch. 7th. Do. a Tartan Plaid. 8th. To the Boy under 14, the best Dancer of the Sword Dance, a set of handsome Dirk Handles, cut; also a Plaid. 9th. To the boy, the best dancer of Highland Reels, a Philibeg. 10th. To the member who shall compose the best Essay or Song in Gaelic, Ossian's Poems. 11th. To the best thrower of the Putting Stone (which is a bullet 22lbs.) A handsome silver mounted Snuff Mull. 12th. To the best at throwing the Sledge hammer, a large Silver Brooch. 13th. To the best at tossing the Bar, Do. 14th. To the best at the Broadsword Exercise, a large handsome pair of silver buckles. 15th. To the best shot with a plain gun, at a target, 80 yards distant, a handsome Dirk. 16th. To the best shot with a rifle gun (target 100 yards distant), a silver mounted Powder Horn. 17th. To the first Boat, at a Boat Race, a handsome

Silver Cup.' Other minor prizes are given to the second-best performers, making the whole number, 30, and the names of the donors of each are specified. Then follows a minute specification of the Regulations to be observed by the Competitors and in the distribution of the prizes.

The virtues of St. Fillan's spring had turned our conversation to the general prevalence of superstition, particularly among the inhabitants of mountain districts, and to a discussion of the causes which will probably always operate to keep it alive. Whether the Patron Saint was determined to punish our incredulity for setting his powers at defiance within his own territory, we knew not, but our horse, after many stumbles notwithstanding the improvement in the road, came down again and broke the crupper and other parts of the harness, throwing me a second time out of the gig! I caught hold of the splash board and threw myself from under the wheel, providentially without sustaining any injury. Dovaston this time kept his seat. The poor animal in fact was quite knocked up; I was nearly so; but to avoid farther risk, was determined to walk the remainder of the stage to Luib, though it was distant between eight and nine miles, and leave my friend behind to toddle on with the gig at a funeral pace. There was an additional motive for this; we saw just behind us, three pedestrian tourists who were probably bound for the same quarters; and as we understood it was only a solitary change house, it was expedient to ensure beds before their arrival.

I therefore pushed on; and the first thing I observed was a great quantity of the trunks of large fir trees plentifully scattered over the turbaries and on the uliginous sides of the mountains. They are the remains of the ancient forests which originally claimed so large a portion of Scotland, and are supposed to have been cut down by the Romans when they first crossed the Forth under Agricola. Though this will admit of very strong doubts, they evidently bear marks of having been felled by the hand of art. The bitumen they have imbibed from lying so long in the mosses makes them so inflammable that the Highlanders here dig them up for fuel and use them instead of candles; and it will be recollected that the torches which lighted up McAulay's Castle when the Cumberland squires came to decide the wager of the Silver Candlesticks, were of 'split bog pine.' I now came in sight of Loch Dochart, a narrow weedy lake about three miles long, into which the river Fillan flows, but on issuing out of it at the eastern extremity, assumes the name of the lake. Strath Fillan also terminates here, but the same glen continues far to the eastward under the name of Glen Dochart. Immediately south of Loch Dochart on the opposite side the road, rises Ben More, one of the loftiest of the Grampians, his highest peak being 3,903 feet above the level of the sea: the diameter of his base measuring north and south, is from seven to eight miles. On his opposite or southern side, is the forest of Glenfinglas, which extends to Loch Katrine and the Trossachs. Ben More was formerly a deer forest, but is now degraded into a sheep walk, not bearing a single tree on his northern side; but it is intersected by deep gullies formed by the wintry torrents. The little water they might now contain was lost amidst the huge rolled stones that choked them up, and was only known to exist by the richer verdure it imparted to the neighbouring vegetation; but it was evident from their width and depth, the vast bare stones and the rocks ground into holes, what furious uproar awakens the wintry echoes of these glens. I observed as I walked along, in the lower parts of these gullies, that the sand and gravel which forms their sides, has been deposited by the same causes which have formed the beds of gravel over the marl near Wrexham. I have also noticed it in many other places, and this adds another proof of the certainty and extent of some remote and vast catastrophe, not the effect of one, but of many successive inundations, though some geologists assert the contrary.

In point of scenery, Loch Dochart has few pretensions to offer to the passing traveller, except by contrast with the general features of the glen. Yet a few trees are scattered round it; its northern bank is occasionally precipitous; and at its western end stands a ruin of one of the many castles belonging to the ancestors of the Breadalbane family. It is nearly divided into two parts by a narrow strip of land, and over the vacant space, a large bridge is now building. It is supposed that it was on this narrow pass that Robert Bruce, by a desperate act of valour, narrowly escaped death by some of the followers of the Lord of Lorn, after an unsuccessful battle with that chieftain, in attempting to pass from Breadalbane into Argyleshire.

The aspect of the valley appeared to improve after I had passed Loch Dochart. The soil was a brown loam, lying on a gravelly or sandy bottom, and very fertile. The farms seemed well managed, and each had a portion of every description of land, as arable, meadow, green pasture, and moor. The mountains, as far as I could observe, were composed of micaceous schist, but of a very different appearance to any I have hitherto seen, being generally full of the common garnet, in octagonal, or dodecahedral crystals. I selected one specimen which I carried between four and five miles. Of plants, the only ones I observed of any interest, were Polypodium phegopteris and P. dryopteris, Pteris crispa, Plantago coronopus, and Saxifraga aizoides, the latter so common in Scotland, that it requires no farther mention. At length, weary and exhausted I reached Luib; but my anxiety was relieved when I found we could have beds, for the exterior appearance was not such as to inspire much confidence on this head. In about half an hour after my arrival I was joined by my friend, whose spirits, if not his body were as jaded as mine; but the pedestrians got in before him, and got but sorry lodgings. Our late dinner was but an indifferent one, though as good as we could expect at a solitary change house on the northern side of the Grampians. We ate it in high good humour, and when we had finished our notes, we talked over the events of the day and discussed our future plans, not without anxiety over a glass of whiskey. So large a portion of every evening was necessarily devoted to the business of the Journal, that it became excessively laborious, after the unremitting exertions of the day, and it certainly required considerable resolution to persevere. But we were aware that if we relaxed but for a single day, the constant succession of new objects would render it difficult, if not impossible to recover it. I had this day walked, as near as I could calculate, from twenty three to twenty four miles, a large portion of it over very uneven ground and during the heat of the day. The direction of the valleys lay nearly north and south, and the reflection of the sun's rays from the southern slopes was sometimes excessively oppressive. In the room where we wrote our notes, appended to the bell-rope, was the foot of an enormous eagle judging 'ex pede Herculem,' shot in the heights of Ben More; and we were told that a neighbouring laird had a pair of them then in confinement. They are so destructive to the sheep and lambs, that rewards are offered for killing them; but they build their nests in such inaccessible situations, that it is frequently impossible to take them.

Sunday, 24th July Being compelled to leave Killin and the scenery of Loch Tay unseen, we were in the gig before six o'clock, intending to breakfast at Loch Earn Head. The valley in which we slept here opens to the north, stretching into a wide plain, partially cultivated and interspersed with cottages, but the greater part of it in broad extended marshes and turbaries, or moory tracts equally unproductive and covered over by the Myrica Gale (bog myrtle) dwarf willows, and alder bushes. Beyond it were the mountains round Loch Tay, their outlines clearly defined through the hazeless atmosphere. The ambrosial scent of the Myrica exhaling with the dew which hung upon it; gave to the other beauties of a fine morning, a fascinating freshness. We gathered large quantities of it and placed it under our feet in the gig enjoying a perpetual fragrance. We soon left the Killin road, and turning to the south, began to ascend into the Pass through the Grampian range, which we were about to cross. The road was so steep that it was necessary to walk, to relieve the horse; but the bracing coolness of the air, and the ever-varying forms of the craggy precipices between which it winds, soon made me forget the stiffness I felt from yesterday's exertion. These precipices were generally perpendicular, rising to a great height on either hand, and appeared to be rent asunder by some great convulsion of nature; but standing firm upon their eternal bases, –

> There to remain,
> Amid the flux of many thousand years,
> That oft have swept the toiling race of men,
> And all their labour'd monuments away!

Full of these sentiments, and of the adoration they must inspire, I sauntered along, the pass becoming more wide and awful. The vast sunny solitudes were animated only by the alighting of a wheatear on a stone, or a falcon hovering among the cliffs; and the universal silence was only broken by the 'murmurs of the mountain bee' ere he hung his grey form dangling from the purple heather bell, by the feeble chirp of the red breasted linnet, or the cries of the eagle. All the way, the rare and beautiful Saxifrga aizoides (for I cannot help naming it) fringed the sides of the trickling gullies of the rocks, and the tall foxglove and the golden ragwort enamelled the margins of the road, changing the desert into a parterre. The rocks were altogether of micaceous schist, perfectly warty with the common garnet, the mica on the surface friable and glittering in the sunshine like silvery black lead.

My attention was now arrested by another and a very different object. Two figures approached me, dressed in the full Highland costume, of a brighter and richer hue than any I had yet seen. They were both on foot, and the one who walked first, was from his bearing and his gait, evidently a gentleman. His Tartan Plaid was thrown gracefully over his left shoulder, the colours being blue, green and black; his kilt or philibeg was gathered or frocked, and low enough just to shew his naked knees, the colours bright scarlet and green, and the crossing lozenges of his hose were rich scarlet and pale pink. In his bonnet he wore an eagle's feather, and his shoes were pierced round the soles with two or three rows of holes, to give a free passage to the water which enters them in wet weather, or in passing through bogs and streams; and which if it could not escape, would very much incommode the wearer. I bowed to him, and he touched his light airy bonnet, bending very politely. Behind him walked his servant, in a similar, but inferior dress, and carrying a leather knapsack of a peculiar make. The Tartan Plaid thrown gracefully over the shoulder, and indeed the whole dress, has a very captivating effect, and is very splendid.

I overtook my fellow traveller near the summit of the Pass, who feeling himself better than he had been since we left Glasgow, now got out, and walked on before me. It was wearisome beyond anything to drive our poor horse, as he could be urged beyond a very slow walk. When I had attained the highest part of the road, and began to descend, Loch Earn lay before me, and beyond it, the huge Ben Ledi and 'Benvoirlich blue' reared their towering heads into the sky and seemed to stop up the entrance of the Pass, though the filmy intervening atmosphere shewed they were at a considerable distance. The meadows and pastures on the borders of Loch Earn wore a more fertile and cheering appearance than those of Glen Dochart; and the sides of the lake were agreeably diversified with trees. After I had passed the defile, and within about a mile of Loch Earn Head, I came up to Dovaston, who was sitting on a stone waiting for me and posting his notebook, for to save time, we always carried them in our pockets, with pen and ink. He said he had seen an Eagle on a high precipice, which

sat alone,
Majestic on his craggy throne –

and had placed a large stone in the wheel track opposite to it, that I might look about me when I came to it; but I neither saw 'the stone of memorial' nor the eagle. Altogether after a tedious crawl of three hours, and a stage of rather more than nine miles, we reached Loch Earn Head; and enjoyed an excellent breakfast in a small parlour of the neat and comfortable inn, which looked out upon the lake, to which we were indebted for some delicious trout which formed part of the repast.

The small village of Loch Earn Head stands in a secluded and quiet spot at the western end of the lake. The surrounding landscape is not marked by any very striking features, but it possesses a sweetness and simplicity of character, strongly contrasted with the desolate valleys of Strath Fillan and Glen Dochart, and particularly with the wild Pass we had just traversed through the Grampians. The lake is about eight miles long and one and a half broad; the hills which rise above it, especially Ben Vorlich, are lofty, bold, and rugged, & the lower sides of the glens are frequently clothed with a profusion of natural forests of oak, with occasional copses and woods on other parts. There is something in the grouping and combination of the objects, not easily to be ascertained or described, which gives to the whole a bewitching expression of calmness and repose.

For several miles before we reached the village, we were overtaken by many well dressed persons, and while we were sitting at breakfast, we observed numerous groups, some on foot, but principally in carts or on horseback going along the road, or traversing the mountain paths which skirt both sides of the lake, and all moving towards the same point. On enquiry we found they were going to Balquhidder kirk, a village about five miles to the south, and a little to the west of the road we were going to Callander, to attend the Sacrament. We also found that this rite is generally celebrated only once a year in country places in Scotland, and that it is attended by a large proportion of the population of the neighbouring parishes, whose ministers also are present, and assist in the service, which continues for many hours. The annual celebration of the Sacrament is a peculiar feature of the established religion of Scotland; and has probably originated in the great extent of many of the parishes, which forbids attendance in the winter; and even in summer great inconveniences must often arise where the climate is so rainy. It is said the meetings are generally characterized by propriety and decorum, though it is not denied that they are sometimes attended by scenes peculiarly inconsistent and disgraceful. It is not surprising that these should occur among so large an assemblage of persons who have seldom an opportunity of meeting together and who consider it as a holiday; and where

The lads an' lasses, blythely bent
To mind baith saul and body,
Sit round the table weel content,
An'steer about the Toddy.

It is to be hoped however that the picture which Burns has given of the attendant circumstances, in his 'Holy Fair' (as the Sacrament is generally called) is rather caricatured. It is nevertheless drawn with inimitable spirit, and shews a deep knowledge of the human heart; while it displays many striking traits of Scotch character and manners.

We were much struck by the crowds that were continually passing; many of the young women very elegantly dressed, either in white or tartan plaid, without bonnets, and their caps bedizened with ribbons; but all bare-footed, carrying their clean thin shoes and white stockings in one hand, and an umbrella or silk parasol the other, the day being very hot.

It is highly gratifying to observe the strong and doubtless sincere religious feelings of these simple mountaineers whatever may be the articles of their creed, the Scotch are a highly moral people, and we ought not to doubt, the sincerity of their devotion will meet its due reward, even were their tenets less pure than they are. The sublimence of nature in these alpine regions is highly favourable to devotion; and a tour through Scotland would be made to little purpose, were not its ardour increased in our own breasts, amid scenes where the vast Spirit of Nature breathes aloud to the 'Universal Lord.'

We left Loch Earn Head about half past eleven, passing directly under the eastern side of Benvoirlich, and having Mealaonah (sic) on our right, both very lofty mountains; but 'fallen is Glenartney's stateliest tree,' for we could see no remains of the ancient forest of that name, near Ben Vorlich. The scenery is wild and sublime, and the land but little susceptible of cultivation, all that is not mountains being covered with heath and bogs. We passed through a line of wretched huts, called Raschachans, near which the road divides; and on calling at a house to enquire our way I found it was the village schoolhouse. On lifting the latch, for there was no lock on the outer door, I saw forms and desks in a room on one side, and a kitchen on the other, in which was some rude oaken furniture, and a good deal of bacon suspended from the ceiling. The house was quite deserted, the inmates no doubt were at Balquhidder, but it shews the simple and honest feelings of the inhabitants, that it could be left exposed so near to the public road.

In a wide opening between the mountains to the right we saw at some distance the 'heathery braes'* of Balquhidder, and beneath them, the little kirk, now surrounded by the population of the whole country. We were now traversing the district in which some of the scenery of the Lady of the

---

* *Brae* is a little hill covered with brushwood, and synonymous with the Welsh, *Bryn*.

Lake is laid, and passages from that delightful poem were continually occurring to us. This part of the stage is the country through which the Fiery Cross passed, to summon the 'Gathering' of the clansmen, and it will be supposed that we did not omit the opportunity which our slow progress afforded, to repeople it with the ancient Gael; to conjure up the frenzied Brian, sending forth the blood-stained emblem, and the male population simultaneously rushing towards the place of muster. Nor did we fail to contrast this imaginary scene, with the happy change of times and manners which has since taken place, when we saw the people moving from every quarter to Balquhidder, to perform their religious rites; – that people whose ancestors had so lately congregated for deeds of blood and revenge.

A little farther, at Innervoirlich, we came in sight of the long and narrow Loch Lubnaig, and passed along its eastern shore. It is about four miles long, and immediately from the foot of it, on the opposite side, the massive and lofty Ben Ledi rises, and gives a dark and gloomy tinge to its waters. The scenery here reminded us of the matchless Ullswater, though it is not so rich in trees, and the mountains and lake are on a smaller scale, except Ben Ledi. This mountain, from its outline, must be of the trap formation, but there is a quarry of chlorite slate, with a good deal of mica, on the opposite side the road. In Loch Lubnaig grows the Nymphaea alba, the leaves and flowers very small, and the large handsome Epilobium angustifolium; and on its sloping banks near that road, Geranium phaeum and Alchemilla alpina. I had already walked a considerable part of this stage under a burning sun. The horse made such wretched progress that we feared we should not reach Callander in time to see Loch Katrine and the Trossachs, and return this evening, so we determined at the foot of Loch Lubnaig, that I should walk on and order dinner, and procure a fresh horse for the purpose, and leave Dovaston to bring in the gig. I had scarcely left him, when I came to an enormous and powerful waterfall, just below the road on my right, on the opposite side a very lofty precipice, clefty and romantic, and well wooded from the summit to the bed of the river with brush oak. It was the far-famed Pass of Lennie; the entrance into the southern Highlands from Callander, named in the notes to Sir W. Scott's Glenfinlas. It is scarcely possible to conceive anything so grand and romantic; I had seen nothing equal to it in magnificence or similar to it in character; Rhaider y Wenol may perhaps be called a miniature and vague resemblance of it; but the magnitude of the Pass of Lennie, or Lenny, the wild and horrid shapes of the rocks, and the impetuous rush of the water, give it more of an alpine character than anything of the kind I ever saw. But this is not describing it; and though language cannot do so, I must attempt it. Midway up a very precipitous defile, a space is cut for the road out of the face of the rock; above it, the rended crags rise to a frightful height and pierce the skies; while below, the whole water of the river Balvay which issues from Loch Lubnaig, rushes impetuously down between the crags of the very highly inclined bottom of a narrow glen, which scarcely allow 'a passage for its pride.' At the top of the face, the rocks rise in a very sharp angle; and here the river is stopped by a huge block of slate, the stratification nearly perpendicular, and broken into keen edges and sharp points, which cut the body of water, forcing it into playful plumes of every size, light and feathery at the top, and falling with cool and coloured spray, into the black dismal and thundering gulf below. After passing the fall, the river hurries down, through many rapids and smaller falls, to Callander; near which it unites its waters with the Teith.

Callander is pleasantly situated amid verdant fields, so few of which we had lately seen, that the sight of them was very cheering. The screen of stupendous mountains which shelter it on the north, and through which we had just penetrated, give a peculiar interest to the scenery. But I had little time for observation. It was now nearly four o'clock; and in about half an hour after, Dovaston crawled in with the gig, having been four hours and three quarters on the road, and the distance from Loch Earn Head only between thirteen and fourteen miles. By the time he arrived I had dinner in readiness, but had not succeeded in procuring another horse – all were in requisition. The day had been so wasted upon the road that no time was to be lost; and as it was indispensable we should be in Glasgow the following day, we began to despair of accomplishing our wishes. At length, while we were at dinner, a man came in to offer us a pony, but doubted whether our harness would suit. The pony was at grass; and when brought and put in the gig, he was lame and unwilling to go. He reminded us of the one, Andrew Fairservice got in exchange for the horse he stole from Osbaldistone Hall, 'an animal with so curious and complete a lameness, that it seemed only to make use of three legs for the purpose of progression, while the fourth was meant to be flourished in the air by way of accompaniment.' But the owner of it assured us, as Andrew did Francis, 'the string-halt will gae aff when he's gaen a mile; its a weel-kenn'd ganger; they ca'it Souple Tam.' The prospect appeared so inauspicious that we refused to have him, and he was taken out and partly unharnessed, when Dovaston, said he would at all events make the attempt. It was half past five when we set out from Callander; the distance to the inn at Loch Katrine* was ten miles and the road very hilly. By dint of great exertion we contrived to reach it in about two hours; keeping the pony at a tolerable pace by alternately getting out at the steep parts of the road, and running alongside. The road branches off to the west, and till it approaches Loch Venachar is rather tame and uninterest-

* The orthography of this far-famed Lake is so unsettled, that a few words may be said to explain its meaning. The wild recesses by which it is surrounded, from their contiguity to the Lowlands, were long the lurking place of banditti, who issued forth into the cultivated plains of Menteith, and carried off the cattle &c of the farms, and hence the name. *Cateran* is a Gaelic word, signifying *banditti*, commonly pronounced Cathearn. Its similarity in sound to Catherine, or Katerine may have occasioned the common orthography.

ing. This lake is about five miles long and one and a half broad, and out of it issues the river Teith at its eastern end. Here is Coilantogle Ford, the point to which Roderic Dhu conducted Fitz James under his guarantee of safety and where the conflict between them took place. At some distance on our right was Ben Ledi, under which we passed this morning, and round whose base are many Druidical remains. Its name is derived from the Gaelic, Benledia, or, the Hill of God; and tradition says that the population of the neighbouring country assembled here during the times of Druidism, to worship the Deity. It would have been difficult to select a more magnificent temple. Its height is 3009 feet above the level of the sea; and *it is said* that from its summit, the borders of England may be seen. Before us, a glimpse of Ben Venue, and that group of rocks, in the heart of which Loch Katrine and the Trossachs lie, is now first obtained; the bold outline above, and the tree-tufted rocks below, which form the entrance to them, prepare the mind for the extraordinary scenery that lies beyond.

About two miles after leaving Loch Venachar, we came to the 'Bridge of Turk,' which crosses the Finglas river where it enters the eastern end of Loch Achray. This stream runs through Glenfinglas, an ancient deer forest of the Scottish kings, which lies between this spot and the southern foot of the Grampians. Before I reached Loch Achray, Dovaston had got out to walk, or rather to run, for his enthusiasm so hurried him along, that I soon lost sight of him, and we did not meet again till we had both been through the Trossachs. He was so totally absorbed by the scenery, that he missed seeing the inn where we had agreed to leave the gig, and went forward through the Trossachs till the precipitous path at the foot of Loch Katrine brought it to his recollection that the gig could not possibly pass along it. Thus had we the mutual misfortune to be separated in this wonderful spot.

By this time the scenery had assumed a more varied and rich appearance, and as I skirted the northern side of the small Loch Achray, I had a full view of its opposite bank, thickly wooded from the verge of the water to the top of the rocks which rose above it. Here I caught a distant glimpse of the Trossachs, which look at first but as little woody crags, scattered very wildly, and in great confusion, across the western extremity of the lake. Before them, several rocks of a round form and inferior height, well clothed with wood, stud the gloomy surface of the water, and form 'the native bulwarks of the pass.' If the brightest tints of their summer dress did not give to the trees which clothe these rocks, a mantle of inexpressible beauty, the outline of the scenery would be awful and terrific, overshadowed as it is by the enormous bulk of Ben Venue rising just above it. When I reached the inn the precipices rose around in such fantastic and bewildering forms, that I appeared to be at once transported into the regions of romance. Here I could learn nothing of my friend. There was no time to be lost; and I hurried alone into the Trossachs, whither I doubted not, he was gone before me.

A Nineteenth-Century Tour

The glen, called the Trossachs* is a very narrow and irregular natural defile, through which the river Teith, issuing from Loch Katrine runs with a wild and foaming impetuosity over a deep and rocky bed, overshadowed by picturesque trees which give a gloomy tinge to its angry waters. Its whole length, including the labyrinth of windings, is nearly two miles, but the huge rocks which project into it from each side prevent the eye from seeing much of it at once.

This wonderful pass is a combination of all that is wild, romantic, and sublime; as though Nature had collected here, in the greatest profusion, every production of her power, and grouped them with the utmost fascination of her fancy;

Crags, knolls, and mounds, confusedly hurl'd,
The fragments of an earlier world.

The road which winds through the pass is in some places artificially cut out of the rocks, sometimes raised, various methods having been resorted to, to effect a passage along it. The walls of rock generally rise perpendicularly from the bottom, often to a great height, crags being piled upon crags, and tier upon tier, receding or projecting, stratified or massive, rugged or smooth, and assuming every fantastic form of castles, turrets, towers, or battlements, and rising in the very confined and lofty horizon of the sky, in pyramids and pinnacles. Some of the masses project far into the defile, bald and grey with lichens, their fissures clothed with shrubs, and their more prominent parts interspersed with tufted knolls of purple heather, golden furze, and the light, blue harebell,** which caught the sunbeams, and blazed like particoloured gems. The intervening recesses are fronted with oaks, ash, and large ancient birch trees, that wave their venerable tresses over the dark and gloomy clefts and foaming torrents which they conceal. The scene changes at every step, and as the road winds in sudden sinuosities, sometimes presents dark and yawning chasms, and sometimes the open face of a broad rock, feathered with birch trees of every size and form, light and airy as the clouds, and fretted with peeping fragments up to the sky. These now resign their office of sentinels to other rocks, similar in general character, but ever varying in detail, and often broken into smaller parts, thrown out in high relief, or running back in all directions into little glens of a more lively appearance, and often of incomparable beauty. It seems as if multitudes of mountains had been shattered into immense fragments, and thrown about at random by some capricious power, and piled upon each other with all their appendages of heaths and trees, ferns and wild flowers. It

---

* In the Gaelic, *Trossach* signifies a rough and rugged region.
** Campanula rotundifolia, the harebell of poets, but not of botanists.

is at once a wilderness and a paradise, and may be conceived to be the vestibule of some gigantic enchanter's palace. It is such a mixture of sublime magnificence and exquisite beauty, that so far from being made tangible by any description, imagination could not have conceived it; no magic, not even that of poetry, ever embodied or delusively presented to the delighted eye, so enchanting a region of wildness and sublimity. Many of the rocks are of stupendous height, and the defile in some places, is so narrow, that the trees which crown their summits, seem almost to meet and to exclude the sky.

At length I reached that part of the defile where Loch Katrine first appears, and on whose margin a small boat was moored, with a crane hanging above, whose use I could not discover. The bold rocks from both sides approach so nearly to each other, that the lake seems only like a little creek or harbour; some of them rise so precipitously as to overhang their bases, and tower so high above it, that the water is thrown in to deep shade and has a gloomy and horrible appearance. These rocks are, I apprehend, a part of the vast Ben Venue, whose summit appears towards the south, overlooking the varied scenery beneath, in awful sublimity. Some of them are barren and naked, others beautifully fringed with trees, shrubs, and purple heather, disposed into innumerable groups, and bending over the projecting promontories which almost choke up the lake. But below, every object was wrapped in gloomy shade and death-like stillness, which gave to the whole a spell-bound and almost supernatural character. The road is a rocky footpath, cut with great labour along the northern side of the lake, sometimes skirting the shore, and sometimes ascending by a rude staircase to a considerable height on the top of inferior precipices or terraces, with a glacis of rock springing above and encroaching so much upon it, that 'There scarce seemed footing for a goat.' Before the present road was formed, the only mode of visiting the lake was by a path down a steep descent, and with the assistance of a rope made of osier or birch twigs fastened to the trunk of a tree. I proceeded along this dizzy and dangerous path for upwards of a mile; among a perfect wilderness of ravines and precipices, heights and hollows, for ever varying, presenting suddenly new objects before, and different combinations of those behind. At every turn the lake appeared to widen; but its shores were again indented into every form by jutting masses of rock and black caverns, over which the shrubs that anchored in the clefts above them spread their fanlike branches and formed an inverted and softened landscape on the glassy surface. We learned that after sudden and heavy rains, thousands of spouting torrents rush down the fringed hollows and toss their spray in wanton airiness, curling on the dark surface of the lake with silvery foam, and rolling in impetuous thunder among the dismal caverns.

This road extends along the whole northern border of Loch Katrine, but I had understood the scenery became less romantically wild as it proceeds to

Head of Loch Katrine

the westward. The day was now fast wearing away; and not knowing where my friend might be – for I kept continually calling, and was answered only by the echoes – I thought it right to turn back, as I knew he would regret our separation equally with myself. The sun was now fast sinking towards the horizon; and the curling and graceful tops of the pendant birch trees catching his rays through some of the openings in the rocks, were turned into a bright golden fringe, and formed a glorious contrast with the darker trees, brown rocks, and black water below. Shortly after, I saw him sink behind the vast curly mountain Mealaonah; watching him till he disappeared in a spot of burning light. At once the mountain became of a purple shade, having its ridges tinged like the edges of a massy and accumulated thundercloud; while through many of its splintered clefts the sunbeams shot out in long misty rays, and flashed on the woods and

Ben Lomond from Loch Katrine

wild flowers in golden splendour. The more confined parts of the Trossachs were now become darker and more dismal, and when I reached the inn, the twilight was coming on apace. Here I was soon joined by my friend, who had been altogether before me, and had proceeded as far as the Lady's Island, which he described as large and covered with heather and graceful birches, many of which dipped their tresses into the water. Beyond this spot the lake widens towards the west, and is seen to a great distance, being closed by Ben Lomond and the still farther mountains of Argyleshire.

Of all the fairy scenes which Scotland had hitherto presented to our observation, the Trossachs and Loch Katrine must undoubtedly be set down as the most enchanting. The views are altogether foregrounds, but there is more wood, and it is more beautifully and variously grouped on the surface of the rocks than I ever saw before. The effect of the warm evening sun upon the pensile foliage of the elegant birches and upon the flowers, was excessively brilliant and striking, and just as it is described in the first Canto of the Lady of the Lake. Who that has a mind the least sensible to the charms of Nature and of Poetry, can fail, while rambling here, to bear testimony to the spirited fidelity of the picture which Sir W. Scott has drawn of it in that bewitching gem of poetry? Though the scenery is new and enchanting, we recognize it at every turn, by his luxurious touches, and when we attempt to describe it, it is in his glowing language.

The house where we rejoined, is called Stuart's inn from the name of the landlord, who, I am since told, is a descendant of the royal race, and a staunch defender of their religious and political principles, and openly avows them to any gentleman who converses with him upon them. We were not then aware of this, or should probably have taken the opportunity which a note we had brought for him from Callander, to forward a book belonging to a Mr. Salway, afforded us, of drawing him out a little.

After a hasty snack, we immediately set out; the natural twilight of the season, and the moon, now about ten days old, afforded sufficient light to distinguish our road and her beams played gently on the surface of Loch Achray and Loch Venachar as we passed them. It was nearly midnight when we reached Callander, having once missed our way for about a quarter of a mile. We again took some refreshment and hastened to our chambers, but not to bed; we had still a laborious but indispensable task to perform – the writing out into our journals the scrap notes we had taken since leaving Loch Earn Head. To arrange and to embody them, in our present exhausted state, was neither an enviable nor an easy occupation; but in the morning we had to seek out a fresh horse to take us to Glasgow, and there was no alternative but either to write them out now or to lose them for ever. Our enthusiasm supported us, and these pages are now a pleasing record of our choice, and of the resolution and exertion we were compelled to summon up. Any attempt at description of the Trossachs, flung off by the most gifted mind, under the happiest opportunities of ease, leisure, and inspiration, can at best give but a faint idea of their rich labyrinths and enchanting beauties; much less could notes written hastily after midnight, under wearisome fatigue and drowsy inactivity. When I recollect the inauspicious circumstances which attended this part of our journey, I feel rather disposed to be satisfied with what was done, than to regret that more had not been performed. I continued writing till two o'clock, when falling asleep in the chair, I was roused by Dovaston, who was still plying at his task, and bent upon completing it. Nature was quite exhausted, and I found it necessary to recruit her by a few hours' repose.

Monday, 25th July   I rose at five o'clock, and before seven had posted up the arrears of my Note Book. Dovaston shewed himself a more complete man of business, and finished his before he went to bed, which was near four o'clock.

Our first care was to provide another horse; for we were so completely wearied with our own, that we determined if possible to be rid of him. The distance to Glasgow was thirty-six miles, the road very hilly and the day likely to prove very hot, and we felt certain the one we had, could not perform the journey. After a good deal of trouble, in which the waiter at the inn very kindly and feelingly took a part, we engaged the only one that seemed likely; the owner undertaking to ride ours and bring his own back the following day. It was half past eight when we left Callander, intending to breakfast at Port Menteith and to pass through Fintry. After a few miles driving, we had the mortification to find out that the horse was not much better than the one we had left behind. But a still worse misfortune befell us; from our imperfect knowledge of the country, we were induced to bear too much to our right, in order, as we thought, to wind round the western end of the Campsie hills; in consequence of which, we missed our road soon after leaving Callander, and did not discover the mistake till it was too late to rectify it. The country was most inhospitable and barren; made up of low black-looking hills and intervening bogs, and is very faithfully described in the following words, taken principally from Rob Roy: 'Huge continuous heaths spread before, behind, and around us, in hopeless barrenness, now level and interspersed with swamps, green with treacherous verdure, or sable with turf, or, as they call them in Scotland, peat bogs, and now swelling into huge heavy ascents, which wanted the dignity and form of hills, while they were still more toilsome to the passenger. There were neither trees nor bushes to relieve the eye from the russet livery of absolute sterility. The very heath was of that stinted imperfect kind which has little or no flower, and affords the coarsest and meanest covering which mother earth is ever arrayed in. Living thing we saw none, except occasionally a few straggling sheep of a strange diversity of colours; the very birds seemed to shun these wastes, and no wonder, since they had an easy method of escaping from them. The few miserable hovels that shewed some marks of human habitation, were of still rarer occurrence.'

The distant scenery was of a more cheering character. Behind, was the lofty and magnificent range of the Grampians, stretching along the distant horizon from the Ochill and Lamont hills on the east, to Ben Arthur and the Argyleshire mountains on the west, throwing up their vast conical masses into the sky, and appearing in the burning atmosphere, of an uniform blue grey tint. We could now recognize most of them by their peculiar outlines and call them by their individual names. Before us, the view might be said to be almost boundless;

> Commanding the rich scenes beneath,
> The windings of the Forth and Teith,
> And all the vales between that lie,
> Till Stirling's turrets melt in sky.

This wide open plain, seen over the low moory hills about us, is 'the varied realm of fair Menteith,' and extended to the foot of the Campsie Fells,* whose long and level ridge bounded the view to the south. We saw the beautiful Lake of Menteith, on whose banks we were to have refreshed ourselves, lying far beneath us in this plain to the east, surrounded by trees, while we were compelled to toil through the labyrinth of cross roads in which we were entangled without being able to escape from them. They were so full of steep pitches, so rough and rutty, and so scattered with large stones, that every now and then we were obliged to draw the gig out of the wheeltracks, to escape being overturned. Beyond the Lake of Menteith we saw the barren and desolate flat, called Moss Flanders, covering many thousand acres, and said to be the most extensive peat moss in Britain, lying in a valley. The depth of the peat is about fifteen feet, and in the solid alluvium which lies beneath it, the roots of oak trees are found fixed in their natural position, with trunks of immense size lying beside them. This district exhibits the most decided mark of having been covered by water; at an earlier period it is on record that it formed part of the ancient Caledonia Sylva of the Roman historians.

We passed through several mean villages, but could not in any of them see a clachan or a change house that could furnish us with a breakfast, or our jaded horse with a few oats. Aberfoil was but a few miles to our right, but we could not afford to lengthen our tedious journey by any deviation, and had already sufficiently proved the truth of our Dumbarton landlady's description of these wretched roads. On crossing the Forth, here a very insignificant stream, we distinctly recognized, to our right, the finely wooded round hill on its banks, where Baillie Jarvie said 'the Fairies wonned' (dwelt). It was also but a short space from this spot, where Rob Roy escaped from the English party in the twilight of evening. But we were weary and out of humour, and toiled up and down the dreary hills that rose one above another in interminable succession, with scarcely enough of animation to converse together. Our poor horse was so distressed by the great heat and the miserable roads, that out of sheer humanity I walked a large portion of this long stage, without my coat, and protected by my

---

* These rise 1500 feet above the level of the sea.

umbrella from the scorching sun. Never can I forget the labours and fatigues of this day. At length about two o'clock we came to the pretty village of Balfron, where after a toilsome journey of full twenty miles, we first broke our fast, and were much cheered by learning that the remainder of the road to Glasgow, a distance of nineteen miles, was very good. We were also consoled a little by hearing that if we had gone through Fintry, we should have found it no better. We had been much annoyed while bewildered in the cross roads, at the ignorance of the few inhabitants we could see, when we enquired our way, we were several times misled. One told us it was only three miles an'a bittock to Balfron; when we had gone this distance, and enquired again, it wanted five miles and a bit; and thus we were tantalized. We had often remarked before, that when the Scotch give directions to travellers, they do it by the points of the compass, saying, turn to the east, or to the south, &c as the case may be. This is more significant than the English mode of right and left; they also give the distances in English miles, because the Scotch miles are longer; but in this instance they were the *longest* miles we ever travelled.

The heat was so excessive that we remained at Balfron till half past four o'clock, when we made a short stage to Strathblane, and baited again, passing through Killearn. This latter village derives celebrity from being the birthplace of George Buchanan, the elegant poet and historian of Scotland, and in it, near the road, we saw a substantial obelisk, one hundred feet high erected to his memory, but without any inscription. This celebrated man was tutor to the Regent Murray, the natural son of James the Fifth, who when he came to power, nominated him to be preceptor to James the Sixth. Buchanan had previously renounced the Romish faith. He was opposed to Queen Mary, and made a virulent attack upon her character, charging her with the murder of Darnley, and with a criminal passion for David Rizzio. His History of Scotland, written in Latin, is said to combine the brevity of Sallust with the perspicuity and elegance of Livy.

Strathblane lies at the western foot of the Campsie Hills; and when we had passed them, (having kept them in sight since leaving Callander) the country improved both in cultivation and in trees; as a proof of which, the largest oak we had seen in Scotland, stood by the roadside near Strathblane. It has a short sturdy trunk and branching arms, and must be at least two hundred years old. Soon after leaving this place, we took our farewell of the towering alps among which we had been winding so many days. Ben Lomond and the frightful Ben Arthur (Cobbler) shewed their superior height and grandeur to the last, the latter retaining his peculiarly craggy outline till we finally lost sight of him behind the Campsie Fells.

I have little else to record of a tour which has afforded such a variety of pleasure and disappointment, of recreation and excessive labour. It was our misfortune to be impeded by a horse worn down when we set out, but the grandeur of the scenery inspired us with an enthusiasm which enabled us to surmount every obstacle, and with an ardour which rose superior to fatigue. Our minds were in a state of continual excitement. The delay, and the consequent anxiety lest we should miss the opportunity of seeing Staffa, occasioned some temporary unease and my feet and ankles were very much swollen with walking; but the only permanent regret arises from our not having seen the borders of Loch Tay: while the impression of the beauties of Inveraray and Loch Awe, the grandeur of Glen Croe, the Passes of the Grampians and of Lenny, and above all, of the Trossachs and Loch Katrine, where beauty and sublimity are combined, will remain upon the memory for ever. We were highly favoured by the weather, and were content to endure the oppressive heat, so long as we continued to enjoy the advantage of the cloudless atmosphere which accompanied it. For though there are intervals in a rainy season when clouds and storms give to mountain scenery its highest magnificence and sublimity, more leisure than we could afford is necessary to watch for these effects, and days and weeks frequently pass away without obtaining even a view of its outlines.

We reached Glasgow about nine o'clock, and alighted at the door of our friendly and goodhearted landlord, honest Mr. Neilson, with feelings such as a weary traveller entertains on returning home after a tiresome journey. This part of our tour had occupied five days, and embraced a circuit of about one hundred and ninety miles through the interior of the Southern Highlands of Scotland.

We had this day a striking instance of the strong contrasts of Scotch scenery. The former part of our journey lay between two of the most enchanting spots in Britain, Loch Lomond and the Trossachs, and the absolute distance of each was but a few miles; yet they were concealed from our view by the surrounding mountains, and the intermediate space was occupied by a bleak and desolate tract which denied subsistence to the hardiest animals. We afterwards experienced that sudden contrasts generally prevail in the Highlands; and give additional charms to the favoured spots. The most picturesque views lie in sheltered situations along the rivers and the lakes, and upon the coasts; and between them the traveller has frequently to pass over long dreary districts, which are fatiguing from their uniformity and repulsive from their sterility.

Tuesday 26th July In the course of yesterday evening we told our adventures to our worthy landlord over a glass of toddy; and he was of the opinion that MacFarlane ought to make some deduction towards the additional expense we had incurred in hiring another horse, and proffered his friendly interference. The wily horse dealer was with us before breakfast, and was quite prepared for our complaints; but far from paying any attention to honest Neilson's arguments in our favour, he fortified his own case by accusing us of having worked his horse hard and withheld his feed. This we could disprove by our Note books and several of the bills we found accidentally in our pockets; but he threatened to take us before the sitting magistrate if we did not immediately discharge his full demand. Dovaston was very much disposed to accompany him there, feeling confident he should obtain redress, but several gentlemen present told him it was very doubtful. Even had we been successful, this remedy would have been worse than the disease; for the delay would have deranged all our plans, and have prevented us from seeing Staffa, one of the grand objects of our northern tour. We were aware the fellow was a rascal, I thought the only way to be rid of him was to satisfy his rapacity. The owner of the Callander horse also attempted an imposition, but this we successfully repelled. We had agreed to pay him a guinea on our arrival in Glasgow, which was to include every expense of his own journey; he now said we had agreed to give him twenty four shillings and to defray his charges. By the time these unpleasant altercations were ended, and we had settled our accounts at the Prince of Wales, it was ten o'clock, the time for the sailing of the Highlander Steam Packet, which was to carry us through the Hebrides. We hurried down to the Broomielaw, and got on deck just as the Bagpipes gave the signal for her to get under weigh.

As we dropped down the Clyde and watched the towers of Glasgow recede finally from our sight, we could not help contrasting the ease and pleasure of this mode of travelling with the extreme toil of our late journey. It was delicious to recline on deck, and to gaze on the clear and expansive estuary, with the sweet landscapes on its banks gliding before us, and to watch the summits of the rocky islands as they hove successively in sight. This was the third time we had sailed along it; and as I have already described its beautiful scenery as low down as Dunoon Castle on the Argyleshire coast, and the Lighthouse of Cloch on the opposite northwest coast of Renfrewshire, I shall now resume my account of it from the ferry between them.

The company on board was rather numerous and very respectable, and I shall have occasion to introduce some of the individuals by and bye. The heat was very great, and the atmosphere so hazy, that we could only distinguish the outlines of the Argyleshire mountains before us. It gradually cleared as we rounded the Cloch Lighthouse and changed our course from west to due south. When we had passed Dunoon Castle, it appeared to project into the estuary on a green undulating slope, and to be still more a ruin than before. The view from it is said to be one of the most extensive and variegated on the Clyde, stretching from near Dumbarton Castle to the rock of Ailsa – comprehending the coasts of Dumbartonshire, Renfrewshire, Ayrshire, Argyleshire, and Bute – displaying an immense expanse of ocean, animated with the ever moving vessels of commerce and pleasure, and exhibiting all the diversity of mountain, valley, wood, rock, and coast scenery.

The Argyleshire coast from Dunoon to Toward Point, is generally bold and high, varied by more sheltered spots, sprinkled with houses, and skirted with patches of cultivated land and of natural wood, which run up the indented sides of the hills. The opposite coast of Renfrewshire is everywhere characterized by cultivation, by woods, towns and villas, displaying with all the marks of wealth and dense population, many scenes of picturesque effect. We were particularly struck with the beautiful situation of Ardgowan, the seat of Sir M. Stewart Bart. near Inverkip. The low green island of Great Cumbray lay before us to the south, and we were making directly for it, when on approaching Toward Point, the vessel suddenly veered about, and took a westerly course. The view here became very extensive, and the estuary very wide, and the high craggy summits of Arran were seen overtopping the lower and somewhat more fertile lands of Bute. On the mainland, opposite Cumbray is the village or town of Largs, in Ayrshire, stretching along the beach. The climate here is so remarkably mild, that it has been termed the Montpelier of Scotland. Near it was fought a very celebrated battle in 1263, between the Scots and the Norwegians, in which the latter were defeated; this event put an end to their predatory expeditions, and caused their rapid expulsion from every settlement which they forcibly held in the Scottish dominions. The issue of this battle was no less important to the nation than the overthrow of other intruders was at a subsequent period; for, had the Norwegians been successful at Largs, and the English at Bannockburn, it is probable that the very name of Scotland would have been annihilated. Many vestiges of ruined castles, fortifications, and encampments, are visible in this neighbourhood, evidently distinguishing this part of the coast, as a frequent point of attack at an early period, and before Scotland became wholly subject to the sway of one monarch.

About the Point of Toward the coast is lower and less interesting; upon it stands a Lighthouse, which is to guard vessels making for the Clyde, from sailing into the Kyles of Bute; while another is placed on the isle of Little Cumbray to direct them to avoid the sound between Bute and Arran. Near Toward Lighthouse is the ruin of Toward Castle, which like every other habitation of chieftainship, was the frequent scene of local war, as well as a defence against marauding banditti. How happily have times and circumstances since changed! Behind it, stands upon a rising ground, Castle Toward, an elegant square stone mansion, facing the south.

The scenery of the estuary of the Clyde has long been celebrated. The extremely diversified character of its shores, lofty rugged and bold, or covered by luxuriant herbage, thick woods, and the motley habitations of every class of society, either standing detached, or congregated into towns and villages, and interspersed with the castles of ancient times, cannot fail to keep the attention of a stranger continually on the stretch. The intricate inlets of Loch Long, the Gare Loch, Holy Loch, and Loch Striven offer almost every variety of mountain scenery. Those narrow straits are often peculiarly striking from the height of the land immediately enclosing them, and from the picturesque disposition of the rocky and woody precipices so often occurring along the shores; while their tortuous courses produce an ever changing variety of scenes. The islands alone present objects of endless diversity, whether by coasting their shores, or, when forming parts of the distance, they combine with the perpetual variations of the surrounding land. After all this, adding the effects produced by the variable atmosphere of the western coasts, and the life and movement of the shipping that navigate the Clyde, it may without exaggeration be said that no portion of Scotland presents greater attractions to him whose pursuit is that of picturesque beauty.

After leaving Toward Point, we again pursued a southern track across the channel which separates this part of Argyleshire from Bute, and made directly for the town of Rothesay, situated in the most sheltered part of a little bay on the north east coast of that island. I was much struck with the beautiful and secluded situation of this spot. The land rises round it on every side like an amphitheatre; seems fertile and well cultivated, and interspersed with brushy oaks. The remains of its ancient and royal castle are a very picturesque feature in the view, independent of their historical interest. It was the residence of several of the early Scottish kings, and gave the title of Duke of Rothesay to the heir apparent of that monarchy.* It stands on one of the low bold cliffs which rise from the shore, and which are of the old red sandstone, having the character of a coarse red conglomerate. The view of the Argyleshire mountains from the quay is particularly magnificent; the sun shining through the partial haze, produced a pleasing effect upon their rugged sides and heaving summits.

The pleasant and healthy situation of Rothesay, and the facility of water communication with Glasgow, have made it a place of considerable resort in the summer months. The climate is so mild that the snow seldom lies upon the ground, but it is often deluged with rains; in sheltered situations, timber grows to a very large size. The pier was crowded with gay company, and we both landed and took in several passengers. The rocky nature of the coast, (and this remark will apply to the whole of the Hebrides that we saw) renders the water brilliantly transparent, and while the vessel was lying in the bay, I observed large quantities of the long ribbon like leaves of the Fucus ligulatus, waving over the bottom far below the keel like a submarine field of green corn. We also observed for the first time great numbers of Medusae, of a variety of brilliant colours, glittering in the sunbeams below the surface of the green and glassy sea, sometimes at a great depth. One species was very large, some of the individuals being from two to three feet long, semicircular above like a vast mushroom or small balloon, the other end forming a tail divided into many tapering points like a comma or long beard. Their colour was buff, yellowish green, or bright

---

* And still does to the Prince of Wales.

flame colour. Another and much smaller species, totally unlike the last, and without a stem, was of a beautiful opal colour, and in the centre of its convex side had four circles touching at their circumference, and in the middle of each, a smaller circle of a fine rose or purple colour, and surrounded with a broad fringe of filmy transparent membrane, so delicate that it was only visible when the sun shone full upon its whole length. This latter species, I think, must be the M. purpura; the former I cannot identify. I was much delighted with their beautiful appearance and motions, and took a sketch of each in my original journal; but I have not sufficient confidence in their accuracy to introduce them here.

When we left Rothesay, we took a northern direction but on passing the entrance into Loch Striven changed to the north west, and began the passage through the Kyles or Straits of Bute. The north east shore of Bute, after passing Kames bay, has some appearance of cultivation at the bases of the hills, every spot not covered by rock, being converted into pasture ground, but the herbage is scanty and ill coloured. The angle in which it declines from the sun is an unfavourable circumstance, but where nature has been so niggardly of her gifts as she is in these inhospitable regions, man must be content to receive them with all their disadvantages, and to suffer proportionate privations. The few solitary mountain farms, and the habitations scattered along the shores at widely separated intervals, serve to mark the general poverty of the country which borders on this singular strait. The hills are low lumpish rocks, and under any other aspect than a summer's sun, must appear dreary and inhospitable. Yet few scenes exist in the Hebrides of a more romantic character than those which occur in the fairy mazes of the Kyles of Bute, presenting throughout an intricate combination of promontories, rocks, and islands. While the navigation is peculiarly dangerous, at every turn all farther progress seems to be denied through the intricate mixture of land and water, the steam packet all the while winding among broken rocks and woody shores, or under overhanging cliffs and loftier hills. We seemed to be threading a perfect labyrinth; and the perpetual shifting of the scenery from the constant alteration of our course, had a novel and pleasing effect. This was particularly the case off the northern point of Bute, where the narrow channel is studded by several rocky islets. We appeared to be sailing upon an island lake; and but for the sea tang on the rocks, which pointed out a high water mark, a person unacquainted with our geographical position, could not be persuaded he was upon saltwater. On one of these rocks is a small vitrified fort, whence the group have probably derived their name of Burnt Islands.

While we were making our way through this perplexing passage, our attention was diverted by a number of porpoises (Delphinus Phocoena) shewing their round backs above the water. They were probably in pursuit of herrings and smaller fish, upon which they prey with great voracity, driving them into the creeks and bays. It is only in warm weather that they approach the shores; they are sometimes taken for the oil they contain, but were formerly eaten as a delicacy. The sailors told us their Gaelic name, which resembled the Latin, Porcus, but I could not catch its orthography; they said it was synonymous with the English word, Pig. As soon as we got disentangled from among the Burnt Islands, our track lay due south, and we appeared to be making a direct course for Arran. I have several times named this alpine island, but purposely avoided saying more, till we had a nearer survey. The characters of its mountains are grand, and their outlines picturesque and serrated, and are said to yield in both respects, only to the superior magnificence of the Cuillin hills in Skye. The northern tract presents an irregular group of mountains, connected by ridges of a tolerably uniform height, and declining towards the shores to which they are nearest, without any distinct set of secondary elevations. They are intersected by deep narrow glens, the declivities of which are such as in most places to afford a constant drainage without suffering lakes to accumulate. The granite of which they are composed, rises into spiry forms, frequently bare of vegetation and extending downwards in faces of naked rock into the intricate sections that divide these complicated ridges. The deep and rugged hollows thus formed, afford passage to the almost perennial torrents which rush with violence along them, forcing their way through the enormous fragments that strew their sides and encumber their surfaces. The sun seldom penetrates these deep recesses, which exhibit all the sober and harmonious tints of reflected light, as it is reverberated from rock to rock, and from the clouds that occasionally rest on their lofty boundaries. The highest mountain is called Goat Fell, which rises very nearly three thousand feet above the sea; but there are other summits in its vicinity which nearly rival it in altitude. From the circumstance of their rising immediately from the sea, the mountains of Arran appear more lofty than others of equal altitude in the interior of the mainland. When the base of a mountain stands on very high ground, the eye is wonderfully deceived in the extent of its absolute elevation.

When we reached Ardlamont Point the whole eastern coast of the promontory of Kintyre came in sight, stretching its long line of low barren hills far to the southward. Having doubled this point, we immediately veered to the north west and entered the noble Loch Fyne, the largest, though not the most picturesque of the sea lochs of Scotland. Its principal beauty consists in the broad expanse of its clear blue waters, and in the view down it towards Arran. The hills upon its banks are generally low and uninteresting, barren and destitute of timber, particularly those on its eastern side. On the opposite side they are bolder, but without either character or variety, frequently running in headlands into the loch, and indenting its shores with creeks and bays. We coasted the western side and touched at East Tarbert, entering a small sheltered bay by a very difficult navigation among sunken rocks. On a near approach, the scenery round it is bold but forbidding; and the ruins of its castle standing on a craggy rock to the south of the village, reminded us of the silent ravages of time and the turbulent events connected with its early history.

The peninsula of Kintyre is here only about three quarters of a mile wide, being nearly separated from the mainland of Argyleshire by Loch Tarbert. I have before named the supposed origin of the word Tarbert, or Tarbet; and Pennant says it is not long since small vessels were drawn by horses across this isthmus, to avoid the dangers of the Mull of Kintyre, so dreaded and so little known was the navigation round that promontory. The narrow channel between it and the north east coast of Ireland being insufficient to allow a passage to the great swell of the Atlantic, produces dreadful currents and great irregularities of the tides along the whole of these shores. The variations of the latter are nowhere more remarkable than on the opposite sides of this isthmus; so much so, that when it is high water at East Tarbert, it is nearly at the ebb at West Tarbert, though they are not a mile distant. The spring tides at the former place rise from ten to eleven feet, at the latter only from four to five feet; sometimes there is neither ebb nor flow, while at others it ebbs and flows in half the usual time.

The irregularity and intricacy of the tides throughout the Western Islands in general, is very considerable, often indeed such as to defeat the calculations even of the mariner experienced in these channels. The causes will be apparent, when it is recollected that every tide is, here more especially, the result of a variety of concurring circumstances, some of which are liable to changes that do not admit of observation or calculation, and which therefore modify the others in various unexpected ways. The chief of these are important variations in the direction and force of the winds, which, as they are combined with different lunar or annual states of the tide, influence in various modes, the more steady causes which consist in the directions of the tide's stream, and the intricate forms of the channels through which it passes.

The remainder of this day's voyage, from East Tarbert to the Canal of Crinan, was rendered delightful by the refreshing coolness of the evening breezes. The surrounding landscape was on a very extensive scale, and the objects were softened by distance into the most pleasing harmony. The moon, now nearly at the full, hung her pale lamp over the towering rocks of Arran, and threw a broad line of silvery light upon the glassy surface of the loch. It was lovely in the extreme; and I expressed my regret to Dovaston, that *one* who in this world is everything to me, and has been my companion through so many years of comfort and of happiness and my best solace under occasional afflictions, should not be present to enjoy it with me. It was a scene of placid beauty, well calculated to remind me of the uniform serenity of her own mind.

Her absence however might have been less agreeably supplied. The passengers on board were very numerous, but being exclusively a ship of pleasure, they were all people of respectability, some indeed of superior understanding and manners; many of them English, but chiefly Scotch or Hebrideans. It is with great and satisfactory pleasure I remember and record the influence my friend Dovaston had over the whole party; his conversation and versatility of talent, abundant in historical recollections, imaginative in fanciful effusion, or brilliant in facetious anecdote, was in continual display, not only to my delight and information, but to those of the whole company. In whichever part of the packet he chose to be, a crowd of attentive and enraptured audience collected round him, and had their countenances continually fixed upon him; insomuch that sometimes the captain found it necessary to request them to disperse more equally, to preserve the proper equilibrium of the vessel. Before we had left the estuary of the Clyde, on his enquiring the name of one of the old castles, the answer elicited from him a narrative from Scottish History, in which among other observations, he remarked that Dr. Robertson, in addition to his own sweetness and urbanity of style has softened into it much of the perspicuous keenness of Hume and enough of the luminous blaze of Gibbon, and he formed a model of historic composition equal to either and inferior to none. An elderly gentleman who stood near my friend Dovaston at the moment of this remark modestly informed him that he was a son of that Historian; that in consequence of some acquisition of property in the Hebrides through his wife, he had taken the name of MacDonald, but that from respect to the celebrity of his father he still liked to be called Robertson. He solicited us to join a small and select circle of his friends and introduced us to several of them and to his two daughters. We then each gave him our names and address; and to this fortunate incident, we owed much future pleasure, information, and convenience. On Col. Robertson enquiring of me the aspect of the country around Wrexham, a lady of the party who was going to spend a few weeks with a relation on one of the islands, asked if I knew Lady Cunliffe, who was in early life a friend of her family and lived in Edinburgh. She represented both her and her sister (Miss Kinlochs I think she called them) as most benevolent and amiable ladies, always seeking out opportunities for the exercise of charity and kindness. I replied that though I had but recently removed to Wrexham, I had frequently understood that she fully supported that character.

Col. Robertson told us he perfectly recollected, when about eight years old, Dr. Johnson's dining with his father, Principal Robertson, on his way to the Hebrides. He has since passed much of his life in India, is a very intelligent and modest gentleman; and in the lower part of his face, bears a considerable resemblance to the portraits of the historian. He now resides at Kinloch Moidart in Morvern, near Strontian, whither he was returning with his daughters from a visit to Edinburgh. Among the friends of the good Colonel, was a fine young Chieftain of the Isles, called Donald McLean, of Drymnen in Morvern, who possessed extensive property both there and in Uist, a part of Long Island, where he manufactured a large quantity of kelp. The small isle of Boreray, one of the most distant of the Hebrides, lying to the north east of St Kilda, belongs to him. It was at Drymnen that Sir Jos[h]. Banks and the celebrated French traveller Fanjas St. Fond (sic) were entertained by his grandfather on their way to Staffa. This amiable and interesting young man was particularly delighted with Dovaston's copious and animated recitations from Burns and other Scotch Poets, which he gave in the broad Lowland dialect, and with his conversation on Music, and seemed, by the attentive, fixed, and intellectual expression of his countenance, eager to catch even every syllable. To the courtesy and exertions of this gentleman, we shall ever feel indebted for very numerous and considerable comfort and accommodations; his attentions and kindness were constant and unabating till, with regret, we saw him depart on board his elegant shallop in the Sound of Mull. As a single instance of his benevolence, I mention the first. As our vessel neared the bold and rocky shores of Crinan we observed him poised on the side of the ship, from which he sprang ashore and ran up the slippery tang-covered crags with the bounding elasticity of a gazelle, disappearing in a moment over their summits. On our landing in the small bay of Lochgilphead for the evening, we saw him on the strand, where he politely received us and his party, and conducted us to apartments which his haste and activity had secured for us. Beds had been secured here for himself and Col. Robertson's party before; and the latter gentleman told us the following morning, that but for McLean's influence, we must either have lain on deck, or have walked on to the village of Lochgilphead, as all the other beds were engaged when he first went ashore, which he did on our account. He very much reminded us, and particularly among these isles, of young Coll, the laird who so warmly obtained the applause of Dr. Johnson. When we reached this little solitary inn, which overlooks Loch Fyne, we shared all the accommodations provided for the party, without the least trouble on our parts, and enjoyed clean and comfortable beds. After supper, Dovaston happening in the most casual manner to say he smoked ocasionally, the young Chieftain, silently, and unknown to all, even sent out and procured a bundle of cigars, which, however, after just lighting one in complaisance, my friend declined using, and entertained us with many a merry tale, and animated poetical recitation, chiefly the rich effusions of the Caledonian Muse, and with copious passages from the Poems of Ossian. To the ladies he discoursed on Music, and told them the anecdote of Gemminiani's having acknowledged that he in vain blotted many quires of paper and spent many years, in attempting to compose a second part, for that lost, of the 'Broom of Cowden-Knowes;' and they much approved my friend's suggestion, after playing the melody repeatedly, with a fine bass, of simply ending with the two first bars. In this circle was also a Mr. John Thompson, son of the celebrated Dr. Thompson of Edinburgh, who joined Dovaston in very learned conversation on Music and Poetry, and told him the melancholy fate of Young Everard, a friend of Mr. McLean's, who was drowned in the Irish sea, while passing from his own to a Norwegian ship.

The evening was spent in the highest enjoyment, for much of which I was, as usual, indebted to my excellent friend. It was midnight before the company reluctantly retired, and *only then*, because we knew we were to resume our voyage at four o'clock the following morning.

While the company was separating I turned to the window to enjoy the serene evening air, and my attention was arrested by a beautiful Aurora Borealis, which extended like a vast sweeping arch of curved lines from the eastern quarter of the heavens across the Pole even to the west. The arched appearance was no doubt owing to the laws of perspective, which frequently give to the clouds the same shape. We went upon the beach to obtain a better view of this novel phenomenon. Within the arch, the whole sky seemed to be in glittering confusion, vivid corruscations of light shot up perpendicularly, like vast columns, now expanding, then collapsing, or bending into various curves and other fantastic figures, which quickly moved off like the scenes of a theatre. In a moment these were succeeded by a filmy stream of light, resembling a silvery shower, through whose misty texture the stars were seen, as through the vapoury form of Ossian's ghosts. These evanescent and fleeting forms then changed into others of varied size and intensity of light, principally of a yellow cast, and often of great brilliancy, which the imagination might easily transform into

– Armies in meet array,
Throng'd with aerial spears and steeds of fire.

After this, again, the arch contracted into curved indentations, according to the play of the electric fluid, seeming as though the immense drapery of Heaven were at once drawn up, spangled with the stars which glittered through its gauze canopy.

The landlord of the inn – a tall, raw boned, and light-haired *Goth*, said they were called the 'merry dancers,' and the indifference with which he viewed them, showed that they were not uncommon in this latitude. He said they always predicted stormy weather; no pleasant news, had we believed it, when we thought of the rocks and currents of the sea we were now visiting.

Wednesday, 27th July At four o'clock we were melodiously awakened by the indefatigable bagpiper, who with his eternal fifths gave us several pibrochs and strathspeys. On board the Scotch steam packets everything is performed when he gives the signal, meals are announced, and the various business of the ship is conducted by this national instrument, and though so late last night when we retired, he gave us a serenade.

A Nineteenth-Century Tour

The packet was lying in the basin at the entrance of the canal of Crinan, and before I went aboard I went down to the beach and selected two specimens of chlorite schist, the beds of which are unusually undulated. We were detained nearly half an hour in taking in a fresh supply of coals, and I occupied it in botanizing upon a steep craggy rock which over looked Loch Fyne, and the summit of Goat Fell in Arran to the south. I saw nothing new, but brought down some fine bunches of heather which I distributed among the ladies, and young McLean placed some of it in his hat. I afterwards understood it was the ancient badge of his clan.

The canal of Crinan was cut about thirty years ago, and by it, vessels avoid the tedious and dangerous voyage round the Mull of Kintyre, the length of which would be about 120 miles up to the same parallel on the west side of the canal. Its length is only about nine miles, its width 60 feet, and the height of its summit level above the tideway, 62 feet. It has 15 locks, each 96 feet in length and 24 in breadth. It is private property, and a tonnage is paid by all vessels passing through it. On account of the numerous locks, the passage is tedious; it took us three hours in getting into the salt water again, which I employed in the cabin, writing my notes, leaving instructions with Dovaston on deck to call me up, if there was anything worthy notice.

On re-entering the sea out of the Canal of Crinan, we got among the hundreds of sunny isles and islets that stud the Western coast of Scotland; the prospect was varied and extensive, and to us novel. On our right was Loch Craignish, spotted with many little green knolls covered with patches of coppice and interspersed with fine trees, while the shores of the loch are rendered highly ornamental by being interspersed with houses and woods on irregular ground. It is not easy to account for the luxuriance and great size of some of these trees, considering the bleak and stormy situation they occupy. Before us was the long island of Jura with its three obtusely conical mountains, significantly called the Paps of Jura, rising from the southern part of it to the height of about 2,500 feet. This island seemed little more than one continued rugged mountainous ridge. To the south lay the fertile island of Islay rising from the water in gentle undulations, green and bright in the morning sun. We sail'd through the passage of Dorishmore, (great gate) which lies off the Point of Craignish, and is dreaded on account of the strength and rapidity of the tides and short cross sea produced when their course is opposed to a fresh breeze.

We breakfasted in the northern part of the Sound of Jura, on fresh herrings as white as snow. They who have not eaten herrings immediately after being taken, cannot conceive their excellence. Returning up on deck, we had before us

– Scarba's isle, whose tortur'd shore
Still rings to Corryvreckan's roar,
   And lonely Colonsay;

the latter seen only in the distant offing between Jura and Scarba, and the scene of the lamented Dr. Jno. Leyden's beautiful ballad of the 'Mermaid'.

Approaching Scarba, the whirlpool of Corryvreckan was pointed out to us at the comfortable distance of about a league to our left, lying in the narrow strait between that island and Jura. The flood tide rushes through this rocky channel with the tremendous force of 8 or 9 miles an hour, and is accompanied by a succession of currents and eddies which render Corryvreckan the Charybdis of Scotland, and realizes the dangers with which poetry seems in former times to have invested the Sicilian Gulf. The whirlpool is produced by a rock of a pyramidal form rising with a steep acclivity from the bottom, which is here about 600 feet deep, to within about 90 feet of the surface, and diverting the rapid course of the tide already described. The stream being thus obstructed, assumes numerous intricate directions, which, interfering with each other, cause the water to break with considerable violence. If there be a fresh breeze, and more particularly if the motion of the wind be opposed to that of the sea, this agitation is increased to a frightful degree; frightful at least to a seaman who knows its dangers, although, to a landsman, it may seem less terrible than the long surging roll of the Atlantic wave. It is this breaking sea which constitutes the real danger of the Corryvreckan, as, when considerable, it will in an instant sink a vessel, unless everything is made secure on deck. The impulse of the stream against the rock above described, produces also a long and rapid counter current or eddy on the side of Scarba; which, returning into the principal stream in an opposite course, causes the chief separation, or the whirlpool; the danger of which is comparatively trifling, since the only effect of it is to prevent the steering of a vessel: the real danger is in the breaking of the sea. Yet even Corryvreckan has its periodical seasons of repose, which take place at the change of the tide, after which the current is renewed in a contrary direction. It is more rational to suppose that the celebrated Maelstrom, off the coast of Norway, if not all whirlpools, originates in a similar cause, and not in a subterraneous passage for the water, as is commonly supposed. But the dangers of Corryvreckan were only described to us by the captain; our distance from it and the quiescent state of the water, divested it of its horrors, and we could only distinguish it by a darker shade upon the surface accompanied by occasional waves.

From this point we had a perfect panorama of islands, not appearing as such, but apparently linked together, and forming a continuous circle of mountains, with the exception of a single break to the south of Jura. The island of Scarba is about three miles long, and consists principally of an enormous rock rising precipitously from the sea; the broken crags, which are clothed with beautiful heather and fine natural woods, render it a very picturesque object. We sailed close under its eastern side and in the bright sunshine could distinguish every flower which enamelled its rugged rocks and covered them with beauty. We were now in the Sound of Luing, having the long hilly ridge which forms the island of that name on our right, and Scarba and Lunga on our left. The two last are separated by a very narrow strait, and diverted at the eastern extremity by a rocky islet, the tide running through both passages, and generally through the whole sound, with a turbulence and impetuosity as great as that of the far more celebrated Corryvreckan. There is more real danger comprized in one day's sailing in a boat among these islands, than in a whole East India voyage. On account of this dreadful current, the steam boat generally goes through the sound of Shuna in boisterous weather. Shuna is a low fertile island, well wooded with birch and alder, between Luing and the mainland.

Leaving the Sound of Luing, which is about five miles long and very narrow, we emerged into a perfect archipelago, called the Slate islands, appearing like rocks rising abruptly out of the sea, in every variety of shape and size; some bleak and serrated, others slightly tinged with verdure and tufted with heather, small and formed entirely of slate, enlivened by a few diminutive huts, and so flat as only just to be seen like black spots studding the smooth azure surface of the deep. This varied foreground of sea and islands was backed on the east by Ben Cruachan seen over the rugged and barren mountains of Lorn; on the north by the blue peaked hills of Appin and Morvern; and on the north west by the long rocky shore of Mull, from which rises a group of high mountains, visible from their great elevation, throughout all the western shores of Scotland, and the fertile parent of the rains and storms, which, according to all travellers, seem to have erected their throne in this cloudy and dreary region. There are many peaks in this group, of which the highest is called Ben More, 3,097 feet high, smooth, and covered with grass nearly to the summit. Great quantities of roofing slate are exported from Seil and Easdale, where we saw many quarries; its quality seemed to differ little from the coarse graywacke slate of Cumberland.

The cross tides and currents that so frequently threaten destruction to the navigators of these stormy seas, are in no part more complex and puzzling than among the Slate Islands. They are so excessively rapid, and the times of high and low water vary so much from local and accidental causes, that the utmost caution and unwearied vigilance are necessary to ward off the danger that perpetually haunts small boats. The steam packets are from their superior size better able to contend with them, and afford facilities to travellers, unknown before their introduction. Desolate as distant strangers may imagine, and dismal and rugged as poets have described "the storm-vex'd Hebrides", to us, under a clear sky, in a safe and commodious vessel, amid courteous and intelligent society, these regions of romance gave an impression of delight, that with life will live in our luxuriating recollections. Sailing among the sunny sides, golden in blossomed furze, or purple in the bonnie bell healther now shooting their high pikes into the blue heaven, and now receding into dim and softened distance, the eye was keen and quick in arresting each object of intrest, the heart alive to every impulse of delight, and the soul basking in silent and grateful adoration of the Great Spirit that moved on the face of the waters. Nor were the waters themselves devoid of inhabitants: Nature, abundant in production, beautiful in formation, and infinite in variety, in plentitude of power from the exuberance of her profusion, peoples all apace with animation. Millions of sea fowl clothed the expanse of ocean: the light and snowy gull rode weightless, as it were, on the ridgy waves; the flapping puffins streaked the surface in lines of light, and the various divers plunged in their circles and reappeared afar in the centre of others. The gannet and the cormorant rose in spiral gyrations to mere specks in the sky, then dropped like stones into the depths of ocean, each rising with a fish glittering across his beak, which flinging into the air, he caught perpendicularly in his capacious throat. The very notes of these tribes, discordant in any other scene, were here in harmony with the whole; and their sleek and silvery plumage, shining in sunny glossiness, kept tone of accordance with the splendour of the rolling waves.

Numbers of Medusae, of both the species already named, passed continually along side the vessel, shewing their brilliant and delicate lines in the bright sunshine, even at a considerable depth. The sailors caught one of enormous size and we hauled it on deck; it was of the larger sort, and must have weighed at least thirty pounds, and its circular transparent top, fringed with lunules of brilliant violet, was nearly three feet in diameter. From its central stem, it had five long members branching out, thickly and irregularly wasted on their inner side like a cauliflower, of a bright brown, beneath each of which was a long cartilaginous opal-coloured substance, with three deeply indented edges like a triangular sword. The central stem was hollow, and its interior surface was coated with a very delicate membranous network, and within it were several small crustaceous animals *alive*, one very much resembling the Cancerstagnalis, with prominent eyes of a golden green, as brilliant as those of the Hemerobius perla. The branching members were probably arms, and the warty substances, so many papilla or tentacula, for the purpose of catching its prey, and conveying it to the central stem, or stomach: they might also serve as rudders to direct its course. I saw other vessels imbedded within the substance of the cupola, which might be branches of the alimentary canal, but so tender that they could not be separated from the transparent mass. Indeed it appeared to be little more than organized gelatine. The sailors called them Sea Nettles; and I was repeatedly cautioned by them and by several of the passengers, not to touch it, but having handled other species upon the Welsh coasts, I disregarded their silly prejudices. I pulled it to pieces and examined its interior, and (like Paul, when he shook the viper into the fire,) felt no harm, though my hands were imbued in it for a considerable time.

After doubling the Point of Ardincaple and inclining to the north east, we first saw the interesting and beautiful island of Kerrera; and looking back on the mainland of Lorn, the ruins of Ardmaddy castle, and a modern house the property of another young and chatty Highland laird whom we took on board at one of the locks of the Crinan canal. His name was MacDougal, and to his politeness I owe some of the notes of my Journal. Kerrera is only separated from the mainland of Argyleshire by a narrow strait about four miles long and half a mile wide called the Sound of Kerrera. Its surface is extremely hilly and ragged, and its shores, abrupt faces of rock finely fringed with low brushwood, and very profusely tufted with bright ivy. At the southern extremity these cliffs extend to the seashore in a variety of intricate and rugged forms well suited to the character of the boisterous sea that so often breaks against them, forming with it a dreary scene of wildness which is rendered more impressive by the ruins of the ancient castle of Gylen, perched on a rocky cliff amid the contention of the winds and water. In this strait is a small but secure harbour, which is celebrated as the spot where Alexander king of Scotland took shelter from a storm: a hut was erected on the shore for the monarch, the site of which is still called Dallreigh. He died here in 1249, and his body was carried to Melrose Abbey.

The northern end of Kerrera is opposite to the small, though lively little town of Oban, which stretches along the shore of its deep and sheltered bay. Here we touched about 1 o'clock to make exchanges of passengers, and saw thousands of Medusae playing gracefully in the pellucid water like globes of opal. The hills which rise from the shore, surround it like an amphitheatre. Oban will be named again on our return from Staffa. We now bore to the west, and sailed close under the fine ivy-mantled ruins of Dunolly castle, standing on a high precipitous rock of red coarse trap conglomerate, overhanging the bay, and near it the modern house of the descendant of its ancient chief, surrounded by a few trees. Dunolly castle was originally a Danish fort, and subsequently a stronghold of the Lords of the Isles. It is a fine picturesque ruin; the walls are of a great thickness, square and broad, but have been barbarously mutilated by a late proprietor to build the modern house. Venerable by its antiquity, it is somewhat surprising that a person still tenacious of the title of Chief, should destroy the most lasting monument of his boasted ancestors.

I scarcely know how to describe the scenery which surrounded us as we steered westward for the shores of Mull. Before us was a fine expanse of water, guarded by many venerable ruins of ancient castles, and hemmed in by bleak hills, above which rose the pale peaked tops of Mull, Morvern, Appin, and Lorn, forming a circular back screen of great magnificence and grandeur. We were now in the regions and scenes of Ossian; 'and the silence of noon sleeps on an hundred isles, the sun glitters fervid on the curving sea, yet desolate is the dwelling of Morna', and we called up in our fancy the deeds of other days, a tale of the times of old. Among these vast mountains, we distinguished Ben Nevis, Ben Cruachan, and those of Glencoe, the highest Britain can boast. The long island of Lismore seemed as the centre round which they rose; while nearer to us, the sea was studded with rocky islets fringed with tang and covered with puffins and other sea fowls, which reminded us of our venerable friend Bewick, whose inimitable tale pieces, – full of imaginative genius – so faithfully portray the habits of these birds, and the scenes they love to haunt. A gentleman from Leeds who was on board, knew our kind friend and his amiable family, and spoke highly of his domestic virtues and cheerful heart. The mind was quite bewildered by the sublimity of the scenery, and the multiplicity of objects that pressed upon our attention – Dunolly, Duart, Aros, and Dunstaffnage castles were all in sight; while the pale ghosts of Ossian slept up on the hills of Morvern and of Lorn – every name, every object, awakened some recollection, enshrined in history or embalmed in song.

As we advanced into the strait that divides the coast of Lorn from Mull, we saw the broad square ruin of Dunstaffnage Castle, so much larger and more entire than any of the surrounding fortresses, that at the distance we saw it from, it might easily be mistaken for a modern mansion. It stands nearly insulated on a narrow promontory of the mainland which guards the entrance into Loch Etive, and is surrounded by the magnificent scenery already named. It has derived an adscititious interest from being considered one of the oldest edifices in the Hebrides, and the seat of royalty during the early ages of the Caledonian dynasty. Here, it is said, was kept the Palladium, or black stone of Scotland, after it came from Ireland, and before it was sent to Scone,* by which is literally fulfilled the remark, "Ubi Palladium, ibi Scotiæ Imperium". All this, however, rests on too doubtful authority to be admitted as the real history of Dunstaffnage.

We passed very near the south west point of the isle of Lismore,* near which is the Lady rock, seen only at low water, and so named from the following circumstance, which forms the ground work of Miss Baillie's beautiful tragedy, entitled the "Family Legend". Duart castle, where the principal scene is laid, was just before us on the shore of Mull, and will be named presently.

McLean of Duart castle was married to a daughter of the Earl of Argyle; but they had no children, and he was unfaithful to her bed. In a fit of jealousy, his lady mixed poison with the medicine he was about to have taken; a servant, however, who had accidentally tasted it, died in consequence, and, as a punishment, the lady was placed upon this rock at low water, to perish by the return of the flood; drowning being in those days the death inflicted upon ladies for a capital crime. She was rescued and taken off the rock by four brothers named McLean, who conducted her in safety to

---

* It was subsequently taken to London, by Edward 1st, and is still used in the Coronation Chair of the Kings of England.

* From Lios more, the great garden; on account of the great fertility of its soil.

her father, but dared never return to Mull. McLean of Duart, when eighty-nine years of age, was murdered in Edinburgh while in bed, by his wife's brother, the first Campbell of Cawdor, who obtained that estate, by the forcible abduction of the infant heiress.

We made the ferry house of Achnacraig, the most eastern point of the isle of Mull, and afterwards skirted the shore, sailing immediately under Duart castle above alluded to, which guards the southern entrance of the Sound of Mull. It is boldly situated on a rock of considerable elevation, and is larger than many of the castles which are scattered along these shores; its ivy mantled walls are of immense thickness. During the existence of Clanship it was the frequent scene of discord, and like every other ancient fortress in the Highlands, many interesting incidents of local history are connected with it. It was, till lately, garrisoned as a royal fortress by a detachment of soldiers from Fort William, but is now fast hastening to decay. Notwithstanding the stormy elements to which the ruined castles of the Hebrides are exposed, and the injury they must formerly have sustained from predatory attacks, they have long survived the purposes for which they were erected, and though now in a state of dilapidation, may no longer remain, to mark to future ages the barbarous manners of the ancient Highland chieftains, before the all subduing hand of time levels them with the base of the eternal hills on which they stand.

Opposite to Duart, on the northern entrance of the Sound, are the picturesque ruins of Ardtornish Castle, on a little promontory of broken basaltic pillars, sloping gently into the sea, combining to throw a gleam of historical interest over the passage of the Sound of Mull.

Of this castle little now remains; but its site is very romantic, having an extensive sea view along the Sound. Originally of Danish formation, it became the inheritance of the Lords of the Isles after the expulsion of that people. From its peculiar situation on a point of land easily defended, and readily communicating with their other possessions on either hand, it was often the rendezvous of their numerous vassals, assembled to receive their arbitrary laws; to be marshalled for the field, or to display the pomp of lordly power.

After leaving Ardtornish, the bagpiper summoned us below to dinner; but unwilling to lose any portion of scenery so novel and so interesting, we hurried over it, and when we returned on deck, found ourselves off Aros,

– where a turrets' airy head
Slender and steep, and battled round,
O'erlook'd, dark Mull! thy mighty Sound,
Where thwarting tides, with mingled roar,
Part thy swarth hills from Morvern's shore.

Aros castle overhangs a little bay of that name, and is backed by rising rocks, characterised rather by dreary sublimity than by beauty. Its chief interest arises from its history; it was another princely residence of the Lords of the Isles; and, during the period of their independence, was the frequent seat of their councils, as well as the stronghold which ensured their personal safety. Here Robert Bruce after his final establishment on the Scottish throne paid a visit to the Lord of the Isles; and there is still extant, a Charter, dated at Aros, and signed by Robert, bestowing upon one of Macdonald's vassals, who had assisted at Bannockburn, certain lands in Ardnamurchan.

While Dovaston was delighting the ladies with animated conversation on Handel, Corelli, and Purcell, I was eagerly exploring the scenery, and gaining information from Col. Robertson. The only object I have to name between Aros and Tobermory, is a very extensive whin dyke, which rises, as it were, out of the sea to an enormous height, and traverses the hills to a considerable distance. While we were all merry and happy together in most pleasing conversation, the hour of our parting with young McLean and his companions, arrived. A light sailing boat appeared, which the chieftain, by the flying pennon and the pibroch of his bagpiper, recognized as his own. He shook hands with us heartily and tenderly, much pressing us to partake the hospitality of his residence; but our time was measured, and we were bound for Staffa. The party descended into his skiff, which bore away, and disappared from our view before it reached the Morvern shore. Drimnin, his residence, was pointed out to us by Col. Robertson. I had previously asked him, if ever he should visit Wales, to allow me an opportunity of testifying more substantially than I now could, my sense of his disinterested kindness to us. Another loss too, soon awaited us: our respected fellow traveller, Col. Robertson and his chatty daughters left us on landing at Tobermory for their residence already named, near Strontian, bidding us an affectionate farewell. 'Tis pleasing to reflect, that similar and congenial minds sometimes meet together; but it is melancholy to lose a sunbeam the moment it has gleamed; for at that moment the shade seems darker than if it had never shone. May every comfort attend these kind hearted people! whose conversation has brightened this portion of our voyage, and added much to our information; and whose kindness softened down the inconveniences we should otherwise have felt at Lochgilphead.

It was about half past seven when we landed for the evening at Tobermory, a village lying a little to the east of the north point of Mull, and consisting, like Bridgnorth, of two portions, the lower, modern and stretching along a pier, the upper consisting only of some mean huts perched upon a perpendicular hill above it. It lies within a small, but very secure bay, which it is dangerous to enter on account of some sunken rocks. These seas are difficult of navigation, even in the day, without most skillful and experienced pilotage, on account of the strong currents, heaving swells, and points of rocks that lurk below; but in the night they never dare to sail among the isles.

If I were to dignify the only house which Tobermory can afford for the reception of travellers by the appellation of an *inn*, I should not convey an idea of the inconveniences we suffered during the two nights we were destined to sleep in it. It resembled an inferior village alehouse in England; but both the house and its inhabitants were filthy in the extreme, and the combination of effluvia from the peat smoke and other things of no delicate recital, aggravated by the heat of the weather, rendered it intolerable under any other circumstances but necessity. The utensils, the linen, and the victuals, were tainted to loathsomeness. The only beds we could secure by entreaty, were in a room belowstairs, having an earthen floor, and a door without even a latch. Everything was in great confusion; for in addition to our own party from the Highlander, that of another packet on its return from Staffa, was in the house, and it was a long time before we could get anything to eat.

We afterwards sallied out in search of a pretty lake which one of the passengers had named to us; and walked about two miles over a strong hilly road whose surface was the naked unlevelled rocks, and over bogs, now from the long drought, as thirsty and elastic as a dry sponge. We could not find the lake, but saw some pretty waterfalls, one, near the town mill in a vast glen, running over a bed of *columnar* basalt, that after rain must be forcibly broad, broken, and grand, by the indications of ravage which its banks exhibited. It was now diminutive, and gurgling almost unseen through the interstices of its black *tessellated* bed. We went through some fine coppice woods which overlooked the bay and a cliffy glen of great beauty rising in terraces immediately from its edge. Mull was formerly celebrated for its woods.

On our return to the village, we met a bevy of Mull lasses who were enjoying the cool of the evening; they were very neatly dressed, and had prettier faces than we had yet seen in Scotland; and what was more pleasing to our yet unreconciled eyes, they wore clean shoes and stockings.

Tobermory (St Mary's Well) is so called from a spring in the neighbourhood which has the reputation of possessing sanative qualities. One of the ships of the Spanish Armada was wrecked in the bay, pieces of which were brought up many years ago in an attempt to weigh her, under the expectation of recovering reported treasure. In this bay also the unfortunate Earl of Argyle effected his first landing, when he invaded Scotland with the view of supporting the cause of the Duke of Monmouth. This village was built under the auspices of the Society for the encouragement of the Fisheries in 1789, but from various causes the project has failed; and the place, though lying in the direct track of the numerous vessels which pass from the more southern ports to the northern countries of Europe, does not consist of more than thirty houses, and perhaps twice as many small turf huts. Before experiments of this kind can succeed, a great change in the dispositions and habits of the people must be effected.

At the *inn* we met with several Italian gentlemen who had just returned from Staffa, and had been highly gratified. One of them spoke excellent English and was a man of superior manners and attainments. They were very warm in their admiration of Scotch Scenery, and allowed that except in some peculiar features, it was not equalled on the Continent. The gentleman named above had walked through Switzerland with Mr Hutchinson a few months before he effected the liberation of Lavalette; had ascended Etna &c, &c.

It was eleven o'clock before we could get our wretched chamber cleared from a party of Mull fisherman who had been drinking in it from the time of our arrival, though we were very anxious to retire for the business of our Journals. We had been so disgusted with the place altogether, that we silently sought for other lodgings in the village, but without success. "Necessity makes men acquainted with strange *bedfellows*"; and we had them here in abundance.

Thursday 28th July Being occupied till two o'clock this morning embodying my notes, I was in a sound sleep when the bagpiper of the steam packet gave the signal for preparation at five o'clock. We were glad to escape from our filthy quarters, and went on board as soon as possible. The morning was as usual, bright and tranquil, with only sufficient breeze to ripple the surface of the sea:– a most important circumstance for a voyage to Staffa and Iona, towards which we were now sailing. Before we left the Sound of Mull, we passed on our right, Loch Sunart, which divides Morvern from Ardnamurchan; and just beyond it, saw the broad, low tower of Mingarury Castle, standing on the beach. Through an opening in the rocks behind it, we saw the very sharp points of two high mountains in the isle of Rum,* which are about 2,300 feet high. As we doubled the northern point of Mull and left the Sound, a fine expanse of ocean opened upon us, less thronged with islands, and they more distant than what we sailed among yesterday off the coast of Lorn, but of greater extent and more magnificent outline. To the north, over the Point of Ardnamurchan, rose the fine conical hills of Rum, and the black ridge of Egg** capped with a perpendicular basaltic rock called the Scuir of Egg, looking like an immense broad tower; while between them, faint and blue in distance, but far succeeding them in altitude and grandeur, rose the high and battered peaks of the Cuthullin hills in the isle of Sky,† peering over each other like masses of clouds. After proceeding a little farther we saw Muck‡ and Canna, two small and low

---

* From the Danish, meaning wide, ample, *roomy*.

** Egg, an edge, Danish, a name very expressive of the appearance of this island. Scuir is a rock; hence the English scar, and scaur.

† Sky, clouds, Scandinav[n] The isle of mist of the Gaelic Poet, Ossian.

‡ Muc, a hog, Gaelic. Kanin, a rabbit, Swedish, 'the isle of rabbits'.

islands lying at the feet of the elegant isle of Rum; the former nearer to us on the eastern, the latter beyond it on its western side. Right west of us was the long and low isle of Coll,* stretching along the distant horizon for a considerable space, its red cliffs of descending perpendicularly into the ocean, giving it very much the appearance of a long wall. Not a tree nor a shrub was seen upon it, as might have been expected from its etymology.

The Point of Ardnamurchan is the most western part of the mainland of Scotland, and from the check given by the isle of Mull to the full current of the Atlantic as it rushes past it, there is here a tremendous sea. Thousands of white gulls were riding on the ridgy waves, and seemed like flakes of snow floating on the azure main. The western shores of Mull are here very uninteresting, rising in shapeless rocks, without any covering of soil, and consequently without vegetation or trees to break the sterile uniformity of their appearance. The soil in the interior is very fertile; and we learned from gentlemen on board, that though from its perpetually dripping atmosphere it is not calculated for the cultivation and ripening of grain, it is well adapted for pasturage. It is celebrated for its small black cattle, of which several thousands are annually exported into the Lowlands of Scotland, and even in England. He told us they yielded on an average from two pints of milk a day. The climate of Mull is considered more rainy than that of any of the Hebrides; which may arise both from the altitude of its own hills, and from its being in the vicinity of the range which extends from Ben Cruachan to Ben Nevis. These are all influential in precipitating the clouds that arrive from the western sea, which fall in undiminished energy in gales of wind and rain, of which the inhabitants of the more favoured climate of England can form no conception.

We were now summoned down to breakfast, but obeyed the call rather reluctantly, the increasing swell having made us mawkish and giddy, and given as weighty reasons for supposing it probable that necessity would soon order us up again. We were a little relieved on returning into the open air, but I felt unhinged and unable to write out my notes. As we pursued our southward track, the Isle of Tiree appeared very far out to the west; low and dim, but much more level than Coll. Both these islands are of gneiss, but at their distance from us, they were not to be distinguished from the neighbouring basaltic cliffs. To the north of the latter is a cluster of cliffs consisting of detached rocks, called the Cairns of Coll, having much the appearance of towering castles whose foundations lie buried beneath the waves.

The swell of the sea, which had been considerable since we left the Sound of Mull, increased very much as we approached the Point of Treshinish, or the Kaylock (sic) of Mull, the most western part of that island, where the

---

* Coll, a hazel, coil, a wood, Gaelic. Colm, or Colum, is also a pigeon.

captain told us there is always a heavy motion and broadswell in the calmest weather, but that during winds, the contention of the elements is dreadful, and the navigation more rough and dangerous than in any of the straits of the storm-vexed Hebrides. He relieved our anxiety by telling us that it would not prevent our landing upon Staffa, nor probably from entering the cave in the boat. The sea had to us a very singular and grand appearance. Its surface was as smooth as glass, yet the vessel pitched so much as to produce a very unpleasant sensation, and I soon perceived that though *smooth*, it was not *level*, as water at rest is, but that large fields of it, were inclined in different directions, giving to the whole expanse, a wide undulating surface, like sloping and uneven ground. Was it the reflection of the sun's rays from these large sloping waves, elevated by the mirage, that caused the singular play of lights upon the rocks?

Under the cliffs of Mull were several of the most diminutive huts we had yet seen, so small indeed, that they might easily have been overlooked among the large masses of rock that lay scattered about them. A person accustomed to the habits and pursuits of civilized society, might justly deem it little better than banishment, were he compelled to lead the amphibious and monotonous life of these secluded beings. These cabins place in a striking light the words of the poet, 'Man wants but little here below,' yet notwithstanding all the privations and hardships these poor fishermen are doomed to bear, their attachment to their native rocks is insuperable, no advantages afforded by other situations appearing to have any power to create a wish for change.

Off the Point of Kaylock lie the Treshinish islands, a group of basaltic rocks whose shores are precipitous cliffs rising perpendicularly from the stormy sea which lashes their base. Their tops are obtusely conical, and covered with grass, affording pasture to a few cattle and sheep; but not one of them is inhabited. Their general appearance is very singular; one is called by the sailors the Dutchman's Caps and another looks like a prodigious brick kiln rising out of the sea, an idea favoured by the red colour of the cliffy sides. On one of them are some insignificant ruins, said to have been erected by the Danes when they occupied Mull; but Dr. MacCulloch has proved them to be of more recent origin. It is not easy to conjecture what could be the motive for placing a fortress on a solitary rock in a remote and boisterous sea which in fact nature had fortified long before. We passed between this group and the coast of Mull, and it was evident from the perfect correspondence of the rocks, that they must all have been originally united.

After doubling this Point, we caught the first glimpse of Staffa and Iona, appearing as specks in the vast sea and of Gometra, Ulva, Colonsay, Inch Kenneth and others lying within a large bay evidently hollowed out of the isle of Mull by the ceaseless action of the eternal waves: the whole of them are basaltic.

A Nineteenth-Century Tour 107

> Merrily, merrily, goes the bark
>   On a breeze from the northward free,
> So shoots through the morning sky the lark,
>   Or the swan through the summer sea.
> The shores of Mull on the eastward lay,
> And Ulva dark and Colonsay,
> And all the group of islets gay
>   That guard fam'd Staffa round.

The shores of Mull which surround this bay are precipitous and picturesque, rising into high cliffs which are occasionally columnar and possess considerable grandeur, backed by the lofty group of cones named in yesterday's voyage. Ulva and Gometra are composed of repeated ranges of terraces rising in succession from the shore to the summit which is covered with a fine verdant surface. The cliffs present rocky faces of dark bluish trap, sometimes marked by a columnar tendency not less regular than that of Staffa, though on a much smaller scale.

Inch Kenneth has a claim on the notice of everyone who visits this country, since that which Johnson has described, is esteemed classical ground by the tourist. The ruins of Sir Allan Maclean's house with the chapel, the cross, and the tombs are still to be seen; the decayed walls of the chapel reminding us, (to borrow a sentiment from that author) of the superstition of those by whom those structures were erected, and of the piety which has suffered them to become the habitation of the nettle and the toad: the cemetery uninclosed, unprotected and forgotten, the haunt of the plover and the curlew.

All these islands, as well as the numerous and nameless rocks that skirt these shores, are covered with verdure and tenanted by sheep or black cattle: even the rock which can maintain but one lamb is not unoccupied.

Staffa,* at first sight, offers nothing interesting to the traveller who has braved the dangers of these stormy seas to visit it. Its size is diminutive, and its northern end, though occasionally precipitous, generally runs down in an inclined plane dipping towards the east. As we approached it however, its eastern side presented ranges of columns of great elegance and regularity, which revived our expectations.

We dropped anchor off the south eastern corner of the island, wondering at its miraculous construction and shapes. It appeared like a huge ark floating on the sea, the sides, as it were, composed of multitudes of strait, angular shafts or narrow pilasters clustered together, and covered with an irregular thick stratum of alluvium, which gives it a heavy appearance. It is

---

* Staffa, from the Scandinavian Staf, a staff or pole, significantly 'the island of columns'. This shews, that though the modern discovery of this island is due to Mr. Leach in 1772, the ancient Northmen were aware of its peculiarities, as well as of its existence.

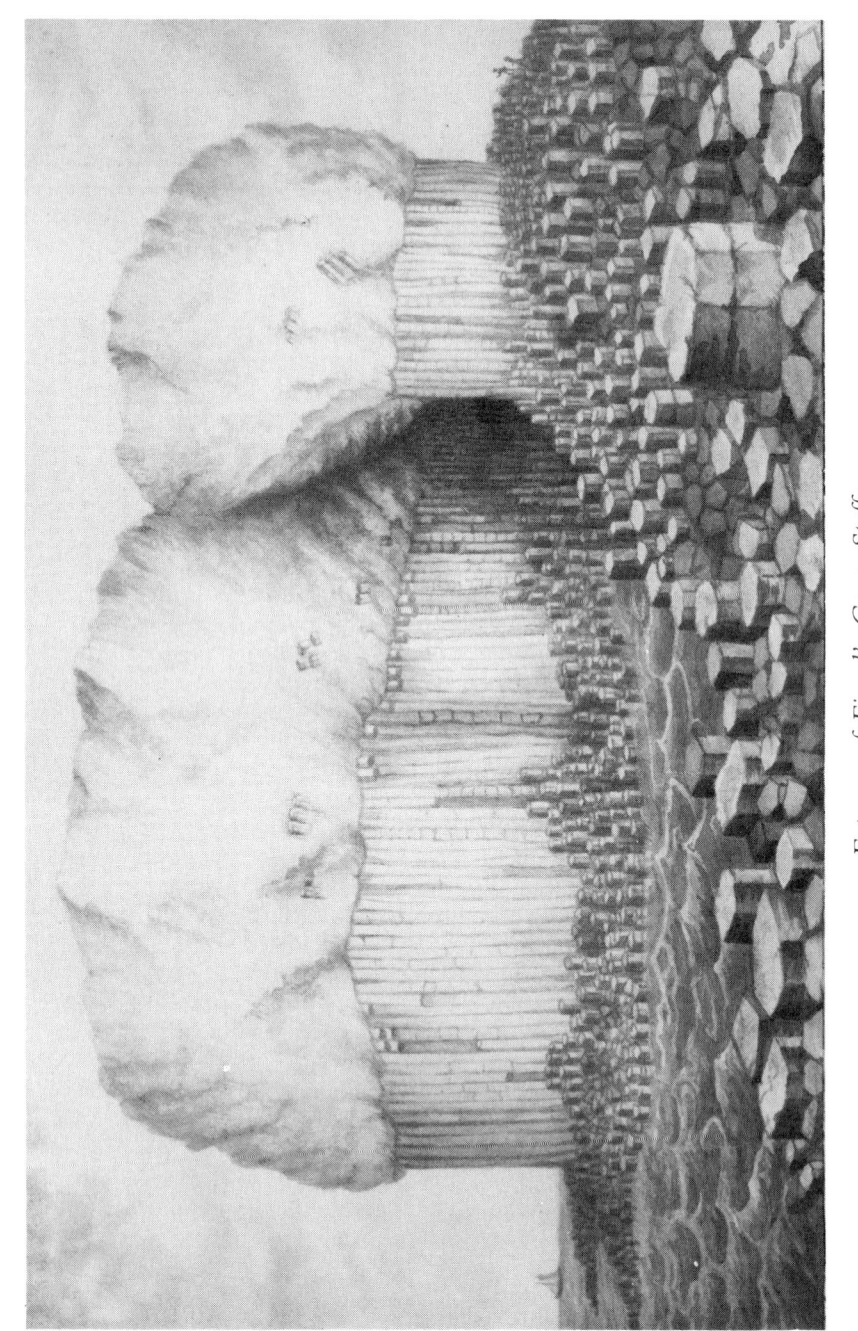

Entrance of Fingal's Cave, Staffa

so totally different from every other object in nature, that it is difficult not to believe it a work of art, though its magnitude at once repressed that idea. The company got into two boats, and over a heaving surf we made the south front, which bore a great resemblance to a long and bulky Doric Temple having three grand entrances. These are the Caves, which have been formed by the action of the sea through countless ages dashing against the pillars, and dislodging them from their places. Fingal's Cave,* which is by far the most magnificent, was now before us; its length is 227 feet, breadth 42 feet, its height from the top of the cliff to the centre of the arch 30 feet, and from the latter to the surface of the water at mean tide, 66 feet. The pillars appear the highest on the west side, on account of the greater length of the broken columns which form the causeway on the east side, and conceal the lower parts of those belonging to the front. The stratum which covers the pillars and forms the surface of the island, is much thicker here than in any other part, and has a heavy appearance, though somewhat relieved by a sharp contrasted arch which springs immediately over the portal. This stratum is strewed with patches of the lichen parietinus and the broken ends of detached columns which project out of it in different directions. The height of the cave diminishes a little within, while the mean breadth is nearly the same through its whole length.

We entered it, riding upon the breakers, which can rarely be done on account of the deep and heavy swell and the sharp points of the broken pillars which form the bottom of the cave, and would swamp the strongest boat. There was even in this calm day, a considerable elevation and depression of the surface, as each successive wave rolled in; the tide was about mid height, and the water about three fathom deep at the upper end. On entering this august and solemn Temple of Nature, which God has built among the roaring billows, and filled with the pealing anthems of the ever surging sea, it instantly reminded us of the great aisle of some ancient Gothic Minster, the sides being perfectly columnar and clustered, some in projecting groups and others as pilasters on spacious walls, the roof fretted and studded with thousands of polygonal sections, like corbels, groins, and armorial escutcheons, the bases resting on or having before them, others, broken off at all heights, as though they were stalls, niches, and steps. I stayed some time in the boat, which heeled and rocked as each gigantic wave heaved itself into the cavern, alternately raising and lowering it very considerably; for the water, having no lateral means of escape, rose, perpendicularly ten or twelve feet with every wave. It rushes in so suddenly, that it confines a portion of air within a little cave at the extremity of the vault, and compresses it to such a degree, that when it is relieved from a portion of the pressure on the subsidence of the wave, its elasticity

---

* Its ancient name was Uaimh binn, or the 'Musical Cave', a term probably derived from the echo of the waves. Fingal's, is a modern name.

causes it to explode with a tremendous noise, and dashes the water with howling hisses up the sides of the pillars to a considerable height. The sailors had great difficulty to prevent the boats from striking against the sides of the cave, or against each other; they had a peculiar method of keeping them steady, by short poles bound round at their ends with bossy balls of pitched tow, which they pushed against the pillars on each side. Though the day was perfectly calm, we had some difficulty in keeping our seats; and the captain, a pleasant communicative man, told us we were singularly fortunate, for not one day in fifty, even in summer could any boat presume to enter, and there was always some danger, as many have their limbs crushed between it and the broken columns.

On entering the cave, we could barely see the pillars at the farther end; but when we had been in awhile, it melted into 'a dim religious light,' solemn and awful, yet enough to distinguish the angular segments and hanging pillars that fretted the roof like massy stalactites, or the pendants of a Gothic building. The chaste and softened harmony of the colours delighted me very much. The surface of the pillars was a dark russet red, and the broken parts a cool greenish grey; they were studded with patches of different coloured lichens, limpets and other shells, pink and purple, white, green and yellow, looking 'like pearls upon an Ethiop's arm,' and the interstices and joints of the sides and roof were filled with a white infiltration of carbonate of lime, which intersected and entwined them with a rich and curious tracery. The transparent water had acquired a dark green cast; yet it revealed the rude mosaic pavement over which it flowed, while it curled in snow white foam round the bases of the columns, and lashed their sides with its feathery spray. Every person in the boats seemed to feel the influence of the sublimity which reigned in this profound and fairy solitude, where

> Nature herself, it seem'd, would raise
> A Minster to her Maker's praise!

Not a word was uttered, and full effect was thus given to the deep and hollow echoes of the swelling surge which met the ear on every side;

> That mighty surge that ebbs and swells,
> And still, between each awful pause,
> From the high vault an answer draws,
> In varied tone prolong'd and high,
> That mocks the organ's melody.

In looking outwards, the portal alternately assumed the form of a circular and of a pointed arch, the dark outline on the bright light being studded and notched with the projecting and broken points of the prisms. Over the heaving surges, at a distance, was seen the sacred island of Iona, sleeping softly on the bosom of the sunny deep.

It must be borne in mind that this wonderful cave has been formed by the loss of some of the columns of which the whole island is a solid mass. They have been undermined, and finally washed away by the stormy waves and by the action of frosts, during perhaps thousands of years. On looking attentively at the roof, it may be observed to be deeply channelled in the middle by a fissure, parallel to the sides, and prolonged from the point of the exterior arch to the end; and I have no doubt but it has been the primary cause of the excavation. The sides have not a regular surface like a wall, as represented in all the engravings I have seen, but in some places the pillars project in colonnades, in others they recede, while others are broken off at all heights, and the roof is composed of the ends of those which have filled up the body of the cave. This irregularity of surface produces a great variety of direct and reflected lights and shadows, and forms a more perfect combination of the chiaro oscuro than is generally seen.

On the eastern side there is an irregular terrace or elevated causeway of broken pillars, which runs nearly to the upper end, and rises about mid-height between the roof and the water, varying in width from one to three feet. It may be walked upon with tolerable safety by stepping on the tops of the pillars, but they vary so much in height, and are so slippery from the smoothness of the basalt and the splashing of the waves, that the greatest coolness and caution are necessary to prevent a false step, particularly in one spot where there is only a single pillar. Several of the passengers took an opportunity, while the boat was raised on the top of a wave, to step upon this terrace; I did so; Dovaston remained in the boat; and said afterwards, he thought the effect there, was more sublime, and that the heaving and rolling excited high and somewhat fearful pleasure. While I was gazing in wonder at the boat, now far beneath me, and now nearly on a level, our bagpiper had also climbed the staircase, and before I was aware of him, struck up a tune. My own feeling at the effect it produced, was that of deep astonishment which I could not define.

Having remained within the Cave as long as the captain thought our other arrangements would permit, the boats backed out, and I made my way over the rude staircase to the exterior portal. The immediate effect upon the eyes, when we issued out into the glaring sunshine, was painful, and the transition from solemn sounds to a comparative silence, affected the ears very sensibly. I again got into the boat, and we rowed along the south front of the island, till we came opposite the Boat Cave, which is the middle one of the three, and formed entirely out of the lowest bed of amorphous basalt. It has a double and rudely square portal, about twenty feet high and twelve broad, is very dark within, and looks like the entrance of a gallery of a mine. It cannot be entered except at high tide, on account of the shallowness of the water. The columns which rise above it are more lofty and magnificent than even those of Fingal's Cave being about fifty feet high, and over the centre of the opening, they retire from the general face of the range with a gentle concave sweep, and produce a shade that sets off the more prominent portions. The whole appearance is like the vast Proscenium of a gorgeous theatre. When we had examined it we went on to Mackinnon's or the Cormorant's cave, the most westerly of the three, which is concealed from the east corner of the island by a projecting point of the rock. Its height and width differ little from the great leave, but being also excavated out of the lowest and solid bed, its sides do not possess the same beauty and magnificence. The face above the cave, is however, more richly decorated, and consists, as the Boat Cave does, of ranges of perpendicular columns of great size and symmetry, hollowed out over the centre into a recess which hangs over the opening like a geometric ceiling. This cave is generally easy of access, but the captain would not allow our boat to enter on account of the strong breakers which shot up the rocks in angry spray, and trickled down their furrows in hundreds of silvery skeins. The sea was as transparent as an emerald, and, as we glided along over the tops of the broken columns, of which the whole shore is composed, we saw the large pinnated fuci and algae which adhered to them, waving in the agitated water like streamers at the mast head. Out of each of these Caves we saw fly many of the Wild Pigeon, or Stock Dove, (Columba oenas which were nearly altogether blue, and are probably the origin of most of those beautiful varieties which in a state of demestication are dependent upon man. The great scale of the front of Staffa and of the Caves, was strikingly exemplified when we were at the western end of it, by the diminutive size of some of the company who had remained in front of Fingal's Cave, and who seemed to be crawling like spiders round the projecting basaltic pillars.

We now rowed back and landed at the South east corner of the island upon the broken pillars which form the front or foreground of the Great Cave, and are of different heights and various diameters. Their tops are sometimes convex, but more generally concave, forming perfect shallow basons, in which was some good tasted white crystallized salt formed in them by the evaporation of the sea water. From the quantity of these broken pillars which we saw under the boat, both in the Cave and as we sailed along the south front of the island, I conceive the effect is not so complete when the tide is in, because it both diminishes the height of the cave, and the breadth of the curiousy tessellated foreground. Here a gentleman, who had come for no other purpose but to shoot at the poor gulls, obliged us, at Dovaston's request, by discharging his musket into the cave. The percussion at first was smart and crackling, as though it would have sent the rocks to fragments; but it soon returned with tenfold reverberations, rolling along the cavern, and catching the impending masses with tremendous thunderings.

On proceeding to the eastern side, the appearance of the columns is perfectly astonishing. They are bent into the most graceful and perfect curves, forming segments of very long circles, yet preserve their angular form and parallelism and are as compactly fitted to each other in the mass as the upright ones. Some of these masses of columns lie in a horizontal, and others in a sloping direction, towards different points of the compass. The concave sides are generally uppermost, and it seems as if some supernatural power had pulled them down in the middle, while in a soft state, and left the side pointing upwards. Looking at them in the direction of the axes of the columns, the appearance more resembles the surface of a honeycomb than anything else. In some of the groups, the convex side is uppermost, in others the incurvation lies in two different planes.

I employed a portion of the short time we remain on the island in sketching this most wonderful appearance into my original Journal; and felt as great a difficulty in doing it justice with the pencil, as I now do by description. If future leisure should permit, I may still introduce it here. The sketch embraces the small conical island of Buachaille, which is only separated from Staffa by a very narrow but rapid channel, and has doubtless been connected. Its shape is that of a tolerably perfect cone; its height is about thirty feet. It is one complete mass of the curved pillars, the concave sides sloping outwards forming the eastern face of it and the broken ends or transverse sections of them, the side next to Staffa. Some of them however lie with their sides towards the north, their upper ends pointing to the apex of the cone, and appearing foreshortened in the sketch.

These bending pillars exhibit a still more wonderful appearance in the Clamshell, or Scallop shell cave, which is very near this spot, and behind Fingal's Cave. It is approached by a cleft concealed between the second or third range from the front of the sketch, but its situation may be traced by the part in shade. The entrance into this cave may with great propriety, be compared to the skeleton of a ship while building on the stocks, the prisms gracefully curving each way like her ribs, with others of the same curve beneath, inverted. On one side, an irregular wall is formed by the broken ends, which looks, as I have before said, like the surface of a honeycomb. The length of this cave is about 130 feet, the height 30, and the breadth at the entrance 16 or 18 feet; its lateral dimensions gradually diminishing to its inner extremity. The incurvation of the pillars extends still farther towards the north, but no new features are presented.

When I had finished my sketch I mounted up the rude staircase represented in it, to the surface of the island, which is about a mile long, uneven, and covered with rather a luxuriant grass, now giving pasture to fifteen small black cows and a few sheep, but without a bee or a shrub, or even a hovel to shelter those who may be so unfortunate as to be overtaken by a storm, and detained all night upon it. A family formerly lived here; and our young friend McLean had told me, that in heavy gales of wind the

Bending Pillars, Staffa

whole island was shaken by the storm. In several places I observed that the ends of the columns projected through the covering of soil, and looked like a tessellated pavement.

There is little on Staffa to interest the botanist. The only plants I saw, were the Anthyllis vulneraria, Plantago maritima, Statice Armeria, Asplenium marimum and, in inaccessible situations, Ligusticum Scoticum. Not being able to reach the latter, I brought away plant of the Asplenium for my Hortus siccus, as a memento of this wonderful spot. I also collected a few of the beautiful little shells which adhered to the columns at the mouth of Fingal's cave.

The west and north sides of the island exhibit some perfect specimens of the columnar basalt, but the cliffs are low, and without peculiar interest. There are, round the whole coast, twenty six natural caves, all, except the four already named, insignificant and diminutive, being only remarkable for the explosions they cause from the collapsing of the air by the waves, which are equal to the discharge of great guns or culverins. The captain told us the Gaelic sailors give the island a name, signifying, 'Over the stormy surf'. God of mercies! what must this sea be to mariners in a midnight storm?

Having spent two hours upon the island, we returned to the vessel, weighed anchor, and bore away southwards for Iona.

As we sailed under the precipitous shores of Mull I observed in several places, instances of the great difference in the waste of the rocks above and below high water mark. Those portions which lay within reach of the diurnal action of the tide, were much less affected by the disintegrating process of the atmosphere those above them, and appeared in the shape of low platforms skirting the bases of the cliffs; while the latter often receded a considerable way from the shore, thus indicating the different degrees of rapidity with which those parts exposed to the air only, and those subjected to the vicissitudes of the sea and air together, have undergone decomposition.

Iona is about twelve miles to the south of Staffa, and lies off the south west promontory of Mull, from which it is only separated by a narrow strait. Iona, or Strona, means the 'Island of Billows', for here the vast Atlantic ocean bears on it with all its force, and no land to the westward is seen to streak or stud the interminable expanse of waters. It is about three miles long and one broad, and consists of rocks of inferior elevation, which are principally of grass. It owes its celebrity to St Columba, an Irish devotee, who fled in disgust from his native country in the sixth century; and after him it was named Icolmkill, or the island of St Columba's cell. It was anciently called I, (the Gaelic word for island, pronounced like the English, ee) or 'The Island,' a distinctive appellation derived from the sacred functions of the Saint.

Though the sanctity of Columba and his successors has doubtless been much exaggerated, there is sufficient proof that this little island was, during the dark ages, the seat of such piety and learning as monks generally professed and practised, while Western Europe was immersed in ignorance and barbarism. It is also certain that it has been considered through many succeeding centuries, a place of extraordinary sanctity; for in it repose the ashes of many of the early Scottish monarchs and chieftains, as well as several from distant countries. It is therefore not easy for a philosophic mind to approach its shores and tread the royal and pious dust which it contains, without feeling the influence of the recollections they are calculated to excite. He who can here abstract himself from the living objects around him, and abandon his mind to the visions of the past, will long after recur, with feelings of pleasing melancholy, to the short time he has spent among the tombs of Iona.

Boats, as at Staffa, were waiting our arrival, and we landed on a beach, very horrible, being composed of very sharp and highly inclined projecting rocks of black and very hard clay slate, which it is difficult to walk over without danger. On the shore, lay blocks of a covered granite, hornblendes late, mica slate, and grass. Ragged filthy children thronged round us, offering for sale pebbles and crystals, but I saw nothing among them of the least value. The heat was now become very oppressive, and we proceeded with slow and weary steps, to satisfy our curiosity under the conduct of a very learned personage, the schoolmaster of the island, who, though an Irishman, had the same antipathy to that witty people, as his patron saint Columba.

The buildings of Iona originally consisted of the Cathedral, two Monasteries, and six small votive chapels. We first went to the Chapel of St. Oran, who was one of the twelve saints that accompanied Columba from Ireland, and lies buried here. In our way we passed by a great tall Cross, called MacLean's Cross, sculptured with devices, and through a rudely inclosed ground, still used as a modern burying place, and all overgrown with thistles and gigantic ragwort. This sacred spot is called Reileg Oran, and has been the cemetery of personages of high distinction from distant lands. It is said to contain the remains of no less than forty-eight Kings of Scotland, four of Ireland, eight of Norway, and one of France, besides knights and heroes whose names, debaucheries, and murders, are now, like themselves, forgotten.

> Here lie the mighty troublers of the earth,
> Who swam to sov'reign rule through seas of blood,
> Who ravag'd kingdoms, and laid empires waste,
> And in a cruel wantonness of power,
> Thinn'd states of half their people!

The short time we were on the island would not allow us to note down

A Nineteenth-Century Tour

particulars, but they may be found copiously detailed in Pennant's Second Tour in Scotland. The oldest inscriptions are in the Saxon character; the sculptured effigies on the tombstones of the kings consisted of warriors, seaships, armorial bearings, and intricate tracery in bar relief characteristic of the low state of the arts in those periods, yet not devoid of spirit, when the refractory nature of the stone (mica slate) is considered. The ships are the most interesting, as serving to give us an idea of the knowledge which these Islanders possessed of navigation. The prow and stern are alike, and protracted into long curves upward like many of the galleys of the Romans. The latter is formed with a well constructed rudder, but there is no provision for rowing, nor is there any bowsprit. It is probable that these ships, or rather boats, were but of small dimensions. The outline on the following page represents one of them and I have accompanied it by another, equally curious, copied from one of the maps in the Bologna Edition of Ptolemy's Geography printed about the year 1470. This latter is rendered still more interesting, as shewing one of the earliest specimens of the art of Engraving upon Copper.

Left: ancient boat from Iona
Below: ancient ship from Ptolemy, about 1470

The Chapel of St Oran is in the Saxon style, with arcular arches and richly zig-zagged mouldings, and is doubtless the most ancient building in Iona, though far more modern than the age of Columba, to which it has been ignorantly referred. It has one pointed arch, and is probably not older than the twelfth or thirteenth century. Its dimensions are very small, being only sixty feet long by twenty. The floor is nearly covered with dark monumental stones, many of them of the Lords of the Isles. The tomb of MacFingon, an elegant piece of sculpture bears the date of 1489.

We went next to the Cathedral. This building must have been erected after the separation of the Diocese of the Isles from that of the Isle of Man in the reign of Edward the First. Much error and confusion existed respecting the title which the Bishops of the latter still retain, vizt. that of Sodor and Man, till Mr. Pennant removed them. During the time that the Norwegians possessed the Hebrides, they separated them into two divisions, the Nordereys or Northern Isles the Sudereys or Southern Isles; the latter being the most important, gave the name to the bishopric, and after the separation above named, the bishops of Man retained the title which has since been corrupted into 'Sodor'.

The Cathedral of the Diocese of the Isles is of a very mixed character as to its architecture, exhibiting various specimens of the Pointed Gothic, which renders it difficult to decide the period of its erection; but it cannot be earlier than the end of the thirteenth century, probably later. Its length from east to west is about 120 feet, and that of the transepts about 70; the tower is also about 70 feet high, supported upon four light and elegant pointed arches, and lighted on two sides; on one, by a window consisting of a single plain slab perforated with quatrefoils, on the other, by a circular light, with diamonds and spirally curved mullions firmly fretted. The Choir is 70 feet long by 27 wide. The shafts of the pillars are cylindrical and plain, like those of the Norman era, their capitals sculptured with spirited equestrian figures of knights and grotesque devices.* These pillars support ranges of pointed arches, of a curvature intermediate between those of the first and the second styles which characterize the two most beautiful periods of Gothic architecture, their soffits being fluted with plain and somewhat rude mouldings. A second and smaller tier of arches is perforated in the wall above these, sometimes circular, and at others terminating in a sort of trefoil head. The roofs have all long ago fallen in, and their rubbish still covers the floors of the aisles. There are some tombstones of kings and warriors and mitred abbots in richly canopied niches in the walls, having their full effigies highly relieved with the insignia of princely power and priestly pride. Near the site of the altar, (of which not a vestige remains) is the splendid tomb of Abbot MacKinnon, on which, under an arch of fine pillars, is a well

---

* Garnet says, one of these, is an Angel with a pair of scales, weighing souls, and the Devil keeping down the scale in which the standard is, with his paw!

executed recumbent figure of that personage with a Latin inscription: he died in 1500. Opposite it, are others of a similar construction. On the north of the Cathedral is the Chapter House, all in ruins, though part of the roof is still entire; some of the Cloisters also may still be traced; also a court, called the College, in which is a stone having the effigy of a priest in his robes, which is named the Black Stone of Iona, over which the Chiefs were wont to swear their most solemn oaths. This ceremony was considered as more sacred than any other obligation, and the oath could not be violated without the blackest infamy. In the churchyard are two very large crosses, one of which is a well sculptured block of red granite, fourteen feet high; the other is much mutilated. History or perhaps tradition says there were formerly 360 crosses in Iona, most of them were probably of a votive character. Near the Cathedral is a small cell where it is said the founder, St Columba, is interred.

We now proceeded southwards to their Nunnery,* which is also in ruins, and is apparently from its plain circular arches, of an earlier date than the Cathedral. The chapel is pretty entire, and contains, beneath sculptured stones, the corpses of many a beautiful nun and matronly abbess – 'for to this complexion must they come at last,' and mingle in common dust with kings and vassals. One grave was shewn us, now covered with rubbish from the dilapidated roof, where lay the beauteous Prioress, called Lady Ann the Divine, daughter of Donald, Lord of the Isles. She died in 1511. Many of the stones had on them well carved figures of dames of high renown. Thus finished our survey of the ruins of Iona.

The irregular range of huts which fronts the shore near the spot where we landed is the only place on the island that has any pretensions to the character of a village, but it is still dignified with the name of Ballymore, or the Great Town, which it has doubtless retained from the period of its wide extended fame. Indeed the remains of streets may yet be traced, running at right angles among the huts; they have Gaelic names signifying 'Main Street', 'Royal Street', and 'Martyr Street,' the latter leading from the Bay of Martyrs (where all the royal and noble corpses were landed) to the Cathedral. This very humble and dirty village is now the abode only of Hebridean fishermen and Kelp makers; we entered one of the huts to beg a little water to moisten our parched palates; it was smoky, dark, and squalid in the extreme, yet its poor inhabitants wore the smile of content, and were civil and obliging, according to our wishes, expressed by signs, for they did not understand our language. Dovaston detected the Hibernian in our sage conductor, by his brogue, though he persisted in denying it. He told us there was no kirk upon the island, but that a minister from Mull visited them four times a year, and preached on a mountain side.

Thus have we seen what Iona was, and what it now is. Its present abject

* Monachihoc veneno pignora concubitûs aboluisse dicuntur.

View of Staffa from the south-west

and degraded state enhances its former consequence, and allows free scope to the imagination to recall the barbarous pomp, the superstitious piety, and the spurious learning connected with its ancient history; while charity prompts us to throw a veil over the vices which reigned uncontrolled in all the remote monastic establishments. It is however but fair to add, that we did not see the Atropa belladonna growing among the ruins.*

The heat was so intense (Thermometer 82°) that it required all our exertion to take down our observations and before we had finished our survey, the captain reminded us that our allotted time was expired. We immediately went on board, and found dinner waiting on arrival. The principal dish was a large cod caught on the spot by angling with baits of lobster. When we returned on deck we had advanced far on our way to Staffa, having now only to return to Tobermory.

As we neared Staffa, the captain very obligingly at my request, changed the direction of the vessel, and took a sweep along the front of its magnificent columnar caves, remaining off the south west corner while I took a general sketch of the great façade, which has here much the appearance of a prodigious antique building blown sideways, the heavy roof crusted with lichens of the brightest orange. The sun had now nearly reached the west, and the slanting direction in which the rays fell upon the projecting colonnades, threw them out in high relief and rendered them doubly striking by the tranquil breadth of shadow which they cast over the contiguous parts, and finely softening again into a full light by a succession of smaller shadows resulting from the irregular grouping of the columns. The still darker recesses of the caverns, the broad green waves crested with silvery foam that shot in tremendous breakers over the slippery rocks – all mellowed by the warm tint of a summer evening, gave to the whole a richness of tone which surpassed anything of the kind I ever saw. The evening was lovely, and thousands of snowy gulls and other sea fowl were playfully wheeling in the warm reflexion of the sunny rocks, or riding on the evening waves in cleanly beauty and in inoffensive sportiveness: at these some young men on board were wantonly, I may say wickedly shooting, and with broken wings and plumage sprinkled with blood, they floated by our vessel with plaintive shrieks, while their murderers even laughed aloud at them as they reloaded their guns. We observed that when the guns were presented at them, the old birds immediately dived under the surface, while the young remained to suffer the fatal consequences of their inexperience. The isles of Skye, Rum, Egg and Coll, with other groups, appeared graceful, beautiful and majestic, as, like the Symplegades of the Archipelago, they met, crossed, and intersected each other, as our point of view changed.

* It will be recollected that this vessel was unfortunately run down in the Clyde, off Greenock, a few months after the period of our tour.

Clouds of smoke were rising gently from several points of the shore under the cliffs of Mull; and an enquiry, we found it was from the kilns used in making Kelp. Most of the population is employed in this laborious occupation during the summer months. Drift weed thrown on the shores by storms, and consisting chiefly of Fucus digitatus and saccharinus, is used to a certain extent when fresh and uninjured, but the greater part is precured by cutting other plants of this tribe at low water. The method of landing the weed after cutting, is simple and ingenious. A rope of heather or birch twigs is laid at low water beyond the portion cut, and the ends are brought upon the shore. At high water, the whole being afloat together, the rope is drawn at each end, and the included material is thus compelled, at the retiring tide, to settle on the line of high water mark. Soda is well known to abound most in the hardest Fuci, the serratus, digitatus, nodosus, and vesiculosus. On some estates they are cut biennially, on others once in three years; nor does it seem to be ascertained what are the relative advantages or disadvantages of these different practices. The weed is burnt in a coffer of stones, a construction which, however rude it may appear; seems fully adequate to the purpose. The quantity of sea weed required to make a ton of Kelp is estimated at twenty four tons, but varies according to the state of its moisture, and hence a conception of the labour employed in this manufacture may be formed, since the whole must be cut, carried on horses, spread out, dried, and stacked, before it is ready for burning.

It seems singular, though a well ascertained fact, that the cattle of the Hebrides are partial to these seaweeds. It has been supposed, though erroneously, that this practice, as well as the eating of fish, was the result of hunger. It appears, on the contrary, to be the effect of choice in cattle as well as in sheep that have once found access to this diet. The accuracy with which they attend to the diurnal variations of the tide is very remarkable; calculating the times of the ebb with such nicety that they are seldom mistaken, even when they have some miles to walk to the beach. With respect to fish, it is equally certain that they often prefer it to their best pastures. It is not less remarkable that the horses of Shetland eat fish from choice and that the dogs brought up on these shores, continue to prefer it to all other diet, even after a long absence.

Sea Weed is also largely employed in the Hebrides as a manure. Dr. MacCulloch says there is a sort of cultivation occasionally seen on the sea shores of the Highlands, at which a stranger will be much surprized. Sea weed is strewed on the shingle above high water mark and on it is sown barley (bear). As it disappears during the growth of the corn, the crop is in harvest time seen covering a surface of pure rounded pebbles of quartz or granite without even a vestige of soil. This plan may succeed in a climate so perpetually moist as that of these regions, as all vegetables are known to derive a large portion of their nourishment from the atmosphere. The saline particles impregnated with the tang are sufficient to keep up the requisite degree of moisture for the supply of the roots, while its loose and open nature is well calculated to allow what is superfluous to pass through it.

It was about eight o'clock when we landed at Tobermory, and though much fatigued, we took a walk through the wretched village at the top of the hill, which we found little cleaner than the kraals of the Hottentots. We had employed a considerable part of our time on board, in 'posting' our voluminous notes, and though we retired early to bed, could catch but little sleep. Wretched as our accommodations were, things are much improved in the Hebrides within the last fifty years. When Dr. Johnson visited Iona with Sir A. Maclean, the party were compelled to spend the night in a hovel, with no other beds than some clean hay. Tobermoray is now so generally visited by the Steam packets, that it would well repay a public spirited individual to establish a comfortable inn there.

Friday 29th July We left Tobermory at five o'clock this morning on our return to Oban, not a little rejoiced to exchange our filthy chamber, for the clean and elegant cabin of the Highlander. The morning was bright and breezy, and the sea pleasantly rough.

> The curling wave was edg'd with white,
> To inch and rock the sea-mews fly.

As we passed under Drymnen, we were agreeably surprized to see young Donald McLean come alongside in his shallop with his friends, escorting two young ladies who were returning to Glasgow. He and young Williamson came on board for a few minutes, and we had the pleasure of again shaking hands with them. With regret we did then once more push off, and parted with them, probably forever. We retraced our former track through the fast broad Sound of Mull, repassed Aros, Ardtornish, and Duart Castles, and enjoyed, a second time, the varied beauties of this romantic country. The mountain screens which rise in graceful curves and high coned peaks round the bay of Oban, the broad expanse of water, and the numerous ruined towers that sentinel its shores, combine to form a landscape, far exceeding in grandeur and sublimity, anything of the kind I have ever seen. The scenery of the Bay of Naples is universally celebrated; I have only seen it on canvas; but will be bold enough to assert, that if nature had placed that which I am now describing, in a more genial climate, it would rival it in beauty, as it now does in magnificence. As we were leaving the Sound of Mull, we saw at a distance the steam packet that was going to the Isle of Skye, and had we been within hail, would have availed ourselves of the opportunity to visit its romantic shores.

Before we take leave of the Highlander, I cannot help expressing the satisfaction and pleasure we uniformly received, both from her excellent accommodations, and from the civility and intelligence of the captain and the steward, during the whole of the voyage, a distance of 284 miles. The passage money amounted to £2.8.0 for each of us, including the boats which were provided at Staffa and Iona. Breakfast and dinner are regularly served up in the cabin; but these, of course, formed a separate charge. These steam vessels have opened so frequent, so expeditious, and so easy a communication between Glasgow and the whole of the Hebrides and the western coast of Scotland, that they are effecting considerable changes in those remote places. But we understood the facilities they afford are confined to the transport of passengers, and that they are not allowed to carry merchandise, on account of interfering with the established coasting trade.

The Highlander put us ashore at Oban at eleven o'clock on her return to Glasgow; and we expected to proceed to Fort William in the Comet* or the Ben Nevis, which usually touch there about noon the same day.

The pretty little town of Oban owes its existence to its advantageous situation and to the fine bay on whose shore it is built. This bay is of a semicircular form; and has two openings; one to the north and another to the south. It is sufficiently extensive to afford anchorage for 500 sail of vessels, and is well defended from the western winds. The first house of any consequence was built about fifty years ago by a trading company at Renfrew, who used it for a storeroom. The example being followed by other mercantile adventurers, Oban soon became a considerable place; and about ten years subsequent to its first foundation, was made one of the ports belonging to the Custom house. It is much indebted to the liberality of the Duke of Argyle and to the spirited exertions of two brothrs of the name of Stevenson. It seems formed by nature and a combination of many important advantages, to become the principal place of trade for the Highlands and the middle district of the Western Isles.

In the immediate vicinity of Oban are immense rocks of breccia or pudding stone, composed of different sorts and sizes of rounded pebbles of quartz, porphyry, granite, schist, &c cemented together by a matrix of trap or basalt, black within, but on exposure to the atmosphere assuming a red colour. The beach is of schist. The houses in Oban are all modern and whitewashed. The town reminded me very much of Aberystwith as seen from Cardigan bay: it is said to contain nearly 1000 inhabitants, mostly employed in the fisheries and coasting trade.

We passed five tedious hours at Oban in momentary expectation of the steam packets. We did not think it prudent to quit the immediate neighbourhood of the shore, as they merely touch at the quay to exchange passengers, or we could have employed our time very agreeably in climbing the hills which overlook Loch Etive. I therefore sat me down in the shade at the bottom of the pier, and 'inked in' my pencil sketch of the bending pillars of Staffa, while Dovaston made some additions to his Journal.

* It will be recollected that this vessel was unfortunately run down in the Clyde, off Greenock, a few months after the period of our tour.

It was nearly four o'clock when the Ben Nevis steamer appeared within the Sound of Kerrera, and when she stood under the pier at Oban, her deck presented such a scene of tumult and disorder that we were at a loss to assign the cause. She was altogether so unsteady, that her wheels were lifted alternately out of the water. We, however, got on board, and with some difficulty made our way to the stern; where we learned that she had a double complement of passengers (280 were on board) in consequence of the Comet being under repair at Glasgow. The captain also was extremely drunk; the heat and crowd both on deck and below, were intense, and some of the passengers were so much alarmed at their critical situation, that they got ashore and remained at Oban. They gave such an account of their voyage from Lochgilphead, that we determined, though reluctantly, not to go, and with some difficulty got again ashore. Being anxious to reach Fort William, we, with five of her late passengers, contracted for an open wherry manned with four sailors (the whole charge for which was £2.4.0.) under the assurance that we should be landed there in six hours, the distance being forty two miles. When this was arranged, another hour was lost by the anxiety of one of the company – a lubberly Englishman – to lay in a stock of bread and cheese, porter and whiskey, for the single night's voyage. At length, however, about six o'clock, we set sail under a pleasant and stiff breeze, and got out into the bay very finely. The sun gilded our swelling sail, steeping in softest orange, the ivy-mantled tower of Dunolly castle, and the grey walls of Dunstaffnage, seen across the mouth of Loch Etive. In about an hour the breeze died away, the tide was ebbing, and the men were obliged to have recourse to their long oars. We found we should have a tedious voyage, and gave up all thoughts of reaching Fort William before morning, so amused ourselves while it was light, in admiring the majestic piles of mountains heaped mass above mass, and cone above cone. Bulky packs of copper coloured thunderclouds hung stationary in the west; yet the sea was rough from the eddies and counter currents among which we sailed though not a breath of air touched its surface. The astonishing abundance of the beautiful Medusae with their filmy curtains, brilliant colours, and finely sensible vibratory threads, seen at a variety of depths in the green transparent water – with now and then a gurnet or other fish shooting across – the sea-fowl tossing on the sunny waves or instantly coming up like fairy apparitions, and again vanishing from the vacant surface, or wheeling round on light and airy wing in plaintive cry – together with the magnificent panorama of mountains around us – gave the eye a rapturous gratification, and with full soul, we frequently said in silence, 'They that go down to the sea in ships, and have their business among the great waters, see the works of the Lord, and his wonders in the mighty deep'.

We were now between the island of Lismore and the mainland, and doubled the Point of Lochnell – the southern promontory of Appin – on the summit of which is an obelisk of modern erection, rising above a fine plantation. Close to this, is the site of Beregonium, the visionary capital of ancient Caledonia.

The tide was now running against us; and on passing the entrance of Loch Creran, we had to contend against a very powerful current, which generated many strong eddies, and for some time made us rather uncomfortable. But the boatmen seemed so well acquainted with the coast, and so much at ease that we felt no alarm. On the opposite coast of Lismore, near the shore, is Kilchiarn, a seminary purchased by the Catholic body for the education of their priests, after the French Revolution had abolished such establishments in that Country. One of their bishops lives here, and has the superintendance of it, and the funds are principally supplied by some lime quarries upon the estate. Farther on, are the kirk and manse of Lismore.

Here the big and vulgar English gentleman, who had long been setting in for the sulks, and whom Dovaston afterwards called 'Blubber-chops', began to be extremely disagreeable. He was very captious with another of the party, a sly and cautious Scot, and quarrelled with the civil and labouring boatmen for not pulling hard enough. The basket being near him, he doled out the bread and cheese, and gave us the porter in a small tin tot; miserably and wretchedly contrasting his ignorant and noisy talk, with the shrewd and sensible remarks of the elderly Scotchman who sat beside him; who, though of few words, and those oozed out like the last drops of a squeezed lemon, was more than a match for him. The boatmen treated his unfeeling taunts with silent contempt, or by conversing together in Gaelic.

The sun was now just setting; and the full moon rose in serene and silent majesty over one of the ridges of the lofty and bifurcated Ben Cruachan; and Dovaston seemed silently amused in watching whether she would mount the pointed rocks, or disappear behind them by the motion of our boat. As we were likely to be such close companions for the night, he tried every expedient to restore his friend Blubber-chops to good humour, and by his sallies of wit and anecdote, to amuse the party; but all would not do, and we were left at liberty to enjoy our own reflections. Our haughty countryman steered, using sea-phrases, evidently to display his knowledge of nautical affairs; and though repeatedly cautioned by our Gaelic sailors, who were toiling at the oars, run us at length upon a sunk rock, which wheeled our boat quite round, and nearly unshipped her rudder. The shrewd Scotchman now took the helm; and on Dovaston's speaking of Sir Walter Scott, said he should rejoice to see his library; 'and I', said the coarse Englishman 'should like to see his kitchen': then looking to the high peaks sleeping in the blessed moon-light, said 'What multitudes of mushrooms must be lost on these mountains, from the impossibility of gathering them!' One of the rowers was an old man and another about thirty, whom they called Alec (Alexander). He had a most benevolent and intelligent face, and agreeable voice, and never would drink or eat until he had first offered it to the old man, pressing him more by manner than by words. They occasionally sung in Gaelic very sweetly, in parts: and not only most civilly answered any questions, but of their own accord pointed out the situation of objects as we passed them, though now scarcely visible. The disgusting Englishman was aristocratically ignorant, and frequently quarrelled with the quiet Scotchman about naval terms, swearing he would never steer us up the Linnhe Lock – 'aye, aye', said the wary Scot, 'I'll clear the rocks, *rudder* an' a'.'

One of the numerous islands to the north of Lismore, called Innis y Cloch, appeared 'through the dim veil of evening's dusky shade', like towers standing in the sea; among them was a singular craggy rock, very much resembling the colosssal head of Memnon, now in the British Museum. Among other objects indistinctly seen, I recollect the ruin of Castle Stalkir, apparently standing in the loch under the high rocks of the mainland a little beyond the village of Port Appin; and near it the very bold rock of Cloch-awe at the southern end of which, was a large natural perforation, like an immense arch, through which the road from Oban to Fort William passes.

After this, the objects among which we glided in the tranquillity of the night, flitted before us in the partial obscurity of moonlight; nothing was conspicuous but the ever-burning luminaries of heaven, and the scintillations of the Medusae among which we ploughed over watery way.

We amused ourselves for a while with listening to the harsh guttural Gaelic of the boatmen and to their songs, which had a musical effect, as eacch one,

>   bending to his oar,
> With measur'd sweep the burden bore,
> In such wild cadence as the breeze,
> Makes through December's leafless trees.

The rest of the voyage till daybreak, was passed in darkness and broken sleep; so, as a pompous tourist would say, He who sees nothing, has not much to describe; and he who knows but little, has not much to say. Having had but little rest the night before, about midnight I rolled myself into the confined den at the head of the boat, where I found a small quantity of broken straw and a large quantity of fleas; yet notwithstanding the activity of these light infantry, I enjoyed about two hours sleep, and was at length awaked by the tossing of the boat and the rippling of the waves against her sides, a slight breeze having again sprung up, much to the relief of our poor fellows. The vulgar gentleman and the keen Scott were still jarring.

When the morning dawned, we found ourselves at the upper end of Loch Linnhe, entering into Loch Eil, the scenery round which, a good deal resembles that of Loch Long and Loch Fyne, excepting that here, at intervals, we saw through the side screens, the peaked hills of Morvern on the left; and the bulky Ben Nevis on the right, heaving his gigantic brow over the nearer mountain piles, and already tinged with the earliest sunbeams. The dawn was fresh and lovely, yet 'there was not a breath the blue wave to curl'. As we approached Fort William, our attention was excited by the group of lofty mountains surrounding the head of the loch, and at whose feet were the numerous locks at the south-west extremity of the Caledonian Canal. At length, after a tedious voyage of thirteen hours, we came under the walls of Fort William: our companions went on after the Steam vessel, which we saw lying in the basin of the Grand Canal; we were paddled ashore in a coble or coracle, more oblong than those which may still be seen on the rivers of Wales. These frail and precarious barks are interesting from their resemblance to those used by our remote ancestors; for they may be clearly traced back to the 'Vitilia navigia 'of Pliny, which have thus, with a slight alteration in their structure, survived the changing customs of two thousand years. The ancient Celtic boats were made of a frame of wickerwork covered with coria, or hides: hence, in Gaelic they are called curach, in Wesh curan, and in English coracle – names which have outlived their original construction, the *hide* being now substituted by canvas strongly pitched. We were directed to the Caledonian hotel, where we learned from one of the passengers of the Ben Nevis, that she did arrive safely about eleven o'clock last night, but that the voyage had been attended with the most disagreeable circumstances, and not without many painful apprehensions of danger.

Volume II

Saturday, 30th July Fort William, formerly called Maryburgh, is a small and poor town situated on the east shore of Loch Eil, near that point where it bends at an acute angle towards the west. The houses are mostly small and mean; and the place has a dull, deserted appearance, though it is a sort of metropolis for the surrounding district. The extent of this district may be conceived, when we consider that there is no town to the south nearer than Inveraray, which is seventy four miles distant, nor to the east than Inverness, which is sixty miles; and some opinion may be formed of its population by that of Fort William itself, which does not contain more than twelve hundred inhabitants. The aspect of the neighbouring country is cheerless and forbidding; consisting of little else than moors and turbaries surrounded by immense dark and barren mountains of shapeless and unwieldy forms, unenlivened by trees or verdure. The climate is said to be almost perpetually wet and stormy, both on account of its vicinity to the sea and the neighbouring lofty mountains, which attract and precipitate the clouds from the western ocean. It owes its existence to the garrison in its suburbs, which stands on the shore of the loch, and commands the entrance of the Great Glen that runs in a north east direction through Scotland. This fortress was originally built by General Monk to keep in check the restless spirit of the neighbouring chiefs, who adhered firmly to the cause of the Stuarts. It was rebuilt in the reign of William the third; and in the year 1746 stood a siege of five weeks, though by no means a place of strength, and seems to be gradually falling into ruin.

The morning was so delightful that we were very desirous to ascend Ben Nevis, aware that the climate was not to be depended upon for an hour. But as much time would have elapsed in preparation, and we were already exhausted by loss of rest, we reluctantly deferred this arduous excursion till the following day; for in addition to our fatigue, my insteps and ankles were still swollen from so much walking during our laborious tour, that I shrunk from the attempt. We therefore agreed to go to Glen Roy – a valley but little known, though its 'Parallel Roads' exhibit one of the most curious and remarkable phenomena in the world. The description of them had long excited in my mind the most lively interest, and the subject was so near my heart, that had circumstances prevented me from seeing them, the disappointment would have been followed by lasting regret. My friend,

View of Glen Roy taken near Glen Fintec

knowing my devotion to geology, and not having heard of them before, accompanied me under a strong impression that he should be disappointed; but when they opened unexpectedly upon him, his distrust was converted into astonishment, and he has ever since thought on them with increasing delight.

There being no gigs at Fort William, we engaged one of the light carts of the country, with a seat suspended across the middle by chains. For the first five miles we took the military road to Fort Augustus, passing the ruin of Inverlochy castle on the left, which stands on the right or south bank of the river Lochy, and at the extremity of an extensive boggy flat. It has evidently been a place of considerable strength and magnitude, and appears to have been built about the time of Edward the first. It is a quadrangular building, with round towers at the angles like the castle at Inveraray; and is nearly one hundred feet every way within the walls, which are nine feet in thickness and the whole building including the towers, covers above an acre and a half of ground. At the gate between the south and east towers, are the remains of a drawbridge. Long previous to this period, however, the Thanes of Lochaber, and particularly Banquo, the predecessor of the Stuart Line, had their residence at Inverlochy; and in Sinclair's Statistical Survey it is said that a walk below the castle still retains the name of 'Banquo's Walk'.

We passed under the northern side of Ben Nevis, and were perfectly astonished, while broiling under the beams of a burning sun in the Dog days, at seeing many large masses of snow lodged in the clefts and lying on the sides of this mountain, particularly near the summits and appearing like large perforations through which the sky was seen. As we proceeded through the barren and inhospitable district, we observed in the turbaries and on the boggy sides of the hills, very extensive remains of vast natural Fir forests, consisting principally of the roots and lower parts of the trees still remaining in their original position, with some enormous trunks lying prostrate among them, 'over which the wind now passes in mournful gusts; and moves in melancholy unison with the memory of years that are gone.' The few scattered huts were entirely of turf; and the scene of desolation was not relieved by a single living tree or even a shrub – the very heather and uliginous plants which covered the moor, scarcely possessed a tinge of green. Among them I observed the Narthecium ossifragum and Schoenus albus.

We crossed the river Spean near its confluence with the Lochy by a singularly lofty and romantic bridge, emphatically named High Bridge. It is thrown across a narrow and deep ravine, at the bottom of which the torrent rushes impetuously over perpendicularly stratified rocks of a primitive blue limestone, which now rise to a great height above it, and are now hollowed out into deep basins filled with the pitchy waters. The bridge is about a hundred feet above the bed of the river, and astonishes the traveller both by the grandeur of the design, and by his being conducted to it without any

View of Glen Roy taken from below Glen Fintec

previous indication of so striking a scene. Soon after passing it, we left the Fort Augustus road, and took a direction nearly east, keeping near the right bank of the Spean and crossing several tributary streams which had hollowed out for themselves deep beds below the general surface of the country, till we came to Keppock. The small village is about twelve miles from Fort McClain, and stands near the junction of the Spean and the Roy. The space between these two rivers is occupied by a large verdant elevated plain or terrace, whose surface is as level as a bowling green, and which is evidently the remnant of an alluvial deposit, which has once covered the whole opening of the valley. Its present shape is triangular, and its salient angle forms the point of junction of the two rivers, by the action of whose streams it has been reduced into its present form. Its surface is on the same horizontal plane with a solitary Parallel Line on the side of the hill above it, indicating their common origin. Other terraces or deltas of different sizes, but with true horizontal surfaces, skirt both the Spean and the Roy before and after they have united their streams, clearly shewing them to be remnants of a general plain which has been partially washed away. The sloping sides of some of the terraces shew regular horizontal beds of gravel, stones and fine sand, confirming their alluvial origin.

After leaving Keppock, the road became so hilly and rough that we were compelled to leave our jolting vehicle, and as it was yet several miles to the point where the Parallel Roads are seen in their greatest extent, our good natured guide said he would leave the cart in the road and unyoke the horse to browse at large in the wide valley while he walked on with us. We requested him not to risk the time and labour it might require to catch him again, but he would not be prevented. As we toiled along in the burning heat, we saw here and there, high above us, long horizontal lines skirting the sides of the hills and running round the escarpments like the remains of ancient fortifications, but as yet singly, and without corresponding ones on the opposite side of the valley. At length on suddenly attaining the summit of a low hill, we were struck with the singular appearance of three vast horizontal lines, running parallel to each other mid way along the lofty, smooth, and sloping sides of the mountains on both sides of the valley, stretching onwards for eight or nine miles, and only lost at length by a turn in the direction of it. They preserve their parallelism and true horizontal position through every turn and winding of the valley, and whatever curves, ravines, or projections there may be in the hills, they never interrupt the Lines, which run round and are regularly taken up on the other side. The Lines also on each side the valley are in the same horizonal plane; the uppermost or highest is situated rather lower than midway beween the summit and the base of the hills, and there is about three times the space between the lowest and the middle Lines, as there is between the latter and the highest. In the upper parts of Glen Roy, the Parallel Lines, or Roads as they are improperly called, consist of uncovered broken fragments of rock,

View of the terraces at the top of Glen Roy

but towards its opening they are covered like the general form of the hills, with a fine green sward, and are only to be distingished by their singularly horizontal and parallel direction. An inattentive spectator might perhaps disregard them from their apparent insignificance in an immense valley ten or twelve miles long, and five or six wide and seeming only like threads or cords zoning mountains which rise perhaps 2,500 feet high and are remarkable for their uniformity and simple grandeur. He might also be disposed to doubt the singular coincidence in the planes of the Lines on each side of the valley, and also whether those on the same side run parallel where they are interrupted by the gullies, but an eye accustomed to perspective can easily reconcile these apparent irregularities.

At the upper end of Lower Glen Roy, the Parallel Lines are narrower, and the declination of their *surfaces* from the horizontal plane is more considerable than towards the lower end; and wherever the natural rock appears, they are either entirely wanting or are always less discernable and their surfaces have a much greater conformity with the natural slope of the hill, than where they appear upon the gravelly mould which frequently covers the rock. Proceeding down the glen, but not far from its top, a stream enters on the left; and here a great series of terraces is found, the highest of which lies on a level with the third or lowest Line; the rest gradually diminish in height, and fall off, as it were, by many successive stages, numerous small ones descending down to the very bed of the river, skirting its banks and accompanying its course. Throughout the whole extent of the valley, various streams or mountain torrents enter the glen, each accompanied by its own lateral terraces. To form a clear conception of these terraces, it is necessary to state that the whole bottom of the valley has formerly been covered with an alluvial deposit of considerable depth, formed of horizontal layers or strata of mud, sand, and gravel, alternating with each other, and having a perfectly level or flat surface. The lateral streams which rush down the sides of the hills in their course towards the river Roy, have gradually worn for themselves beds through this alluvial deposit; and the terraces which now form a singular a feature of the valley, are the insulated portions of it which have not been disturbed by the streams. They wear the appearance of the artificial earthworks of a fortification, frequently occupying considerable areas, their surfaces as level as water, and covered with grass, trees, and cottages. Their salient angle is always towards the middle of the valley, and either acute or obtuse, as the nature of the ground has allowed the tributary stream to join the main river more or less at right angles. It is easy to conceive that the sinuous course of the Roy itself has variously affected these angles; one side of each terrace having been formed by it, and the other by the tributary stream. Many ranges of the terraces are sometimes seen one above another, occasioned both by the successive deepening of the beds of the Roy and of the smaller streams, and by the continual shifting of the beds themselves from local causes.

The lowest of the three Parallel Lines first occurs at Glen Turit, one of the lateral vallies opening into Glen Roy, and all the three are occasionally seen from this point to the opening of the valley. They also occur in very regular and perfect series in Glen Gloy, a small valley to the north, and partially also in Glen Spean, to the south, before the Spean joins the Roy at Keppock, by indicating that they owe their origin to water, and that it must have covered the two last named glens as well as Glen Roy.

I shall here eneavour to explain the manner in which they have been formed. In an existing lake, it is easy to see the very traces in question produced by the wash of the waves hollowing out the alluvial matter of the banks, and forming a gently sloping margin. By the check which the stones that fall from above thus receive, and by the loss of gravity which they suffer from immersion in water, are distributed in a belt along the edge of the lake, a belt broadest and most level where there are most loose materials and where the declivity of the hills is least; narrowest and most imperfect where these circumstances are different, and, wherever rocks protrude, ceasing to be formed. Existing lakes would present all these appearances in similar situations, if drained.

I omitted to mention that a tradition prevails in the neighbourhood of Glen Roy, that the Parallel Roads were constructed by human power, for the purpose of driving chariots by the Fee Inhions (sic) or wild men of renown in the days of Ossian, Fingal, Cathullin &c – an idea too ridiculous for refutation. Our modest and intelligent guide however had heard that a lake had filled the valley and had formed the roads, and at his own request I explained to him how the water had probably acted upon the sides of the hills to produce the effect. His name was Archibald MacDonald, and we were so much pleased with him, than on our return to Fort William, we engaged him to accompany us up Ben Nevis on the following morning. It was half past seven o'clock when we reached the Caledonian hotel to dinner, and were as much overcome by the excessive heat and loss of rest the previous night, that after finishing our notes we returned to bed.

Sunday, 31st July We rose at four o'clock, and were cheered by the prospect of a fine day, though the summits and sides of the hills were muffled in clouds. Archibald soon appeared, and kindly brought with him his grey horse for me to ride to the foot of the mountain, having heard me express doubts to Dovaston when we were in Glen Roy whether my swollen ankles would not prevent me from reaching the summit. He brought with him a companion, who soon ingratiated himself into our favour by his intelligent conversation and by asking many sensible questions about England. They alternately carried our basket of provisions; and thus we set out, crossing the stream of the River Nevis, having the mountain on our right, Inverlochy castle on our left, and Corpach, with the long line of locks at the southwest end of the Caledonian Canal over the head of Loch Linnhe, in sight. After following the Fort Augustus road about two miles, we turned to the right and crossed a very heavy bog, which soon obliged me to dismount. The ascent began beside a 'wimplin burn', and was so steep (as we then thought) that we several times sat down to rest. A few pretty birches fringed the rivulet for a while; but we soon left every shrub and vegetation behind. On gaining the ridge of the first mountain, the lofty, rugged, and nearly perpendicular face of Ben Nevis[*] appeared in black, appalling majesty, and the heart somewhat shrunk at the thought of ever gaining the summit, which, were it unclouded, could not be seen from this point. The view upwards was dismal and frowning, consisting of craggy and turretted rocks; and below us, thin vapoury clouds were sailing rapidly along, as they tore and detached themselves from the mass that enveloped the plain and the head of the Loch, and by their magnificent effects amply compensated for the loss of the terrestrial scenery. The tops of the higher mountains piercing through the stratum of fleecy clouds, appeared like rocky islands in the midst of an icy sea.

After much laborious climbing, relieved by intervals of rest, we came in sight of a small alpine lake, in which the trout are said to be extremely black. Vast ravines now began to present their yawning declivities, down many of which little silvery waters were playing amid enormous blocks of red sienitic granite and huddled wrecks of fragments, plainly indicating

---

[*] From Ben, head, & Nêf, Heaven, or the Hill of Heaven. Nef is Heaven in Welsh.

what uproar and ravage exist here in winter or after thunderstorms. Very bright sunlight occasionally gleamed and shifted on the sides of the distant hills below us, silvering the edges of the aspiring vapours which still enveloped their bases. We assured ourselves of an auspicious day, so proceeded in confidence, but with awe, excited by the wild sublimity of the surrounding scenery. The sun soon rose in gorgeous majesty above the rolling ocean of clouds that in every colour floated below him, 'oër the sky'd mountains and the shadowy vale', as he slowly, but not imperceptibly made his progress towards the canopy of lovely azure that arched the clear vault of heaven. We had now left every trace of vegetation behind us; and on turning towards the north, the ascent suddenly became extremely steep, over one eternally continued mass of sharp fragments. The labour here was much increased by the extreme caution necessary to avoid stepping on the loose stones which, on being displaced would bring down a volley of others clattering after them, and send the intrepid climber downwards. A false step among these angular and slippery ruins would be followed by serious bruises or broken limbs. We had also to cross many broad taluses or slopes of small gravelly fragments which lie in an angle of 45 degrees and render the footing more difficult and precarious than the last, as they sometimes slip down in masses, and the only thing to be done, is to preserve an erect position, and to descend with them till they settle of themselves. The feet then become buried half knee deep, and in extricating them we sometimes set the mass again in motion. Thus much exertion and time were often spent to gain a trifling perpendicular ascent, especially as the high angle of the mountain compelled us to take a very zigzag and circuitous course. Several gullies and craggy ravines were now to be passed, in which we sometimes became enveloped in mist, and had to encounter strong currents of air. Upon the whole however, the clouds above us were becoming more attenuated, and over the distant hills of Mull, the blue sky appeared hung with a long level embattlement of thunderclouds.

We frequently cast our eyes upwards to measure the termination of our labours, but the guides told us it would yet be some time before we should see the summit. They said that many ptarmigans, or white grouse, black game, here called the heathcock, and red grouse called moorfowl, inhabit Ben Nevis and the neighbouring mountains; as well as three species of eagles, foxes, badgers, weasels and polecats. In the glens, wild deer and hares are found, the latter being frequently white in winter.

A black and strongly indented ridge now appeared, which the heart, from the great labour and weariness of the limbs, would fondly imagine to be the uppermost; yet others afterwards appeared, as lofty and as frowning, sometimes struggling with the thin steamy vapours that enveloped them, and sometimes rising like insulated castles hanging in mid air. The floating clouds had a wonderful and even magical effect upon the scenery, which from our winding course was constantly changing, now rapidly coming on and involving us in a misty vacuity, and now as rapidly wheeling off and revealing horrid chasms and overhanging precipices, unseen before, in all their bald and vast sublimity, the sun beaming full upon their white and weathered sides and thunder-splintered pinnacles. Down one of these we looked as far as the clouds would permit, and saw its shelving bottom filled with eternal snow, while on the sides rose up in rugged grandeur, perpendicular piles of rocks like cathedral steeples, serrated and fissured, and raised tier on tier. In another of these dreadful abysses, the rocks appeared through the partial openings of the vapoury clouds which were sailing majestically over them, of a horrid blackness and of immeasurable depth, giving the most unbounded scope to the imagination, and covering them with all the awful mystery of sublime obscurity.

We now reached an insignificant spring, which our guides told us was the highest on the mountain, though it was still two miles to the summit. Here we sat down and broke our fast on a cold shoulder of mutton, bread and cheese, and a mutchkin of whiskey. The water was as cold as ice. Soon after resuming our arduous task, we walked over a broad deep mass of very hard snow, which we broke with our sticks and eat of, for we were sore athirst, and playfully pelted each other with snowballs, though the inhabitants of the world below was broiling under a burning sun. I have since ascertained that Fahrenheit's thermometer on this and the previous day, stood at 83 degrees near Edinburgh, while in London it was only 81, a circumstance worthy of remark. We now got upon a large plain of but little slope, covered with a wreck of rugged broken stones without a vestige of soil in the spaces between them; and were surprised at its great extent, being some hundreds of acres, this is called a Scarnach, and other similar ones are scattered here and there on the face of the mountain. When we had toiled across it, we gained another ridge of rock, and seeing through a sweep of the clouds, a distant black point, exclaimd with satisfactory rapture – 'There's the summit!' but the guides then checked our hopes by saying it was yet more than a mile to the top, and that many of those single rocks appeared at intervals, deluding the hopes of the arduous pilgrim. Our hearts for a moment shrunk appalled as the rolling clouds kindly encurtain'd the object of our disappointment: and after a short snatch of delicious rest, we recommenced our laborious ascent.

Soon after this, the gauzy vapours began to wheel off so rapidly, that Dovaston hurried on, impatient to reach the summit before they were quite dispersed. As I followed him, gaining ridge after ridge, which I successively believed to be the last, I at length looked up, and saw him.

> Perch'd on the point of Britain's topmost height
>   His keen eyed ken to throw
> Around the mighty map that lies below;
>   Or gaze with aching eye

> On all the vast concavity of sky
> Himself an undistinguish'd mite.*

We met at the heap of stones which is piled upon the extremest summit and congratulated each other on having attained the most elevated point in the empire of Great Britain. The sun shone out nobly; the clouds smoking up from the yawning gulfs and abysses below, or curling about like steam from enormous furnaces and craterous cauldrons; and when they cleared the chasms, floating off in mid air, tinged with all the colours of the rainbow, to settle round some neighbouring summit, or gradually vanish in the lower atmosphere. After giving the first moments to a rapid glance at the boundless prospect beneath us, we sat down to finish our prog. We had brought no water to dilute our whiskey, and it was two miles down to the nearest well, but we contemplated no difficulty in dissolving some of the snow by which we were surrounded. When it had been sometime in the glass however, with the spirit, we found it necessary to use artificial means to thaw it, and by turns we held it between our hands till they were benumbed. This proving ineffective we placed the tumbler on a stone inclined to the south and reared behind it two others with as much service as we were masters of, to throw the reflected rays upon it, and were much surprised to find that after leaving it in this position for more than half an hour, but a small portion of it was dissolved. At length we threw it away unthawed, nor had it melted when we left it on the sunny stones. After despatching our mountain fare, I began to make a few notes, and Dovaston wrote part of a letter to his friend Warren; and it is a singular fact, that though surrounded by scenery calculated to cause so strong an excitement, we both insensibly fell asleep, overcome by fatigue. The air was cool and chilly, but the great heat of the day moderated the keen atmosphere of this high region. As we carried no thermometer, we could only judge of the temperature by our sensations; it would probably have ranged from 40 to 45 degrees.

The altitude of Ben Nevis is said to be 4,370 feet above the level of the sea, and thought it has the credit of being the most lofty mountain in Britain, it is supposed to be equalled by some hills in Mar. Its summit is an extensive plain, irregularly circular and nearly horizontal, composed of immense blocks of stone, the fragments of other peaks which have in distant centuries peered high above it, though now laid prostrate by the lightning and the tempest in obedience to that universal law which exposes the most elevated in station and in power to all the vicissitudes of fortune, while it shelters the humble and unaspiring by means of the very obscurity into which they are thrown. Not a particle of soil or vegetable mould can be seen in the wide interstices between the blocks, to support even the

---

* See his own Poems, page 358.

minutest moss. A few crustaceous lichens are thinly sprinkled upon their bleached surfaces, and these first germs of vegetable life are all the traces of organized matter that are to be found here, having vainly attempted to form a mould for the reception of more perfect plants. The shattered fragments on which we stood were a perfect chaos of desolation, bald and naked, and without any variety of colour; while the vast undulated country which lay below, was too remote for the eye to distinguish either its colours or its features: it appeared of an uniform neutral tint, without any beauty. Many of the surrounding summits which from the plain and during our ascent had astonished us by their elevation, were now by the superior altitude of our position, wonderfully diminished, and appeared only like the furrows of a ploughed field, or the rising seats of an amphitheatre. From the same cause also, the valleys were apparently sunk much below the level of the ocean; an effect of the laws of perspective I had never before noticed.

The view was boundless and bewildering; and except the line of lakes leading towards Inverness, it was some time before the eye could identify the most prominent objects, even with the assistance of our map (which we spread out upon the stones) and of our intelligent guides. Looking north east, the whole of the Great Glen which intersects Scotland from the Linnhe Loch on the west of the Moray Firth beyond Inverness on the east, was in view; and the chain of lakes which lie within it, resembled an irregular canal between a double wall of low black rocks, the intervening spaces appearing only as bridges. Our distance from the Moray Firth could not be much less than Eighty miles. In the opposite direction, or south west, the view was equally extensive, embracing the mountains of Morven and Appin, divided by the Linnhe Loch, over which are seen the fine group of Ben More in Mull, now reduced to a pigmy size, and the isle of Colonsay like a faint speck in the extreme offing. The extent of the visible horizon therefore in a north east and southwest direction, could not be less than about a hundred and sixty miles, and embraced at once both the German and Atlantic oceans.

Looking eastward, rose the very bulky and near point of Cairn Dierg, one of the group of Ben Nevis which is named from its singularly red appearance. It is an entire, rounded mass of sienitic granite, and wherever the rock is laid bare by the numerous watercourses, it shews a red streak. In this direction we saw Loch Laggan, and a little to the south of it Loch Rannoch, beyond which was Schiehallion; then Ben Lawers and the Grampian chain stretching to Ben Cruachan, whose three conical tops were directly in the meridian line. A little to the westward our guides pointed out the tops of the not very distant mountains which surround Glencoe, the most desolate and dreadful glen in Scotland, and the pass called the Devil's Staircase, which we could not otherwise have recognized among the interminable ocean of billowy hills which everywhere met the eye. To the north we saw some very distant, and consequently very lofty peak in

Rosshire. While contemplating vast protuberant cumulous thunder clouds that hung in the northwest, such was our amazement to discover, that what we at first glance had taken for other clouds beyond, were the Cathullin mountains in the isle of Skye, seen through and as it were, above the clouds; while to the west we could distinguish others of the Hebrides studding the western region. To go into farther detail would be both tedious and useless.

The north east front of Ben Nevis is perforated and engulfed with prodigious deep ravines, about fifteen hundred feet perpendicular, craggy in the extreme, and absolutely destitute of vegetation. As the misty vapours cleared out of them, we crept to the edges of these frightful and dizzy cliffs, and looked down into the interminable chasms whose bottoms were concealed by eternal snows, which were they ice instead, would be perfect glaciers. On throwing down a stone, we discovered a horribly pleasing phenomenon: it at first bounded on a projecting crag, and the echoes from the opposite side crackled like near thunder, but as it was whirled and dashed below, it awakened innumerable little echoes, and sometimes a thundering crash or hollow sound, till, what with its own fragments and others it hurled down, the effect was like a heavy storm of hail and thunder, or the musketry and cannon of hostile armies. After an interval it was renewed several times with intervening pauses; till at length, reverberating, whirling, and dashing, it reached the bottom with a clattering rattle. We amused ourselves for some time in thus hurling down the largest stones our united strength could drag to the edge of the impending cliffs. I measured by my watch the duration of several of these discharges: the noise generally continued about a minute, or rather more, and one in particular, almost a minute and three quarters.

Having remained on the summit from about eleven to nearly two o'clock, we began our descent. There are but two ways by which this mountain can be scaled, and we determined to descend by the other, which traverses the west side and passes through Glen Nevis. The whole distance from the top to Fort William by this route, is about nine miles, of which the winding course down the mountain itself is about seven. We retraced our former track to the highest well, above which there is but a single path recrossing the field of snow, and looking once more down the deep and dark abysses and upon the lowering precipices that for perhaps a thousand centuries have mocked the water's storms and the lightning's power; and which, when we are sleeping in the dust, will still defy them. Here we deviated to the west, and descended over a broad deep declivity of rugged stones for a vast distance, and down a gully where we saw the most beautiful natural rock work of plants imaginable; the stones covered with emerald moss, the Saxifraga nivalis and other alpine plants; while the Pteris crispa and Cyathea fragilis filled the intervening spaces with their fringy foliage. At length we came to a grassy slope; but this was still more difficult and dangerous to descend on account of the great declivity and the

A Nineteenth-Century Tour

smoothness which the shoes soon acquired in passing over it. Where there were no loose stones intermixed, we slipped down it in a sitting posture, using our sticks to check the increasing momentum. The heat here was excessive, the sun's rays falling direct upon us; and frequent intervals of rest were necessary to enable us to complete our laborious excursion. We found ourselves on a mountain ridge overhanging a glen of great depth, but very narrow; at the bottom of which we heard, rather than saw, an angry torrent, concealed by the birch and alders that skirted its margin. The sides of the ravine were broken banks of earth with detached blocks of stone, their lower half embedded in the soil, and here and there a tuft of stunted brushwood. We soon reached the higher part of this torrent, which is one of the sources of the river Nevis, vastly broad, and choked with ponderous rounded blocks of red granite; scrambled over heaps of fragments with laborious fear; and wearied with heat and fatigue, got at last into Glen Nevis. In this glen lives Peter Cameron Esq. who holds it and the mountain by a singular tenure from the Duke of Gordon, viz. that he should present him with a snowball whenever he should require it. Some years ago during a hot summer, one was demanded under the idea that it could not be given; but on exploring the gullies a bed was found twenty five feet deep. The mountain and forest of Ben Uaish in Rosshire is held of the king *in capite* by a similar tenure, and a clause to this effect is inserted in a charter of the family of Fowlis; and it is said that a quantity of snow was actually sent to the Duke of Cumberland when at Inverness in 1746 to cool his wine.

While we were at dinner, our goodnatured guide came in and offered to take us in his boat across Loch Eil to see the locks at the western entrance of the Caledonian Canal, which we gladly accepted. It was a delightful evening, and we quite enjoyed the smooth sail and the refreshing breeze after the fatigues of the day. From the middle of the lake the whole bulk of Ben Nevis was visible, rising from the plain like several vast rounded hills piled one upon another, and spotted with white patches of sand but without grace or beauty of outline. The keener eye of Archibald distinguished and pointed out to us, two shifting figures on one of the mountain ridges, diminished by distances to a pigmy size; and, having the sky for a background seeming to move in air. They were a gentleman and his guide who we were told at the inn, had begun the ascent about two o'clock. The thin mists of evening were already beginning to rise out of the gullies; and it was often through their gauzy medium that the western sun illuminated the beetling cliffs.

We landed under the sea-lock of the Canal near Corpach, and examined the basin and enormous locks by means of which the various levels are preserved. I have taken the following dimensions from a printed account. Within the floodgates, the locks are 170 feet long, 40 feet broad, and have 20 feet depth of water. The surface of the Canal is 110 feet broad, diminishing to 50 feet at the bottom, its depth is 20 feet, and will thus admit of the passage of a 32 gun frigate and of the largest merchantmen. The whole length of it from Corpach to near Inverness is upwards of 60 miles, of which more than 37 are succesively occupied by Loch Lochy, Loch Oich, and Loch Ness, leaving only about 23 miles for artificial cutting. The difficulties of making the Locks and embankments were very considerable. One of the latter near Inverness is 1,000 feet long by 12 feet high, and the soil was so porous, that in pits sunk for trial, the water rose and fell with the tide. We saw near Corpach a series of eight connected locks called Neptune's Staircase, which raise the water 64 feet to the level of Loch Lochy. A new course has been cut for the river Lochy, the old bed being occupied by the canal, thus raising the loch twelve feet above its ancient level. The whole number of locks on the Canal is 25, the lockgates 38, being many of them in sets.

Near Corpach is the kirk of Kilmallie; and adjoining it we saw a very neat monument in the form of an obelisk, erected to the memory of Col. Cameron who was killed at Waterloo. The woodlands in this parish belong to Sir A. Cameron and are said to cover 14,000 acres. Our guide told us that Corpach* derived its name from being the place where their ancestors embarked the bodies of illustrious strangers on their way for interment at Iona; he also said, that in their progress through the country, they generally contrived to rest at night near an island, on which they placed the corpses to prevent the wolves from carrying them away.

As we recrossed Loch Eil the faint breezes died away and its glassy surface reflected, in their minutest outline, some beautiful weeping birches which hung over it from the projecting crags of its rocky islands, forming a most lovely, though inverted landscape. Before we reached Fort William, the sun had sunk behind the hills in the north west; every object was mellowed by the declining rays of light, giving to the mind a solemn and pensive cast, and leading the imagination towards that mysterious world to which the sun seemed to travel in all his glory.

Monday 1st August Having spent as much time upon the western coast of Scotland as was consistent with our plans rather than our wishes, it was now necessary to think of passing on to the eastern side – 'may be to return to Lochaber no more.' Our journey had hitherto been prosecuted under the most favourable circumstances of weather, with considerable diligence and labour, and without the slightest accident. In the course of seventeen days we had travelled upwards of nine hundred and forty miles, and seen a large portion of the most interesting scenery of this part of Scotland and of the Hebrides; Glen Coe and the romantic shores of the isle of Skye were only omitted from circumstances over which we had no control; but on running over the chapter of accidents and disappointments to which travellers who

---

* Corp, a body or corpse, & Ach, a stranger.

trust to chance conveyances are always liable, we had reason to congratulate ourselves that we had accomplished so much. It was my original intention to have gone to Inverness by the Caledonian Canal; but the glasgow Steam packets only make this voyage once a week, and as no stage coach runs on the fine military road that accompanies its course since their establishment, we had no alternative but to travel across the island in the common carts of that country. We therefore again agreed with Archibald to take us as far as Fort Augustus, but he having another engagement, sent with us a younger brother, a nice open countenanced lad of about 14.

We left Fort William at four o'clock this morning that we might reach Inverness in the course of the day. At this early hour the summit of Ben Nevis was free from clouds, and as we passed close under his shelving sides and gazed at his rugged ridges, clefty precipices, and vast patches of snow, congratulated ourselves with a shrug of combined horror and satisfaction, that our ascent was safely accomplished. The great breadth and rounded outlines of this monarch of the Caledonian Alps take off much from the effect of his great altitude. Inverlochy Castle and the dreary tract of Lochaber as far as High Bridge, have been already described in our excursion to Glen Roy. Before reaching the Spean, I observed a large projecting shelf or terrace on its right bank, which I had not noticed in going to Glen Roy, evidently connected with the Parallel Roads.

Soon after crossing High Bridge, the road descends towards the shore of Loch Lochy and approaches it near its south western or lowest end, not far from the point where the Spean enters it. We were now in the Great Valley of the Caledonian Canal, so often named, which was to conduct us, with a single deviation to Inverness: it is called by the Highlanders 'Glen more na Albin', or the Great Glen of Scotland.* After skirting Loch Lochy for about three miles, we came to Low Bridge, crossing the river Gloy in its passage from Glen Gloy to the loch. This latter valley was named in my account of Glen Roy, as exhibiting traces of Parallel Roads, but we could not discover them from the point where we crossed it.

We broke fast at Latter Findlay, a solitary and wretched changehouse about fifteen miles from Fort William, on kebbuck, oatcake, and eggs; but everything was so disgustingly dirty, that notwithstanding the pure air of the mountains had sharpened our appetites, we found some difficulty in satisfying them. Here for the first time I think since we entered Scotland, breakast was served without Fish: we were indulged, however, with a novelty (and it was the only instance of it during our journey, seldom tasted in the more cultivated districts of Scotland, and exceedingly rare in England. This was a marmalade or jam made from the fruit of the Rubus

---

* From Albin is derived Albion, the land of hills. In the Gaelic; Alb, Ailp, and Alpa, signify mountains, words synonymous with Alp in the continental languages, and illustrating their common origin.

Chamoemorus, or Cloudberry, a plant of frequent occurrence in alpine countries, but elsewhere almost unknown. It had an agreeable acid and rather raw taste, and is considered a great delicacy even in Scotland. Linnæus in his interesting Lapland Tour says the fruit is there preserved fresh for a long time in the snow, and eaten with the milk of the reindeer. The scenery round Loch Lochy is by no means interesting, the mountains rise very high, but are smooth and green, particularly on the south bank, very uniformly concave and sloping down to the lake on both sides, with deep perpendicular gullies, now nearly dry and fringed with the golden Saxifraga aizoides in the richest profusion, but after rains forming the beds of powerful waterfalls. The view is nearly destitute of timber, and almost of human habitations. The valley runs in a strait line and is of equal width for eight or ten miles, the lake occupying the centre, and the road, though extremely hard and smooth, undulating over a succession of little braes and skirting its margin without a turn or a new object to relieve the eye. This vast and naked monotony is wearisome and uncomfortable to the mind; and though we kept rumbling along in our rickety vehicle, and had noise and shaking enough, we seemed to make no progress, and began to speculate whether we should ever pass the shores of Loch Lochy or approach objects that had been long in sight.

The great rise in the surface of the loch, in consequence of the lockage of the Caledonian Canal, was very apparent as we passed it: the trunks of many small trees which grew near it were under water, and their bushy heads, peeping above the suface, had a singular appearance.

About the year 1545, a severe battle was fought near the east end of this loch, between the Frasers under Lord Lovat, and the MacDonalds, in which almost all the followers of the former name were slain. Buchanan says that the whole clan of Fraser would have been annihilated, had not eighty of their wives been delivered of sons who all grew up to manhood. It was on one of the wildest mountains in this wild country, that Prince Chas. Edward Stuart erected his standard in the year 1745, having landed for the conquest of the British empire with seven officers and arms for two thousand men! He immediately on his landing applied to Cameron of Loch Eil, who, on seeing him arrive in a manner so unprotected, entreated him to abandon an enterprize for which he was so ill prepared, and pointed out the many difficulties he had to encounter: upon this the young Adventurer grew warm, and began to reproach him with ingratitude to his sovereign and a breach of honour. This was the right key to the heart of a Highland chieftain; he told him that he would follow his fortunes to the last; and immediately took a tender and affecting leave of his family whom he supposed he should never more behold. The event of this wild project is well known. The income of his estate was not above £700 per Annum, yet he brought 1400 men into the field.

Loch Oich is not more than three miles long, and is situated near the summit level of the Great Glen. It is on this account so shallow, that artificial means are employed to deepen it for the larger vessels: a flat, with a dredging machine for that purpose, was at work when we passed it. The surrounding landscapes are much richer and bolder than those of Loch Lochy, the mountains more craggy, broken, and woody, and often topped with the remains of watch towers or small fortresses, while the road we travelled on the south east bank, though hilly, forms very good foregrounds. The ruin of Invergarry Castle, with its lofty round tower and grim fortresses rising above a wood on the opposite side the loch is a noble and picturesque object, and is rendered more striking by its situation at the entrance of Glengarry, whose richly wooded shelving sides rise behind it. The whole is backed by the elegant and many-coned group of Cairn Scourach, or Scarsough, which mounts in sure and graceful majesty to the height of 3,412 feet, and forms a prominent object for many miles. Invergarry Castle was burnt during the rebellion of 1746. The views looking towards Loch Ness are particularly bold and striking; and 'Vales more wild, and mountains more sublime' opened upon us as we approached Fort Augustus.

This small place lies in the centre of the Great Glen, at the head of the noble and expansive Loch Ness, and takes its name from the neighbouring garrison, which forms the central link of that chain of forts or military stations, which were designed to keep the Highland chieftains in subjection. It has four bastions and barracks for the accommodation of four hundred soldiers. Here is a stone bridge of three arches over the river Oich, the road over which leads to the isle of Skye.

We arrived at Fort Augustus about two o'clock; and our first care was to insure a conveyance to Inverness. We had been told it would be impossible to procure a chaise or a gig, so were not disappointed to find we must pursue our weary way in another cart. The one we had brought from Fort William had a board swung across it by chains, which to a certain extent supplied the want of springs; but here, alas! no such *luxury* could be obtained; and to mend the matter, that, now offered us, had just returned from the lime kiln! For this vile and heavy concern we were modestly asked the sum of thirty shillings. In the hope of being better accommodated, we at first assumed some consequence; but finding we had only 'Hobson's Choice', changed our tack, and civilly begged a little straw and a few horse rugs to protect our clothes. The landlord, though at bottom a good natured bluff fellow, seemed obstinately determined to stick to his price. While they were clearing the cart from the lime, and nailing across it a clumsy, rough, and dirty board for a seat, Dovaston in vain assailed him with all his eloquence to reduce the exorbitant charge he saw our necessity enabled him to demand. My facetious companion, disappointed of his object, and baffled in the display of his persuasive powers, turned round to me, and slyly vowed he would make it as broad as long – for he could actually talk him out of the price of all we should eat and drink. This humourous stratagem he commenced as the landlord waited on us at dinner, by some judicious compliments on the personal appearance of the Highlanders, their costume and graceful manners: in which, to do my friend justice, he scarcely exaggerated, but coloured rather with a warm than a wanton encomium. To this succeeded his remarks on the dinner, all addressed to *me*; how much cleanliness, kindness, and good cooking could enhance ordinary viands. On the appearance of some fine salmon, he was in raptures on the natural productions of these romantic regions. The landlord's health was not forgotten, and my friend and self hob-a-nobb'd with him in a cup of wretched stuff he called porter. The whiskey however was of a more generous quality, and the landlord gave broad hints that we were rather sparing in calling for it. On condition however of his joining us, we acceded to his proposal of another mutchkin. On his going out to procure it, Dovaston gave a broad wink of security; and remarked, on his returning with the bill, that his victuals were much cheaper than his vehicle; and having his note book in his hand, said he would make a few remarks. The landlord now voluntarily offered to remit the charge for all the liquor. 'Highlanders should do nothing by halves', said my loquacious friend; 'bid me tear the bond, and bring us another mutchkin' – to which, with a little if-ing and but-ing on his part, and a few quotations from Ossian and Burns on that of my friend, the doughty landlord consented. We now parted in high good humour, mounted our clumsy conveyance, heartily laughing at our ludicrous situation, and repeatedly wishing that our friends in England were there to see with how much spirit and good humour the Barrister and Banker sat cheek by chowl on a board across a limecart in the Highlands.

Soon after leaving Fort Augustus, we crossed the river Tarf by a flat wooden bridge, and ascended a very long and excessively steep hill which took us for the first time out of the Great Glen. I prevented myself from slipping off the seat, by fixing the hook of my stick on the front of the cart; but Dovaston, having no such support, at a sudden jolt fell backwards, heels over head, into the body of the cart, raising around us an atmosphere of calcareous dust, that not only effectually powdered the counsellor's pate, but rendered our clothes in perfect keeping with our carriage. We were driven by a queer Scotch Sawney, who alternately sat upon the shaft and the front of the cart: his nose was driven flat between his cheeks like the handle of a pewter pot beaten close up to the side, and in profile presented so ludicrous an appearance that it highly excited our risible muscles. After ascending full two miles, we dropped again as suddenly into a romantic and secluded dingle called Glendow, diversified with jutting rocks, weeping birch trees, and a brawling torrent, over which was thrown a light airy bridge, forming one of those minor, though beautiful landscapes we so frequently saw during our tour, but which cannot be particularized by description. Again ascending, we attained a high, barren and moory district, passing on our left, Loch Tarf and several other small lakes, famous for char; and crossing a succession of low eminences of long and tedious uniformity, where our only amusement consisted in watching for plants along the heathy wastes. At intervals the road was lined with lofty poles, to indicate its course when concealed by the snow, and conveying ideas of winter, of desolation, and of death. We were here several miles to the south of Loch Ness; for the mountains rise so precipitously from its edge, that Genl. Wade was compelled to carry the road at some distance from it, partly on account of the labour and expense of cutting through so much solid rock, partly through an apprehension that in the event of another rebellion the troops might be destroyed in their march by the enemy hurling down stones from above. Another serious obstacle presented itself in the width of the chasm through which the water of Foyers rushes down to the lake; as a prodigious arch must have been thrown across it. Loch Ness is twenty two miles long and from one to two miles and a half broad; its depth varying from sixty to a hundred and forty fathoms. In many accounts of it, it is stated as a wonderful phenomenon that its water never freezes; Dr. Johnson displays much pompous ignorance upon this subject; whereas it arises simply from its great depth, the duration of frost being too short to allow the whole body of water to cool down to the freezing point; for it freezes as soon as any other when taken out of the lake. Its surface, on account of the lofty mountains that enclose it, is much agitated by currents of wind, and the waves often rise to a great height. It was affected in a very extraordinary manner at the time of the great earthquake at Lisbon in November 1755, which I have never seen satisfactorily explained. Pennent says the scenery round Loch Ness resembles that of the Lake of Lucerne, especially towards the eastern end.

We now crossed a torrent called the Enrick, having romantic rocks on each bank, and which, after receiving many smaller streams, joins the water of Foyers above the Falls. Previous to this, however, its banks present some very decided illustrations of the different depths below the surface of the country, at which all rivers have run in different periods. Some of its earlier and deserted beds were shallow, exhibiting shelves, terraces, and deltas, covered with gravel and great rolled stones: these were sometimes intersected by its present channel, and cut down to a great depth, plainly shewing that it must have required many ages to wear away the rocks to such an enormous depth.

We saw before us on the left, the craggy mountains among which the river makes its way; and soon entered a labyrinth of dark and deep defiles, surrounded by perpendicular rocks, grey with age and lichens; threading glen after glen, through which the road winds in complicated sinuosities, successively leading towards every point of the compass in its progress through obstacles which nothing but science and perseverance could have surmounted. The scenery here, in addition to its magnificence, possessed the charm of novelty, for nothing we had ever seen bore any resemblance to it, though some of the rocks reminded us of the Trossachs. These picturesque crags were richly interspersed with tufted heather and other flowers in gay profusion; among which rose the most elegant birch trees ever seen, some rising abrupt with knurly, furrowed trunks, some in silvery satin, some grouped in little clusters, and others snugly curving in graceful bends, or clinging almost horizontally in the rocks that impend over the road, and dangling their pendent tresses lightly in the breeze of evening. At length over many crossings of the road below, and also over some gulphy rocks, a bridge of one arch was seen and in the rock above, another arch that carried a footpath over a chasm, and the dell resounded with the roar of many waters.

This was the Upper Fall of the far celebrated Foyers or Fyers; and here we alighted from our shaking *carriage*, sending it on to the General's Hut about a mile and a half farther, to wait our arrival. Standing upon the bridge, we looked down upon a terrible torrent issuing in a single smooth stream through a wide fissure worn in the hard rock by its own force, and falling into a very deep cauldron where it appeared as black as pitch. Its agitated surface reflected the azure sky, and assumed the appearance of blue flakes flickering in the darkness, reminding the fancy of the dismal pit of Acheron. Easily might a warm and poetic imagination conceive scenes similar to this, to be the haunts of monsters and demons, and people them with such dreadful incidents and imagery as Homer, Dante, and Milton have drawn. The cauldron or bason is worn by the eternal waters into yawning holes and projecting masses of various fantastic shapes, scarcely distinguishable through the surrounding gloom; while the torrent slips down the smooth black rock, white as sea-foam severed from the wave, and boils and thunders in the gulf below. We flung down several large stones, and such was the height of the bridge, that we had time to see them very sensibly diminish in size ere they plunged in the dismal depth. On the other side an alpine path zig-zags up the rocks over a dizzy arch thrown across a fracture, and is lost amid fine birch trees and purple heather.

We now followed the course of the river, which is a succession of rapids and cascades rushing and foaming angrily among huge fragments of rock, and concealed by trees for several hundred yards, and descended to the Lower or greater Fall. This baffles and dismays description. The path is narrow and difficult, leading down into a dark circus of one surrounding scene of rocks that frown in horror on every side, except a mere outlet, and that scarcely seen, where the raging and furious waters hurry away to the lake. As though Nature intended a rostrum or shelf whence to view her wonders most favourably, a fragment of rock projects over the deep abyss, about halfway down, upon which with caution we seated ourselves. Looking up, a very little of the sky is seen and filmy clouds floating on its azure, the edges of the skylight, (as it were) fringed with a few shrubs and birches that flung their slender arm across the light. The white torrent at first issues out of a narrow cleft, and for a few feet is shot in a smooth and narrower column; but meeting with a projecting rock, is spread into a broad sheet, widening as it falls down perpendicularly; its sides broken into tangled loops and playful tresses of brilliant silver, at once both grand and graceful. After falling upwards of 200 feet, it reaches the bottom of the vast circular furnace over which we hung, burying itself among foaming eddies, and dashing against the base of the precipices, hurrying confusedly round the sides till it seeks the horrible outlet beyond which it is heard tumbling and roaring in the deep thunder of other dismal and more distant caverns. The aspect both up and down is overwhelming, dreadful, and appalling; and the projecting crag on which we stood, seemed momentarily preparing to rush into the roaring gulf. The sides of this frightful circus are quite perpendicular and seamed with fissures in which cling a few dangling rose briars and trees of large size. We looked so long at the Fall, that it produced a dizzy effect on the eyes, and made all the rocks and fragments appear to separate and crawl upwards, like the gradual drawing up of a scene in some ample theatre. What must be the effect here after a deluge of rain, when in this long, very long dry season, the force of waters was so grand and beautiful?

The river is small and bears no proportion to the vast scale of the surrounding cavity; yet if it were altogether absent, Foyers would be a sublime and striking scene. It is undoubtedly the grandest cascade in Britain, but of a character so peculiar, that it can not be compared to any other. Nothing can exceed the combination of grandeur and profuse ornament here displayed. Yet the first impression is, that it is not so vast, and that the trees are but bushes; nor is it till we discover that we are viewing trees of the ordinary size, one above another in succession from the surface of the water to the sky, that we became fully impressed with the magnitude of the whole. The force of the torrent sends up clouds of curling spray like the mists riding up the chasms of Ben Nevis but so attenuated and gauzy, that the scenery is seen through, and derives from them, that aerial perspective and harmony of colour, which increase its magnitude by creating an ideal distance.

We lingered long and fondly in this wonderful scene but the near approach of evening, and the distance we still were from Inverness compelled us to tear ourselves away. On regaining the road, we walked among scenery the richest and sweetest the most fastidious heart could desire. Each side of it was lined with a luxuriant forest, principally of birch trees, some airy, light, and tressy, and some with graceful plumy tops, feathering the ragged rocks to their very summits, till we came to the General's Hut. At intervals we saw Loch Ness smiling through the trees in calm repose and reflecting the lofty mountains and the azure sky like an immense mirror: its beauty being doubtless enhanced by the wild sublimity of the scene we had just quitted.

The General's Hut is a solitary change house, so called from being built near the site of the hut where Genl. Wade resided when he constructed their most excellent military roads: where, or how, the soldiers who worked under him, were lodged, we could not divine for no other habitation was in sight, except the modern mansion of Foyers, almost concealed among the lofty trees at the mouth of the glen.

Instead of entering the General's Hut, we threw ourselves down, exhausted with heat and fatigue, upon an inviting green knoll before the door, and odered some porter to be brought us, feasting our eyes for the few minutes we had to remain here on the enchanting scene before us. Immediately in front, but far below us, the noble Loch Ness spread its broad and long sheet of blue waters on either hand as far as the eye could reach, its opposite shores rising precipitously to a great height, here and there thickly mantled with dark woods, whose tops only caught the light, and backed by a screen of wavy mountains now clothed in soft purple. On the side we sat, woody promontories curled down into the lake, with group above group of luxuriant birches rising above us, crowned with craggy rocks glowing in the evening sunbeams.

The principal group of hills on the opposite bank is called Mealfourvonie (sic); it rises above 3,000 feet high and is the first land described by sailors on approaching the east shores. A little to the east of it is Castle Urquhart, an ancient fortress now in ruins, hanging on a rocky promontory over the lake. It is said to have been the seat of the Comyns or Cummins, Lords of Badenoch, who acted so conspicuous a part during that series of regal minorities which caused so much distraction to Scotland during several centuries. One of the chiefs of this once powerful family rendered himself so odious by his ferocity and cruelty, that he acquired the surname of the Wolf of Badenoch. Behind the ruin is Glen Urquhart; and still more to the west, Glen Morison; both of which are said to possess scenery of incomparable beauty. But circumstances almost denied our stealing even a distant glimpse – our wretched carriage was waiting – the sun was setting and we had still eighteen miles to travel to Inverness.

The scenery for several miles was the most lovely imaginable, and perfectly novel in its character. The road is hewn out of the precipitous side of a lofty hill which dips down into the lake, running like a shelf in nearly a strait line at a considerable height above it; sometimes shaded by thick groves, sometimes opening upon the peaceful waters, and sometimes guarded by the jutting crags and precipices that soar above it in fantastic and tottering attitudes, on which the setting sun now slept in golden glory. Groups of birch trees of every size and form have fixed themselves in the rocks of this steep acclivity canopying the projecting crags and crowning the knolls which stud its surface – some gracefully drooping over the road and the lake below in every imaginable variety of beauty – and others clambering the mountain or perched on its summit, and receiving from the skiey background, additional airiness and elegance. Their silvery trunks, springing from the rocks, incline at all angles from the perpendicular, the pendent branches droop in elegant forms, and expose their light feathery foliage to the evening breeze. Never before were we so transported with road scenery as in this delicious garden of the wilderness; the road also was smooth, clean, and hard, with scarcely any sensible inclination; and for many miles we might imagine ourselves passing through the most ornamented park. At length the birches were succeeded by hazel, ash and alder; and, occasionally we seemed to be transported into an Engish lane. The sides of the hill were in many places profusely clothed with Juniper, intervened occasionally by large bushes of the beautiful Rosa coesia.

Gloamin (twilight) at length came on; but before it quite 'left the world to darkness and to us' the scenery assumed a more tranquil character; the high cliffs above us sunk down into gentle grassy elevations, and we rode for some miles through forests of larch and pine which enveloped us in total darkness. During the remainder of the journey, the fragrance, in varied odours of the birch, juniper, honeysuckle and heather was exceedingly grateful and refreshing after so hot a day, and tended much to relieve the tedious hours we were compelled to pass in darkness in our cramping vehicle. Our cheeks frequently came in contact with the filmy threads of the Gossamer spider which hung across the road loaded with dew; and though surrounded by darkness and worn down with fatigue, we forgot the inconveniences of our situation in an animated conversation on the habits of this truly surprizing little creature. We distinguished through the birches a large light at some distance high among the woody cliffs across the lake; and our driver told us it was the fire of smugglers who resorted to those remote defiles for the secret purpose of making whisky: they had a very striking and romantic effect. The moon at length rose in the south east, and by the aid of her faint horizontal light, we dimly described the town of Inverness. As we entered it, tremulous floating double lights were seen gleaming on the broad river Ness, dancing like aquatic demons and giving to the agitated water the appearance of lambent fire. As a superior and more permanent Light has long driven the mischievous Kelpie from his watery throne, we concluded they must proceed from the moving coracles of salmon fishers, who take advange of that natural instinct which suffers fish to be allured by luminous objects. The town clock of Inverness loudly proclaimed the hour of two, while we were knocking up the waiter at Wilson's Caledonian hotel. After apologizing for our unseasonable arrival, we hastily took a little refreshment, and retired to that repose which a long and laborious day of twenty three hours, and a journey of above sixty miles in jolting carts, rendered so necessary.

Tuesday, 2nd August We needed rest, and this morning we indulged in it freely; for before we had finished breakast it was noon. Dovaston was down, if not up before me; and very shortly returned to say he had seen his old friend "Blubberchops' in the vestibule of the hotel buttoning his gaiters and quarrelling violently with the civil and intelligent waiter, of whom he was making enquiries about a conveyance to the Orkneys. 'What can *he* want at the Orkneys?' said Dovaston; 'are they famous for *mushrooms?*'

Inverness is the first place worthy the name of a town we had seen since leaving Glasgow. It is large and well built, the streets wide and clean, with less of those offensive smells which issue from the alleys and small courts of that city. Many of the houses are of freestone and lofty; and the place is altogether more lively and respectable than any other Scotch town we have seen. It contains nearly 9,000 inhabitants, and may be considered as the capital of the Highlands; being the only town of any importance north of Aberdeen, for here the chiefs and Gentry resort as to a metropolis, and occasionally wear their peculiar dress. The courts and tolbooth stand in the centre of it and form together a very handsome modern building. The spires here, as in all the Scotch kirks have a light and elegant appearance; not requiring the massy towers of our English churches, because peals of bells are not used. Inverness, anciently written Innerness,* is principally built on the southern side of the river Ness, near its entrance into the Moray, or Murray Firth, and over which is a large substantial bridge of seven arches and of some antiquity, yet a pontage of a halfpenny was demanded from each of us for crossing it. The castle near the river on the western extremity of the hill which covers the town, was destroyed during the rebellion of 1745. Nothing now remains of it but rubbish: it is supposed to have been built by King Malcolm Canmore. The Thane of Calder's Castle was built on the easern extremity of the hill; there is not a vestige of it now to be seen. The memory of the theatre of Macbeth's ambitious villainy is still preserved in the names of the land which belonged to it, and the eminence on which it stood is still called Castle Hill.

After strolling about Inverness, our attention was first directed to the singular oblong conical hill called Tom-na-heurich, or Hill of the Fairies, situated south west about half a mile from the town on the bank of the river. Its very regular shape, and the circumstance of its standing alone on the flat and widely extended beach, render it a very striking object; and almost persuade us into the belief that it has been raised by artificial means, but its great size, and the absence of any contiguous moats or fosses whence the earth could have been taken, render it certain that no human means could have been equal to the requisite labour.

From Tom-na-heurich we proceeded towards Craig Phadrick, a round hill 1150 feet high and about two miles west of Inverness, on whose summit

---

* Inver, or Inner, is synonymous with the Welsh Aber, and indicates the place where a small river discharges itself into a greater, or into the sea; or a town situated at the confluence. Aber, so common in Wales, is sometimes met with in Scotland, as Aberdeen, Aberfoyle, &c.

is a Vitrified Fort in tolerable preservation. We were obliged to take a circuitous course on account of the Caledonian Canal, walking for some distance along its bank and crossing it by one of its handsome swing bridges. This is the place where the long embankment already named at Fort William, is made. In the course of this morning some rain had fallen – the first we had had since the commencement of our tour; and before we reached Craig Phadrick, we were twice obliged to take shelter. Vegetation on the south sides of the mountains was everywhere brown and scorched; and we had been so frequently incommoded by dust and heat that the coolness and fragrance of the air were very refreshing and exhilarating, and forcibly called to our recollection the animated description of the Sweet Singer of Israel, of the effect produced by rain on the parched mountains of Judea – 'Thou visitest the earth, and waterest it – Thou makest it soft with showers; thou blessest the springing thereof – The little hills rejoice on every side; the pastures are clothed with flocks: the valleys also are covered with corn; they shout for joy; they also sing.'

We toil'd up the steep hill, which is composed of old, or lower red sandstone, imbedding large rounded pebbles of quartz, and is in many places covered with plantations of pines. The road has been cut out with considerable labour; and we were sore and stiff in every limb from the incessant jolting of yesterday's journey. The area on the summit is irregularly oblong and tolerably level, about eighty yards long and thirty broad. It is surrounded by a rampart or vallum, apparently of earth, and covered by time with a thick green sward and vegetable mould, which alone is sufficient to shew its high antiquity in a cold climate and elevated situation, where the process of vegetation must be very slow. The height of this rampart within the area is but a few feet; but its outer face where it rises from a foss, owing to the declivity of the hill, has a perpendicular elevation of eight or ten feet. Immediately below the foss, a second, or outer vallum runs round the summit of the hill, intended probably for an outwork to protect the fort. This is also covered with sward, but much lower and less perfect than the inner one, and in some places could scarcely be traced. Under the sward, the rampart consists of a wall several yards thick, formed of small shapeless stones run together and cemented into a solid mass by a semi-vitreous dark grey substance which is honeycombed or carious, and very much resembles lava, or the scoria of an iron furnace. Of this I brought away a specimen. The stones seem to have been collected in the neighbourhood, as they are of the same description with those now lying about the roads, principally of fine grained white sandstone. With some difficulty we removed a portion of the sward on the outer side of the upper and more perfect vallum, and broke through the glazed surface to examine its interior.

The view from the Vitrified Fort was very fine, embracing Inverness and the beautifully varied surrounding country, the eastern end of the Great Glen, with the river Ness and the Caledonian Canal, Loch Beauly and the

Moray Firth guarded by Fort George, and bounded by the distant German Ocean. Fort George is the largest and most perfect of those which guard the Caledonian Valley, and is built upon a promontory, where with the opposite headland of Fort Ross, seems to include the southwest part of the Moray Firth.

It was four o'clock when we returned to Inverness, and while we were standing before the hotel, waiting the announcement of dinner, several bagpipers decked out in full Highland costume, with red and green ribbons streaming from their drones, were parading the streets and screeling away in full fury. Dovaston got into conversation with one of them about national melodies, and said he could catch a touch or two of the celebrated Swiss 'Rans des Vaches' in one of their tunes. The piper referred and introduced Dovaston to his chieftain, which ultimately produced an invitation to us both to dine with some other friends at his table. Indeed I wish here, once for all, to mention that my gifted friend's knowledge of music, Scotch literature, and powerful talent of conversation, have obtained for me many comforts and much valuable information which my own taciturnity and retired habits would not have procured. When dinner was announced we followed the gentlemen into a large room, where to our utter astonishment, 'Blubberchops' had taken possession of one end of the table. Sir James Grant silently but with some dignity, took the other. The conversation at first was very mixed, but seeing we sought information respecting the manners and scenery of their highly interesting country, the chieftains were highly and agreeably communicative. The cloth was scarce drawn when a very young gentleman entered, whom they all seemed to greet with particular regard; and Sir James *spiered* how they all were, and what was going forward in his 'Strath'. A side-table was spread, where he dined, and wine was occasionally sent to him from ours with health and courtesy. To detail the conversation would be tiresome, as accuracy would be impossible; it was animated and desultory. 'Blubberchops' after having abused the viands he had gorged, fell asleep, breathing hard and heavy, like a sow in the sunshine. Some Highland songs were sung, and local anecdotes related. One gentleman, on perceiving us admiring his dirk, politely and good humouredly drew it, and shewed us the rich inlay of silver devices in the ivory handle. He said, in ancient days each stuck his dirk beside his elbow in the unplaned pine plank, but he would not illustrate the manners by spoiling our landlord's mahogany table. The bottle standing with me, (as I had often, so sinned) Sir Jas. Grant facetiously upbraided me with want of the notion of Highland cheer – 'You are resolved we shall not have the honour to carry you "to your heather" in our plaids, Sir' – I pleaded my general habits, and as a stranger threw myself upon the liberality of the company, adding that my fellow traveller would acquit himself to their satisfaction. Dovaston kindly supported me, exclaiming to Sir James, 'Never mind Bowman, he's a philosopher; and I'll soon be one also, if you will but pass the bottle, Sir James'. This caused a laugh – Sir James passed the bottles demanding a toast. Dovaston gave, 'Both sides the Tweed'. This turned the conversation to the Union and the relation in which the two countries stood towards each other; and it was evident, rather from the expression of features and the manner, than from anything that was said, that the old national feeling was not quite forgotten. We made enquiries as to the present state of the ancient Highland customs, dresses, &c; but the opinions of the company did not altogether coincide. Sir Jas. Grant remarked that the Highlanders, before the American war had got very heterodox with the colours of their tartans, one clan promiscuously mixing with his own, those of another, but that they had since rallied and were becoming more strict in this respect. He also observed, what had struck me before, that the colours were originally adapted to the face of the country of each clan, the green and black to the bracken (fern) and the green and red to the heather, for their better concealment. The bottle circulated freely; but I owe it to the politeness of the company, that I felt perfectly free from all restraint; and was tacitly allowed to pass it on, untasted. My friend was (as usually) animated and brilliant; and by his smart sallies of wit and his varied information, riveted the attention of the company. I was unwilling to interrupt his flow of enjoyment; and as we were to leave Inverness at five o'clock the next morning, at length took an opportunity of stealing away, and after drawing up the notes of the day, retired to rest.

It was a late hour, and I had been asleep, when Dovaston entered, a little unsteadily, our double bedroom. 'Bowman', said he, 'where's the ink pot?' The '*ink* pot?' said I, 'why in my coat pocket; but what do you want with that? 'Why to post the Log, to be sure' said he. 'I have enjoyed glorious conversation, and my defects in that luxury have been more perspicuously detected, and more delicately reproved than I have ever felt before or ever may again. If I leave not Inverness a wiser and better man, 'tis my own fault and misfortune – 'So spit i'my face and call me – horse'. And thus mumbling a mixture of Shakespeare, Burns and Sir Walter – he ultimately settled himself at the dressing table, where, with a few libations to the Naiades, it is but justice to my excellent friend to say, that in the morning I found he had composed several of the brightest pages of his journal before he composed himself to sleep.

Wednesday, 3rd August Inverness was the most northern point of our tour; nor had we ever any intention of proceeding farther. In a general sense, the country beyond it is said to have but few attractions, and is seldom visited except by persons who have full command of their time. We would gladly have deferred our progress southwards another day, to see the ruins of Beauly Abbey, and to examine more at leisure the interesting conical hills already named; but finding there was no other day coach to Dunkeld till Saturday, we felt it incumbent on us to proceed. We left Inverness at five o'clock; and on rising the hill south east of the town, were more sensibly impressed with its charming situation and delightful scenery than we had been before. The country was well wooded and highly cultivated; the mountains which rose in the north were very picturesque; and the maritime views of the estuary excelled in beauty, though not in grandeur and magnificence, any we had seen on the western coast. As we left the town, I saw on the right, more of the oblong flat hillocks described yesterday, which, had I been aware of, I would certainly have visited on foot.

We passed under the north eastern end of the Castle hill celebrated as the site of Macbeth's Castle, as already named, and entered upon a part of Culloden moor. Looking eastward, we saw the site of the important battle fought in April 1746, between the Duke of Cumberland and the Highlanders under Prince Charles Edward, which finally terminated the hopes of the Stuart family and its adherents. The mounds of earth which the Highlanders raised over their slain companions remain; and though at some distance, we saw them as green spots among the general dark hue of this bleak and sorry district; also a tree near the sea, where Charles Edward displayed his Standard at the commencement of the battle.

We now traversed a dreary, barren district of moor and peatland, – interesting only to grouse-shooters – both hills and plains being covered with a sombre brown, with here and there a block of weathered gneiss bleaching on its surface. About seven miles from Inverness are crossed Strath-Nairn and the river of that name, the country very irregular, and presenting many obstacles to the direct course of the road. At some distance farther we passed close by a beautiful little lake on the left, surrounded by fine trees; in the middle of it is a round verdant islet rendered more striking by containing a ruin and a modern conical obelisk. It is called Loch Moy, and is a most interesting spot in the midst of so dreary a country. There was formerly a castle upon it, where in turbulent times, the neighbouring chief to whom it belonged, used to retire for security. About two miles beyond, we arrived at Freeburn Inn, a solitary house near the river Findhorn which we crossed. We were told here by a passenger, that Sir Jas. Grant with whom we dined yesterday, resides at Castle Grant near Cromdale on the Spey. He is one of the most extensive landed proprietors in Invernessshire, and his seat is the most distinguished mansion in that county, and also possesses immense natural pine forests on the sides of the hills and in the glens which border the Spey.

Soon after leaving Freeburn, we began to ascend the range of the Monadhliath mountains, a long ridge of black hills which separates the valleys of the Findhorn and the Spey, and which we had sometime seen before us stretching from east to west. They are of the most desolate and repulsive character, alike wearying to the eye and the mind of the traveller. As we descended their southern slope, a more cheering scene was spread before us. The wide irregular valley through which the river Spey winds, called Strath-Spey, opened very finely to the left, showing large tracts of forest lands interspersed with naked hills and grassy plains – not indeed covered with the rich and luxuriant verdure of our English vales, and very thinly inhabited – but occasionally of great extent, and possessing a wild melancholy beauty, which interests the heart, and tells the spectator that man has had no hand in producing it.

As we dropped down into Strathspey, the road kept winding among large detached and scattered groups of trees, principally pines, which had an appearance so novel and striking, and so different from the artificial plantations in England, that we felt convinced they were the Natural Pine Forests we had read of. Trees of all sizes grew intermixed, though at a sufficient distance for each to assume its full character and receive the full influence of the sun and air, and for the larger ones to throw out their broad declining arms in graceful sweeps to a great extent.

Cairngorm had long been in view; and as we kept descending towards Aviemore – a solitary inn on the banks of the Spey, where we breakfasted – we approached so near it that the patches of snow on its northern slope, were distinctly seen, reminding us of Ben Nevis. It is well known for its quartz crystals of various colours, particularly those of a topaz or amber colour; though it is asserted by MacCulloch that smoky quartz is found upon it, and that the brighter ones are clandestinely imported from Brazil in large quantities and sold as Cairngorm stones – they are without any intrinsic value. So much for a name, and for fashion!

A person on the coach pointed out Glen More, a vast valley on the northeast side of Cairngorm, long celebrated for the largest and oldest pines in Scotland; but which were considered of little value, as it was thought impossible to transport them from their native inaccessible forests to a market. At length however the whole was purchased, as a speculation, from the Duke of Gordon for £10,000. A method was discovered of getting the trees down to the Spey and floating them to the sea; and they yielded to the enterprising adventurer, a profit of £70,000. Some of the trees were of great age and of an enormous girth; the Duke has preserved one plank which is six feet wide.

At Aviemore we reached the Spey, and taking a south west direction skirted its nothern bank for about fifteen miles, meeting its stream. Soon after leaving the inn we passed through the middle of a thick forest of pines, which was not protected by fences, and was inhabited by wild deer. It is called the Great Pine Forest of Rothiemurchus. Under the trees the great herculean ant (Formica herculanea) had raised, with the old spines, enormous loose hillocks, that had exactly the appearance of haycocks. These surprising insects are one among a thousand instances, by which we may trace, in the natural productions of our own climate, the kindred habits of families widely dispersed over the surface of the globe.

Soon after we emerged from the forest of Rothiemurchus, we passed

Loch Alvie, not otherwise remarkable than as lying in a district very much diversified with low green hills, partially, though very picturesquely clothed with groups of elegant birch trees, both low and scattered, and intermixed with open glades, producing altogether a scene, at once alpine and artificial, combining the discordant character of wild mountain landscape, and of ornamental park scenery.

The coach stopped at the lodge of a small, though elegant country seat, seen through the plantations at a little distance, to leave several packages of wine, we had brought from Inverness; and also three dogs which we took up upon the road, and by which we had been somewhat annoyed. We learned that the mansion was called Kinrara, and was a hunting seat of the Marquis of Huntley; – that the grousing season was near at hand – and that the medley now imported, and much more that was to follow, was to supply the occasions of a large company the noble lord had invited, to murder the poor birds as soon as the Law would permit; – for strange to say, even the British Nobility are constrained to indulge their pleasures under the control of an Act of Parliament. I may here add, (to dismiss at once the bloody subject) that at Dunkeld and Perth, and at intervals along the road as far as Edinburgh, we met horses, dogs, and servants going northwards – perhaps to Kinrara – and understood that the coaches in that direction were so loaded, that ordinary passengers could not be forwarded.

Such are the pleasures of the Great – of the Sportsman I should say, for unfortunately men of all classes pursue this cowardly sport of death. How immeasureably superior are the pleasures of the naturalist, in season, circumstance, and extent! He is not subject to any of the drawbacks arising from the silent consciousness of cruelty, oppression, or demoralization; and can indulge in his pursuits, without either a License or the attendant expenses of horses, dogs, or servants. He mounts the uplands, brilliant with morning dew; fearless of giving offence to the most capricious owner, or of being visited by Fine or Summons from a jealous or lordly magistrate.

Shortly after leaving Kinrara we passed Loch Inch, through which the Spey runs, and came to Belleville the elegant mansion of Jas. Macpherson Esq, son to the *Translator* of Ossian; standing on a sloping bank on our right. On the lawn is a fine obelisk, erected to the imaginary Gaelic Homer by the translator of the Iliad. It may truly be said, 'His dwelling is calm among the hills, and the fields of his rest are pleasant.' A fine youth, son to the present possessor, came to the lodge and gave our guard a Pound Note in reward for having found a parcel of his father's which had been sometime lost. A little farther, on the left, we saw across the Spey the ruin of Ruthven Castle, belonging to the Duke of Gordon, who has immense property in Strathspey. It has been a ruin since the rebellion of 1745.

We next came to Kingussie, the first village we had seen since leaving Inverness: it consists of widely scattered cottages, principally on the north bank of the Spey, but possesses nothing interesting or striking. After proceeding about two miles, the road crosses the Spey, and gradually winds out of the valley, exchanging the pleasant and variegated landscapes we had enjoyed since entering it for a high, cold, and sterile tract. We were now about to pass the formidable Grampian range we had seen so long before us; but were told the ride would not be enhanced by any of that romantic scenery which characterised the Pass above Loch Earn Head. Indeed it is difficult to conceive anything more cheerless and forbidding than the appearance of the country till we approached Blair Atholl – a distance of not less than twenty five miles. Through the whole of this long and dreary space, the eye in vain wanders about for any pleasing object on which to rest: black sterile moors – alike deserted by man and animals – stretch for many miles without either a hut, a tree, or even a sheep to keep alive the idea that we are still connected with the living world; and these are interrupted only by long flat-topped hills, which rise insensibly from the moors or turbaries, and afford no variety of form or colour. The silence and solitude of death seems stamped upon the scene; and the aspect and situation of the country cut off even the hope of its ever being reclaimed from that eternal barrenness to which it is condemned by a law more irrevocable than the primæval curse. In the middle of this inhospitable region, stands the solitary inn of Dalwhinnie; a caravansera in the desert. It is near the north eastern, or upper extremity of Loch Ericht, whose waters stagnate among bogs and morasses, that in this lovely season of summer scarcely put on a shade of green.

The summit level, or ridge of the Grampians, divides the counties of Inverness and Perth, and the properties of the Dukes of Gordon and Atholl. We had scarcely begun to descend towards the south, before we perceived a sensible change, both in the temperature of the air, and the hue of the dark brown heather which covered the surface. We were now in the ancient Forest of Atholl; but like almost every other part of the Caledonia Sylva, it has long been despoiled of its honours, and with them, of its 'wild bulls with thick manes, its witches and wicked women, and other 'hideous horrors' spoken of by Camden; of all which nothing now remains but the name. The Forest of Mar in Aberdeenshire, and the classic Loch-na-gar, immortalized by Lord Byron, where the Dee has its source, lie to the north east of this district.

We dined at Dalnachardoch, another solitary though spacious inn near the infant stream of the Garry. Both this and the house at Dalwhinnie were built by Government out of the funds arising from the forfeited estates for the convenience of travellers who cross these barren wilds. The landlord, a remarkably strong-built man with high cheek bones, and habited in the full Highland costume even to the dirk, (which he wore suspended from a leathern girdle) had come with us from Aviemore, but we did not recognize him as such till he courteously escorted us into the room where dinner waited our arrival. His speech was very strongly tinctured with the broad

Lowland Scotch. The Highland dress seems to be more generally retained in this part of the country than in any other we have yet visited.

Near the Falls of Bruar, which lay a little distance from the road on our left three miles from Blair Atholl, we passed a Highland funeral, which was attended by perhaps a hundred people, among whom were a few females. None of the company were in mourning, but many wore the fillibeg and hose. The coffin was borne by four men, who carried it at arm's length on hand spikes, and covered with a plaid, not thrown loosely over it as the pall is with us, but wrapped closely around it. The attendants walkd promiscuously before and behind the corpse, accompanied by a bagpiper, who, as we approached ceased playing the coronach. Sir Walter Scott says in his notes to the Lady of the Lake, that the coronach of the Highlanders, like the 'ulutatus' of the Romans and the 'ulaloo' of the Irish, was a wild expression of lamentation poured forth by the mourners over the body of a departed friend; but that it has for some years past been superseded at funerals by the use of the bagpipes; and *that* also is, like many other Highland peculiarities, falling into disuse, unless in remote districts.

The country shewed symptoms of improvement soon after we left Dalnachardoch; the Garry, whose course we followed, was a succession of rapids tumbling over a rocky bed, and occasionally presented respectable cascades; but the scenery on its banks was naked and uninteresting till we came within a few miles of Blair Atholl. Here it became more diversified, its general surface was enlivened with verdure, and its hills and glens were clothed with rich and extensive plantations; forming an agreeable contrast with the wearisome journey across the Grampians, and amply compensating by its fertility and the lively bustle of its streams for the black stunted heather and stagnating shallow pools we had at length escaped from. At a little distance from the road on the left, is seen Blair castle, a seat of the Duke of Atholl, with other respectable buildings near it. It has an incongruous and unsightly appearance, owing to the alterations made in its original plan by the late Duke. It was formerly a place of great strength and very lofty; and being the only fortress of importance in the neighbourhood, and so near the Pass of Killiecrankie, was an object of attention in the numerous feuds which continually disturbed the peace of the country. In 1644, the celebrated Marquis of Montrose besieged and took it by assault a short time before the victory he obtained at Tibbermore near Perth. In 1689, it occasioned, as Pennant observes, one of the greatest events of the time; being the cause that brought on the important battle of Killiecrankie. Its towers and three upper stories were therefore taken down to prevent its being again used as a garrison.

The defile of Killiecrankie is very romantic and striking; lofty and very precipitous hills rise from a deep and narrow glen, thickly clothed with luxuriant woods of birch and pine; here and there craggy rocks jut out; and white foaming cataracts, as if emerging from subterreaneous channels, tumble down their steep slopes in to the river Garry that rolls turbulently below, chaffing and fretting over its rocky bed. The hills on each side the defile approach so closely that the river can scarcely force itself a passage through the mazy windings of their deep bases. The road is cut along that which forms the eastern side, and is so concealed by trees as not to be seen till the Pass is entered. The whole of the ride through it, by the constant changes in the grouping of the trees, rocks, and waterfalls, must arouse the attention of the most indifferent spectator; at every step a new landscape meets the eye, each so diversified in composition yet so similar in general character, as to elude every attempt at delineation, and render description vague and unsatisfactory.

In a military light, the Pass of Killiecrankie has always been considered as a very formidable defile, and may with propriety, be termed the Caledonian Thermopylae. It may be defended by a very small body of men against almost any number, because few of the most numerous army could come into action.

After leaving the Pass, the remainder of the land to Dunkeld lies through a valley which affords a constant succession of the richest and most beautiful scenery imaginable; the hills are profusedly covered with the finest plantations of larch, pine, and spruces, the meadows and plains with the most luxuriant herbage and with corn. The Tummel enters this valley just below the defile, and in this river the Garry loses both its waters and its name. A few miles lower, the sable Tay rolls in its waters from the westward; and after receiving those of the Tummel, flows down to Dunkeld – sometimes in a broad and tranquil stream, and sometimes divided by wooded islands – not pursuing its course in a continued line, but turning and winding in playful mazes through overhanging woods, and flowery meads, and rural scenes. The outlines of the distant mountains which often burst suddenly upon the eye through the openings of the lateral valleys, are highly picturesque, particularly the different views of the Grampians to the north, and a noble group seen in the west over the valley through which the Tay runs before it joins the Tummel – among these, Ben Lawers towered high above the rest. From this point, the views are luxuriant and rich beyond description; the road is carried along a high level on the left bank of the river, crossing the little glens by means of arched walls built up with great skill and labour; frequently overshadowed by woods of the finest ash, wych-elm and spruce, and sometimes overlooking the wide and fertile vale of the Tay – rich in pastures and corn, and enlivened by groups of cattle, cottages, and seats of the neighbouring gentry. As we approached Dunkeld the vale narrowed, and the road passed through a romantic defile or cleft at the foot of towering rocks, fissured and craggy, fringed and mantled with plantations, and the amazingly lofty brows and ridges crowned with pines. This wild spot is called the King's Seat, or King's Pass, and had a magnificent effect, as the red tinged rocks and dark green foliage glowed warm and tranquil in the evening sunbeams. Just beyond it is a little dark and secluded lake, called Loch Palney, surrounded by precipitous rocks, and presenting a fairy solitude in the midst of a very extensive landscape.

At length, about eight o'clock, we reached the pretty town of Dunkeld, embosomed in towering pineclad hills, after a journey of a hundred and three miles, full of strong contrasts in the scenery. The most striking of these, were the natural forests of Strathspey; – the repulsive and barren tract across the Grampians – and the continued paradise which extends from Blair to Dunkeld. The road is uniformly good, though generally narrow, and without a single turnpike till we entered Perthshire. In the course of the day we had seen several Druidical Circles and Cromlechs – one near the inn at Aviemore where we breakfasted – another whose situation I did not recollect – and a third, consisting of two large upright stones, at Dowally, a small village above the Tay, nearly opposite Dalguise. These are common in Perthshire, under the name of 'Stones of Worship', and are still regarded with no inconsiderable degree of superstition by the common people.

Though it was late, we were anxious to snatch a hasty view of the Cathedral of Dunkeld; and within its ruined walls we whiled away the lingering twilight of this delightful evening, nor quitted it till want of rest and refreshment summoned us to retire.

Thursday, 4th August After an early breakfast, we took a survey of the town in our way to the Cathedral. We had read of Dunkeld as a city, and were therefore disappointed to find it only a small place consisting of little more than one principal street, running parallel with the Tay. It is the beauty of its situation, the rich scenery of the surrounding country, the varied attractions of the extensive pleasure grounds of the Duke of Atholl, and the interesting ruins of its Cathedral, which combine to render Dunkeld a place of such general resort and well-merited admiration. Its Cathedral entitled it to the distinction of a City; and was probably the reason why it was noted in the early annals of Scottish history. In the eighth century, one of the Pictish kings founded a monastery here in honour of St Columba; and from that time it became the seat of what was then deemed Religion. That pious prince, David the first, converted this establishment into a bishopric which then ranked as the first in Scotland, and hence Dunkeld was sometimes called the capital of ancient Caledonia.

The Cathedral, in common with most others that I have seen, exhibits a variety of styles, and has evidently been built at different periods. Its dimensions are small, compared with the English metropolitan churches, the Great Aisle, or Nave, being, according to Pennant, only 120 feet long by 60 wide. The choir, though the oldest part of the building, is the most perfect, having been repaired and new roofed some years ago, and is now used as the parish kirk. In a picturesque point of view, it is an eyesore, and spoils the effect of the ruin, particularly the windows, which retain their original gothic shape and shew the modern brickwork by which they have been partially filled up. The Great Aisle or nave is altogether unroofed and abandoned to the slow and silent spoliations of time and the elements. On each side, six massive Saxon pillars separate the side aisles, and support light pointed arches, over the centre of each of which is a small circular arch, and higher still, a range of clerestories with narrow lancet openings. The great west window appears to have been richly mullioned, if we may judge from the side mouldings to which they have been joined; but much of the rich and delicate tracery itself, has yielded to the infuriated zeal of the reformer. Several ancient tombs with mutilated recumbent figures of mitred ecclesiastics in canopied recesses, ornament the side aisles; the grey walls are covered with various coloured lichens, or smeared with damp green moss; while dense ivy richly mantles the pillars or flings its elegant tangles among the graceful mullions of the light and lofty windows. The area is overgrown with rank grass and the Ægopodium podagraria, and is used as a common burial-ground; and to the disgrace of those who might prevent it, vulgar and ridiculous inscriptions and epitaphs are suffered to be painted on the noble Saxon pillars. At the north west corner is a singular octagonal tower or belfry, not usually so situated.

From the Cathedral we went down to the Tay, and crossed its broad stream by an elegant bridge of seven lofty arches, where a pontage of one halfpenny each was demanded, as at Inverness. From the opposite bank we had an extremely rich and beautiful view of the grey ruin we had just left, yellow with golden lichen, and its verdant background of fine tufted trees – above these, rise projecting cliffs masked with blue-green pines – and below, the Tay gliding between banks wooded to the water's edge – all bright and brilliant in the fresh and dewy morning. Some rain had fallen in the night, which gave a transparency to the atmosphere, and greatly heightened the verdure of this wooded landscape. We turned to the left, and soon entered the ornamented grounds of the Duke of Atholl, skirting the left bank of the Braan in our way to the Rumbling Brig – the principal object of our present walk. This turbulent and powerful river is a succession of rapids and cascades for several miles, rolling and forming over a bed of perfectly cliffy rocks, which it has hollowed into the most fantastic shapes, and keeping upon ceaseless and tremendous coil – sometimes lost among the overhanging foliage of these elysian retreats and sometimes bursting forth in the most wild and romantic manner. We proceeded along a fine gravelled walk amid refreshing woods, fragrant and cool, with frequent patches of highly kept rockwork, heaths, rhododendrons, and other plants of lovely beauty, trembling with glittering dew.

After wandering sometime in these secluded walks, where the judicious hand of art was occasionally detected, we got again into the road, following it over an open hill, from which is a sweet view of the evergreen summits and warm rocks we had admired from the riverside. The deep roar of the waterfall was now heard, though still unseen; and by the aid of this invisible guide we soon found ourselves upon the Rumbling Brig. It is a small arch sprung across a very narrow chasm, but of astonishing and appalling depth; about midway down, so narrow that a person, had he hardihood enough, might easily skip across; and widening toward the top, but more toward the bottom. On the east side of the bridge clings a most graceful ash, shooting up its feathery foliage into the sky, and also dangling downwards to the same length below, as pensile as ivy or willow, and even waving to the breath of the torrent: it reminded us of the ivy in the church of Welsh Pool. On the west side a short distance from the bridge, comes down in a contorted series of clefts, a very powerful body of water, with such a stunning and deafening roar that the bridge is very sensibly felt to 'dirl' and vibrate. In the bottom of the abyss a huge rock has fallen, under which the water is lost, but is seen again on the other side beneath the tressy ash, gliding away with its silvery foam, calm as a smooth canal. Above the fall are many great gushes, and the river is seen coming to its cataract over rocks to a great distance. The roar is prodigious; and seems like the Hymn of the loud Water Gods, calling in harmonious thunders, on the Dryads around, to wave their high tops and unite their echoes in praise of the Great Common Spirit whose power has so lavishly displayed and a profusion of sublime beauties.

This fall is of moderate size compared with that of Foyers – not so vast and sublime, but more within the grasp of the mind, and on that account perhaps pleases more. The rocks are of micaceous schist.

The interior of Atholl House being shut up, we were left at liberty to enjoy what was far more interesting to us than the luxuries of art, those luxuries of nature that are displayed round Dunkeld with such lavish prodigality of beauty. As a ducal palace it is insignificant and mean, having no rooms above the ground floor, though it occupies a considerable space. We saw, among others on the lawn, the two venerable larches which were the first ever introduced into this country in 1738. So little was the natural history of this invaluable tree then known, that they were placed in the greenhouse.

After again visiting the Cathedral, we walked to Loch Palney and the defile through which we entered Dunkeld last night. It is called the King's Seat, or the King's Pass, from having been the station where the Scottish monarchs and attendant Nobles formerly placed themselves, during their hunting excursions in the Forest of Atholl, in order to direct their shafts with advantage at the flying deer which were driven that way for their amusement. In this romantic and secluded spot, for the first time since we commenced our tour, we felt ourselves at leisure; and as our exertions had been great and unremitting, we enjoyed it with a proportionate zest.

We had previously ordered dinner; and the clock of the old Cathedral from its desolated tower reminded us that it would be waiting our return;

and on entering Fisher's Hotel, the waiter shewed us to a room where covers were spread for *three*, at the same time soliciting permission for a gentleman to dine with us, who was in a hurry to go on to Perth. Dovaston was at this moment looking through the window; and not hearing the waiter's request, sat down, saying, 'Bowman uncover that Hotchpot, and stir it up "to make the gruel thick and slab".' – It must be recollected that Birnam hill was only across the Tay. I replied that a gentleman was about to join us: – Pshaw! said he – some vulgar Englishman, mayhap. At all events, said I, let us shew what we can of good manners where we find so much. He waited but a moment. A gentleman came in, and as he bowed and sat down, his manner had more of the apology in it than his brief salutation. I helped him to some Hotchpot, on which he, seeing we were Southrons, commented kindly, saying he had eaten better, but it was good. – Fish of course – from the all bounteous Tay, piscocissimus amnis. – Dovaston observing that both the waiter and his own servant called him 'Sir George,' – on taking wine with him, said 'You have a title Sir – we were unaware – but on your favouring us with it, we will redeem our omission of that courtesy.' He then freely gave us each a card, saying, 'Sir George M. Ogilvy.' The same awakened in me the interesting history of the preservation of the Scotch Regalia by a gentleman or rather lady of that name; and on mentioning this circumstance to Sir George, he said it was his ancestor, and gave us, after the cloth was withdrawn, a minute narrative of the particulars – During the time of the Commonwealth, the Regalia of Scotland were deposited in the Castle of Dunottar in Mearns, to secure them from the Parliamentary forces which then overran the country. The governor, Genl. Ogilvie, though repeatedly summoned to surrender, maintaind his post with the greatest resolution; but at length, finding it impossible, from scarcity of provisions and want of ammunition, to hold out any longer, he contrived by the following stratagem, to carry off the Regalia. Mrs Granger, wife of the minister of the neighbouring parish of Kinneff, attended by a maid servant, asked leave to visit Mrs Ogilvie, the governor's wife, and on her return, brought away the crown in her lap. The governor himself set her on horseback; and her maid brought away the sword and sceptre on her back in a bundle of hemp. All Cromwell's efforts could not afterwards induce the governor to betray his trust, or tell him where they were secreted; which so exasperated the Protector, that he kept him six years in confinement. They were sometimes concealed under the pulpit in the church of Kinneff, and sometimes under a bed at the manse till the Restoration in 1660, when they were safely returned to the governor, who informed Charles the second of his trust, and by his order, delivered the whole of it to the Earl Marischal. Sir George told us that he was in possession of an autograph letter of thanks from the king to his ancestor for his fidelity, as well as of many original papers relating to the siege, and the Earl Marischal's receipt on taking charge of the Regalia. He says the royal letter is written in a neat fine hand, and is not much larger than his thumb nail, being conveyed to the governor concealed in a man's stock or shirt collar. For this important service he was created a baronet, but no farther mark of royal favour or reward was given him. The family motto is 'Proeclarum Regi et regno servitium'.

A few years ago, the chest containing those insignia of an extinct race of monarchs was opened with great ceremony at Edinburgh, to satisfy the doubts of some who supposed them to be stolen; and we undertood there was some intention of removing them to London. This would be an impolitic step, and would rekindle the national jealousy of the Scotch.

We had taken places for Perth in an evening coach just established, which was to leave Dunkeld at six o'clock; and as our wine was finished before that hour arrived, Sir George said, that though he also was going there, his time was at his own command, and he would tak ae mutchkin o' moontain dew wi' us ere we parted: the whiskey was accordingly brought in, and as we sipped it, we enjoyed the last of a short gleam from the hearty and honest baronet, born indeed in England, at Gloucester as he told us, but whose heart's gems of truest and best loyalty were bright and pure as ever Aurora hung on the native spines of old Coila's mountain thistle.

The coach was named the Duchess of Atholl, and set out from the Atholl Arms; and as we lounged about the door, waiting for passengers, we saw the following ludicrous handbill announcing its establishment: 'The Duchess of Atholl starts from the Duke's arms every lawful evening at six o'clock.' – Taken in a literal sense, this pithy paragraph would certainly convey no favourable idea of the domestic happiness of the noble pair.

We again crossed the handsome bridge over the Tay; and in passing under the far famed Birnam Hill – which is very near Dunkeld – were caught by a sudden and smart shower. Having a third person between us, we had some difficulty in unfurling and raising our common umbrella, embarrassed as we were 'in thunder, lighting, and in rain,' and but for the courtesy of our fellow-traveller, should have suffered much more inconvenience than we did. It continued to rain the whole of the stage; and cooped as we were under our umbrella, we could see little of the country. It seemed to be generally flat, but the pastures and numerous cornfields bespoke the soil to possess great fertility. About four miles from Perth we passed a straggling village and some factories, called Luncarty bleachfields. There was fought a celebrated battle between the Danes and the Scots at the end of the tenth century, in which the former were completely defeated.

A little farther on, we saw across the Tay, the Palace of Scone (pronounced Scoon) under the well wooded hill of Kinnoul. Here was formerly the Palace where the kings of Scotland were crowned; upon its site stands a modern mansion, belonging to the Earl of Mansfield. The ancient stone, brought hither from Dunstaffnage and used at coronations, was afterwards taken to Westminster Abbey, where it is still appropriated to the same purpose under the feet of British sovereigns.

On entering Perth, being strangers, we requested our chatty friend would recommend an inn, which he did by taking us with him to the Hammerment Hotel; where after drying our clothes, and laying in a good supper, we enjoyed with him, over our whiskey, much very interesting conversation, principally on literature. At a very late hour we retired to bed, and he proceeded in a coach for Edinburgh.

I have now brought down the detail of our tour to the conclusion of the Highland, and to us, the most interesting, portion of it. Our principal objects in visiting these remote districts, were, their wild and romantic scenery, and the traces of primitive manners which might still remain among their simple and secluded inhabitants. The new and interesting objects which the Tour itself afforded, have sucessively passed in review before me during the drawing up of these pages, arrayed in colours scarcely less brilliant, and accompanied by sensations scarcely less delightful, than their originals. Even those inhospitable tracts which frequently separated the richest gems of scenery, and presented nothing to the passing traveller but inanity and desolation, were far from being devoid of interest in a philosophic point of view. Dr. Johnson soundly remarks – 'Regions mountainous and wild, thinly inhabited and little cultivated, make a great part of the earth; and he that has never seen them, must live unacquainted with much of the face of nature, and with one of the great scenes of human existence.' We cannot travel far in the Highlands, without seeing much to remind us, within how narrow a circle the real wants of man are confined, nor without learning that it is possible for Content to dwell with Poverty, to exist, even without a pittance of comfort – much less without riches and honours – things that 'play round the head, but come not near the heart.' The balance of Happiness is adjusted by a nicer and a wiser standard than we are apt to imagine; and He who has seen fit to deny them the comforts which the inhabitants of more favoured countries consider as the essentials of life, has also kindly placed them beyond the reach of those cares and mortifications which so frequently embitter and destroy the substantial blessings of civilized and refined society.

Friday, 5th August Though the 'Duchess started from the Duke's arms at six o'clock' yesterday evening, she seemed to be under no apprehension of being pursued by his Grace: – in other words, our new coach travelled so slowly, that it was quite dark when we reached Perth. I was therefore anxious to see the beauties of this celebrated place, and walked over it before breakfast.

Perth, though it cannot boast of high antiquity was, till nearly the middle of the 15th century, the principal city of Scotland, the frequent residence of its princes and nobility, and the seat of its parliaments and courts of justice.

It rose after the destruction of Old Perth, the Bertha of the ancient writers, which was situated about two miles higher up the Tay, and, with the ground on which it stood, was washed away by an inundation early in the thirteenth century.

Perth is delightfully situated on the west bank of the majestic Tay; and from its commercial advantages, might with great propriety, be selected as the seat of government and the emporium of commerce. The river is navigable up to the quays at common tides for sloops and small craft; and in spring tides, for vessels of considerable burden. It is large and handsome; the streets long and spacious; and the houses altogether of freestone. Though far inferior to either Edinburgh of Glasgow, it ranks next to them in the scale of Scotch towns: the majority of the shops are rather below mediocrity. Here and there, curious old buildings occur, which have been probably the town residences of the nobility, and remain as vestiges of its ancient importance: one of these is the old Parliament House. Near the bridge, is a modern and very elegant Grecian temple of the Ionic order; of a circular form with rich fluted columns and portico, and surmounted by a dome. On the pediment are the words 'T.H. Marshall Cives Grati.' We understood it was a mausoleum erected as a tribute to the memory of a Provost of that name, who had been a great benefactor to the city, and by his public spirit and judicious measures, had considerably increased its revenues. It contains a library and museum.

The bridge over the Tay is the most noble structure of the kind in North Britain, being nine hundred feet long, and consisting of nine arches: it was built by that able engineer, Smeaton. The course of the river from Dunkeld is nearly south; but on quitting Perth, (where though broad, it is not deep) it turns eastward round the hill of Kinnoul, and through the Carse of Gowrie, to Dundee and the German ocean. The Tay is the largest river in Scotland, and may be called the main artery of Perthshire, for nearly all the streams that rise within the county fall in to it. It can also boast, if we incude its various ramifications, a greater display of romantic scenery than any of her other rivers, and besides its own picturesque beauty, is frequently interesting from association with the events of history or the strains of poesy. From the number of its tributary streams and the extent of surface which they drain, there is less inequality in the flow of its waters, than in alpine rivers in general. From one or other of these, it receives a tolerable supply of water; and, except in very dry seasons, is never deficient; and on the other hand, the great distance of many of its sources from the main trunk and from each other, usually prevents the floods from being either sudden or overwhelming. These circumstances may account for the quantity and excellence of its salmon. The various fisheries upon it, including those of the Firth, are so productive, that we were told at Dunkeld, they brought in the amazing annual rental of £22,000 to their respective proprietors. Pennant says three thousand fish have been caught in one morning, weighing on an average, sixteen pounds each, making the weight of the whole capture forty eight thousand pounds. Every four days during the season, which continues from Christmas to the end of August, a smack with a cargo of salmon, sails for London: the spring and part of the summer fish go packed in ice; and when they are plentiful in warm weather, they are pickled and kippered. The process of kippering is performd as follows: After cleansing the fish inside and outside, the head is cut off and the back-bone taken out, but the tail and two or three inches of bone are left in; then laid on a board, well rubbed, and covered with equal quantities of salt and Jamaica pepper. It is then pressed flat for sometime, and occasionally rubbed with the mixture; and afterwards hung up to dry in the sun or by the fire. Kippered salmon is an indispensable accompaniment of Scotch breakfast, and is generally introduced broiled; its flavour is excellent, being between that of the fresh and the dried fish. We seldom broke our fast without 'kipper' as it is called, and before we left Scotland became quite partial to it.

After breakfast we walked to the top of the hill of Kinnoul, celebrated both on account of the rich and extensive view from its summit, and for affording a great variety of beautiful agates and carnelians, commonly known by the name of Scotch Pebbles. It lies about two miles due east from Perth on the opposite side the Tay, and is the most westerly of the Sidlaw chain of mountains, which, like most others in Scotland, runs north-east and south-west. The classical hill of Dunsinane, on which stood Macbeth's castle forms the north east termination of this chain. We crossed the Tay by the fine bridge already named, and leaving the river, turned to the left. The side of the hill looking towards Perth, is a rather steep slope, planted with pines, &c, nearly to the summit: through these we ascended along a winding path cut through the trees, where we saw the golden-crested wren, the smallest of European birds. On arriving at the summit, we came almost immediately to the edge of a perpendicular precipice, at the foot of which lay stretched before us the Carse of Gowrie, a fine flat cultivated country, through the midst of which the bright and broad Tay glided gently, meandering in long and graceful sweeps, studded with many pretty green islands, and enlivened by moving sails. On the opposite bank is the hill of Moncrief, called by Pennant, 'the glory of Scotland', from the richness and beauty of the prospect; it is about the same height as Kinnoul (between six and seven hundred feet) and the view must be very similar. Beyond it, rose the range of the Ochil hills, and more to the east, the Lomond hills in Fifeshire; while the view to the north was bounded by the blue and distant Grampians, among which – by his lofty concave summit – we recognized Ben Lawers. The village and mansion of Scone lay embosomed in luxuriant woods immediately below us; but Perth was concealed by a projecting portion of the hill. The landscape altogether was varied, rich, and lovely; and the atmosphere had a transparency peculiar to showery weather, which gave to the nearer objects an extraordinary brilliancy. The effect was much enhanced by the sudden and unexpected manner in which the view burst upon us on attaining the summit, and reminded us of a similar station on the Blodwell rocks near Llanymynech.

The Carse of Gowrie is a long narrow plain extending sixteen or eighteen miles in length, and containing about 18,000 acres of extremely rich and fertile soil. This district, indeed, may be justly styled the boast of Great Britain for natural productiveness, and yield to no portion of the globe in the intelligence and skill of its farmers. Like the Delta land of Egypt, and those fertile tracts adjacent to the mouths of the Ganges, the Indus, and the Mississippi, the Carse of Gowrie has been formed in a long course of ages, and has grown rich by the spoils of the Highlands. The heavy rains which fall near the sources of the Earn, the Tay, the Tummel, and the Garry, and their tributary streams, have washed down great portions of soil, and have laid bare the rocks of the highest mountains, to give exuberance to the banks of the Tay. The Carse, in fact, is evidently nothing more than what is called in other quarters, sea-mud or sludge, consolidated by time and gradual deposition.

When we had reached the bottom of the hill on our return, I discovered that I had left upon the summit my favourite walking stick, which I had thrown upon the grass while I went to knock off a suitable specimen of rock, and not returning to the same spot, had forgotten. It was then very warm, and the ascent was arduous; therefore after a little deliberation, I determined – as I only should *feel* the loss – to leave it to its fate.

When we reached Perth, we found it full of life and bustle in consequence of a Review of the militia of the County by the Duke of Atholl, on a large plain near the bridge. Dovaston went there, in hopes of hearing a fine Band play Scotch Melodies in slow, full breathing harmonies; but he was disappointed. He represented the Band as feeble and poor; and instead of the heart-melting melodies of Scotland, heard nothing but common English Opera tunes. He had however the pleasure of again shaking by the hand the affable Sir Geo. Ogilvy, who was one of the officers, now in his military dress, attending on the Duke. In his absence, I had engaged to procure tickets of admission to the Library and Museum already mentioned; but on reaching it I found the time of admission was past, and the doors closed for the day. I was directed to a bookseller at some distance, who was one of the trustees; and on informing him I was a stranger leaving Perth early the next morning, he very politely, and without hesitation, intrusted me with the keys. I returned to the Museum where Dovaston soon joined me; and we were both particularly gratified by this mark of confidence and attention to the wishes of strangers, so different from what we had often experienced in England.

The Library was in a circular room below, round which ran also a light elegant gallery, holding books. Above, was a circular domed area, containing the Museum, which was only established last year; yet there is a consists of the usual assortment of Kamschatka dresses, weapons, &c, elephant's heads, serpents, birds, coins and minerals chiefly found in Perthshire. Among the collection we noticed a curious copy of the Bible in Chinese, printed in many thin volumes, each containing two or three of the Tracts of the Old and New Testament; the entire Koran, beautifully and minutely written and emblazoned on a roll of vellum four inches wide and twelve yards long: a white specimen of the Hirundo apus, Swift; and specimens of plants presented by Dr. Fisher, which he had gathered in the Arctic regions on the late expedition.

We spent the evening in strolling about the town and in gazing at the great concourse of people of all classes which the Review had brought together, and who were now collected before the principal hotel to see the Duke and his officers retire from the mess. In the different carriages there was a brilliant display of ladies – now spreading their wings, and fluttering in the beams of Mars – but Venus smiled not there. The generality even of the younger part of the sex among the highest classes, were harsh and coarse featured; yet here and there a handsome face relieved the eye. Those on foot were generally well dressed but occasionally without shoes and stockings; their legs universally thick and strong about the ankles; and they had a masculine shape and gait. Of the lower classes, the women were altogether bare legged; also boys under fourteen or fifteen, filthy in their persons and habits; and the compound of villainous smells that constantly assailed us from the courts and alleys, whispered that they were not less so in their habitations. Notwithstanding these disparagements, there is a decency of behaviour and a feeling of propriety and subordination in a Scotch crowd that gives a stranger a very pleasing impression of their moral respectability. Truth compels me to say, we witnessed nothing of that vacant and brutal gaze, that sauciness and insolence in the men, nor heard those savage yells and disgusting blasphemies among the boys, which are characteristic of the rabble of our English towns, and so lamentably indicative of their demoralized habits and gross feelings. How venial, compared with these, are the national foibles of the Scotch. But let us hope that when the mighty Engine now in motion for educating the lower classes in England, shall have been so long at work as it has in Scotland, it will have produced such effects upon the morals and habits of our poor, as will give the future philanthropist no cause to blush, to censure, or to regret, when they are compared with those of any other nation.

Before we commenced our tour, our venerable friend Bewick had pressed us to spend a short time with him at Newcastle; and Dovaston wrote to him this evening to inform him of our progress southwards, and of our intention to accept his invitation; requesting a reply addressed to Edinburgh, to say if he was at home and at liberty to receive us.

Saturday, 6th August   We left Perth this morning at a quarter before seven o'clock by a coach which travelled at the rate of ten miles per hour. We passed through a finely varied country, rich in corn and the most luxuriant pastures, sometimes bounded by smooth verdant hills, and sometimes opening into lateral valleys of Arcadian beauty. The precipitous face of Kinnoul hill stretched much farther to the east than we had imagined when on the summit. Looking backwards we had a very bright and pleasing view of Perth, the well wooded hills beyond it, and the blue and distant Grampians. We kept the broad and magnificent Tay long in sight and after we had proceeded a few miles, we crossed the river Earn and the eastern end of the long and very fertile vale through which it flows from Loch Earn, designated by the general appellation of Strathearn. It possesses many scenes of picturesque beauty. Near the confluence of the Earn with the estuary of the Tay, is the small decayed town of Abernethy, once the residence of the ancient line of the Scottish or Pictish kings. The country now rises into gentle slopes, but their surfaces are smooth and covered with grass, and interspersed with woods, hamlets, and gentlemen's seats. It soon swells into hills of greater elevation, with intervening flat moory districts, whence the distant views are diversified by mountains and reaches of the estuary, which agreeably relieve the uniformity of the foregound.

The southern face of the Ochil hills is more precipitous than the northern, though, like it, generally covered with a green herbage – now by the long continued drought changed into a brown and withered sward. We were now in the small county of Kinross, the whole of which was stretched before us, and appeared of a basin-like form; its broad central plain gradually rising on every side into verdant hills diversified with woods. We descended into this plain, and on passing the small village of Milnathort, got the first glimpse of the interesting Loch Leven, with the ruins of Burleigh castle on its western bank, surrounded by a group of lofty trees. It was formerly the residene of Lord Burleigh, and a place of great strength.

To a traveller fresh from a tour through the Highlands, the scenery of Loch Leven, if unconnected with historical events, and not associated with feelings of sympathy for the fate of a woman and a queen who suffered here the first pangs of a captivity which terminated only with her life, would of itself possess little interest. Its extent is not considerable, and the surrounding scenery, though composed of hills and fertile plains, has not sufficient character to astonish or delight. In most of the views of it which I have seen, this defect has been supplied by the imagination of the painter; and Loch Leven has been made to repose in the bosom of lofty mountains whose graceful cones and broken surfaces are surrounded by umbrageous woods and picturesque glades – as though the scene on which this captive princess was doomed to look, must of ncessity receive the impress of her own attractions. As we approached the town of Kinross, we saw the small island in the centre of the lake with its ruined castle within whose walls the unhappy Mary Stuart was compelled to resign her crown.

The island on which the Castle stands is small and grassy; the building itself is square, surrounded by a wall and guarded by a circular tower; with a few scattered trees about it. Pennant gives a view of it, which at my request, my daughter has copied upon the title-page of this volume, as an early specimen of her drawing.

Kinross is a well built, though small town, and the principal thoroughfare from Edinburgh to the north east parts of the kingdom. It stands on the western shore of Loch Leven and between it and a large level plain which stretches to the westward. Here we made a hasty breakfast; part of which consisted of fine perch caught in the lake. We were told that Loch Leven is celebrated for trout of a large size, which very much resemble salmon both in taste and appearance and are considered a great delicacy. The red colour of their flesh is attributed to their feeding chiefly on a small shell-fish of a deep red colour which abounds at the bottom of the water. Some of our passengers expressed much disappointment that we were not allowed an opportunity of tasting them.

Soon after leaving Kinross we took a new road which branched off to the east from that to Queen's ferry, and was in parts very hilly. Notwithstanding this, we did not slacken our average rate of ten miles an hour. On passing the top of the Cleish hills, where we entered Fifeshire, we caught the first view of Arthur's Seat near Edinburgh and sometime before we descended towards the Firth of Forth, had a very noble view of this estuary, with the town of Leith on the opposite shore, the new part of Edinburgh with the Calton Hill, Salisbury Crags, and Arthur's Seat. The new city was seen to great advantage occupying the side of a hill which sloped towards us, and had a peculiar appearance from the great width of the streets and the circumstance of their intersecting each other at right angles. Some rain had fallen, and the sun's light reflected from the wetted roofs and white buildings, shewed the dark intersections of the streets and the uniformity of the plan. We came down to the Firth of Forth at Burnt island (so called from the volcanic appearance of its rocks) and immediately went on board a steam packet that waited our arrival. The town has an excellent harbour and pier; and from its manufactories and shipping, and the activity of commerce everywhere observable, seems to be a place of some importance. The estuary is here about seven miles wide; and with the numerous vessels moving upon it in every direction, and the beautiful scenery of its southern shore, forms a very fine picture. The town of Leith with its crowded dock-yards, appeared, as it were, to lie upon its surface: to the west, its rising banks were interspersed with the well-wooded seats of personages of distinction; and in the opposite direction, where it opens finely to the eastern sea, it is variegated by several rocky islets, beyond which is seen, as far as the eye can reach, the singular conic hill called Bass island, & Berwick Law, near North Berwick.

The [steam vessel] 'Thane of Fife' soon wafted us across to Leith, the port of Edinburgh, lying about a mile and a half from the capital. The streets are narrow, filthy, and thronged with sailors; in short a perfect Wapping. We mounted another stage coach, which after driving us along a noble road lined with fine buildings and green fields in about equal proportions, set us down in the modern Athens, the capital of Scotland, and the most magnificent modern city in Europe. We took up our abode at Menzie's Register Hotel, close to the superb Register Office and to the wellknown Archibald Constable's extensive bookshop at the corner of Princess street, and engaged bedrooms and a very comfortable retired sitting room on the first floor.

On first ranging the streets of Edinburgh, the eyes of a stranger, though he has seen London, Paris, or Bath, must at once be struck with amazement. Instead of considering it the metropolis of one part of a great commercial nation, its classic elegance recalls to the fancy, ideas of eastern magnificence. Athens, Babylon, Bagdad, or Palmyra, seem to rise again from their ruins of countless centuries, and to re-appear in all their splendour before his eyes. Porticoes of massive columns, fluted and plain and of every order, pilasters, domes, obelisks, pillars, and temples; streets of spacious width, intersecting each other at right angles and stretching in long and elegant perspective; houses of towering height, richly decorated with friezes and cornices, meet the eye on every side, all airy, chaste, and classical. Every building is of freestone, beautifully clean and light, not a brick or even plaster or cement offends the eye.

Such is the impression which a first view of this Queen of the North makes upon a stranger. We devoted the remainder of the day to a general lounge, without meaning to confine ourselves to any particular object, renewing our wanderings after dinner, and sauntering about the brilliant gas illuminated streets till ten o'clock; when we retired to our clean and comfortable hotel, to record the various scenes that had engaged our attention through the day.

Sunday, 7th August It will perhaps be recollected that among the agreeable party it was our good fortune to fall in with on board the Highlander Steam packet from Glasgow to Staffa, was a son of Dr. Thompson of Edinburgh, a friend of the kind hearted Maclean, who was going to spend a short time with him at Drymnen. Before we parted from him in the Sound of Mull, he pressed upon Dovaston a letter of introduction to another Mr. Thompson of Edinburgh (though no relation) the editor of the British Melodies, and the gentleman whose numerous letters to Burns are inserted in Dr. Currie's Life of that poet.

We put ourselves into the best trim our threadbare clothes would allow – for they were miserably the worse for the journey – and after breakfast went to call on Mr. Thompson in Princess Street with the letter. However much we might have thought last night, this splendid city resembled those of the

Enchanters in the Arabian Nights, the impression was not diminished by what we saw this morning. On ringing the bell at the No. given on the superscription, the outer door almost immediately opened of its own accord into a lobby where no person was to be seen: we walked in; and while we were looking about to understand the meaning of this dumb shew, it as suddenly closed upon us with a loud bang. We saw some machinery behind the door, to which was attached a cord that communicated with the rooms above, and with the apartments underneath. On ascending the first flight of steps, we met a lady, who informed us that Mr. Thompson lived two doors farther. She liberated us by ringing the bell; on which the outer door again opened, and closed as before, the same pantomimic performance was repeated there; and we learnd from a servant, that her master and mistress were over the Firth at Burnt island, but that we might see Miss T. As we went up one flight of stairs after another, we observed that each storey was inhabited by a distinct family whose name appeared on a brass plate fixed to the principal door. At length we were ushered into Miss Thompson's presence, in a very good room hung with excellent paintings, and having a Grand Pianoforte. Dovaston told her briefly an outline of the past part of our tour – the time we spent with Mr. John Thompson and Mr. Maclean, on the voyage to Staffa – and so delivered the letter, which she did not open, but shewed us the pictures, particularly a very spirited one by Wilkie, of Burns's 'Duncan Gray', the story of which led to a conversation on her father's connection with that poet. She regretted he was not at home; but in a very pleasing and affable manner expressed her wish to render us any service in her power.

Leaving Princess Street; we descended through the gardens, and mounted up a very steep zigzag path cut in the castle rock, which here impends over the valley to a great and precipitous height. On our way up, Miss Thompson pointed out an old ruined fortress of much greater antiquity than the castle, and supposed to be Roman. The Castle however is much older than any other building in Edinburgh, and is situated on the western extremity of the central hill on which the High Street is built. It occupies an area of about seven acres, and is accessible only by the above street which runs along the ridge, and approaches it from the east. On every other side the rock is nearly perpendicular. When we reached the summit and stood in front of the building, we overlooked the greater part of the old town, and were able to form a tolerable idea of its irregular site and singular ground plan. The steep side of the central hill towards the south, though entirely built upon, might be traced by the successive rising of the roofs of the houses from the intervening valley, like the huge steps of a great irregular amphitheatre. The loftiest houses we saw in Edinburgh, are in the neighbourhood of the castle but from the steep slope of the hill, the floors which are level with the street in front, are often three or four stories from the ground at the back, where they tower to an amazing height. In many of them we counted eight, nine, or ten windows, one above another, and Miss Thompson said she believed some of them were fourteen stories high. Each floor, or as it is here called, *flat*, or *land*, is inhabited by a separate family, and sometimes by two; and it may be supposed that the inconveniences of those who occupy the upper ones, must be both numerous and great. The former reproach of Edinburgh is however done away with by a severe law; and, except perhaps in an obscure alley or back street, it is now no longer necessary for a passenger to cast his eyes upwards as he walks along, and cry out, 'Haud your hand, lassie.' From this spot we had a fine view of the Cathedral, the Iron Church, Heriots Hospital, and other public buildings, as well as the neighbouring hills.

From the castle we were led by our fair conductress through the wonderful streets of the old town; and coming to an opening on each side, we looked down, and saw below us, as it were, a subterranean street, variant and gloomy, and filled with moving groups of people. This was the Cowgate, which runs along the valley to the south of the central hill; and the point on which we stood, was the South Bridge which runs across it, but which, (though consisting of nineteen arches) from being lined on each side with lofty houses, exactly resembles a common street, and is invisible. The central arch only is not built upon, and allows a view down into the Cowgate, into which run many steep and narrow alleys from the main street on the hill. We passed the Iron Chuch, whose tower was covered with a low pyramid of boards, having had its little spire, then scaled with wooden shingles, burnt down by the great fire which happened here about six months before, and the dreadful ravages of which, we saw when we reached the Cathedral. This, and the Parliament Close, are both situated on the south side of High Street, a little farther up the hill. The old Cathedral or St Giles's, is now called the High Kirk, and is divided into four separate places of worship. It is a venerable and mutilated, but not a spacious structure, nor is its architecture rich: its tower is surmounted by a dome formed of open, converging, groined arches, or flying buttresses, intended to represent an imperial crown; but it is not so tall and elegant as that of St Nicholas's Church at Newcastle-upon-Tyne, which is of a similar design. Near it is the Square called the Parliament Close, because the old Parliament House occupies two of its angles. The tremendous fire just alluded to, broke out in this neighbourhood; and an idea of the fury with which it raged, might be formed by the great space laid bare, and now cleared of the ruins, which before was covered with very lofty houses. The celebrated Tolbooth – known to all the readers of the Heart of Midlothian, as the prison from which an exasperated mob tore their victim, Porteous, on the dreadful night of the 7th September 1736, and dragged him to the Grassmarket, the scene at once of his offence and of his execution – stood close to the Cathedral, but was totally destroyed: not a vestige of it is now to be seen, as the ruined walls have been removed. The statue also of Charles the second, which stood on a pedestal in the centre of the Close, was injured, and is now taken down. Over several doors we observed the memorable name of Porteous, probably relatives or descendants of the unfortunate Captain.

We next came upon the North Bridge, which is thrown across the Norloch. Here we again gazed with astonishment both at the depth of the houses below the street where we stood, and at their height above us; and also at the people who walked under us, reduced to the size of pigmies. This vast dry bridge consists of three ponderous and expansive arches, resting on pillars about one hundred feet high; and the space below is occupied by shambles and a green market, disposed in terraces upon the declivity of the hill. The view of the castle hill, covered with steppy houses rising ten or twelve stories high, and looking like a conglomeration of pinnacled rocks, is here very curious and striking. We were now again in the new town; and turning to our right into Regent Street, passed the Theatre, Post Office, &c, and stood upon the Regent's Bridge, where, through the open balustrades, we saw under us, as before, another street filled with a densely crowded population. These lofty dry bridges, by means of which one street is carried above another which crosses it at right angles at a considerable depth below it, form one of the most novel and peculiar features of Edinburgh; and, from being closely surrounded by very lofty houses, and not rising above the level of the street, the singular scene they present below, bursts unawares upon the stranger, and fills him with amazement. Regent Street is considered, for its length, the most magnificent in the whole city being lined with many public buildings and houses having highly decorated fronts all of fine freestone. It forms the modern entrance into Edinburgh from the south, and has but lately been completed. At the end of it we turned to the left near the new Bridewell, and the kind Miss Thompson toiled with us up the Calton hill, on which is a tall round banded tower, erected in honour of Lord Nelson, compared by our fair conductress to a churn with a staff in it, (the flag-staff). As we approached the summit, we had an excellent view of Arthur's Seat, and below it, of Salisbury Crags, – a long obliquely rising rock with a very precipitous face. Miss T. pointed out a cottage near St. Leonards, that since the publication of the Heart of Mid-Lothian, has been called the cottage of Douce David Deans; shewed us St. Anthony's Chapel, and the imaginary site of Muschats cairn, (which she pronounced Mushat's). We now rounded the Calton hill on a broad public walk, having a noble view over Leith of the Firth of Forth, Inch Keith &c, Bass Island rising out of the sea like the high pitched roof of an old thatched barn, the Fifeshire hills, and in the extreme western distance, Ben Lomond just faintly marking the sky. We still continued to round the hill, passing the Observatory, a burial ground in which are deposited the remains of the celebrated David Hume, a very fine Grecian temple with porticoes and dome. We now came under Nelson's Tower; and she led us to the site of the intended Parthenon, on the first stone of which – laid when the King was here, – we all stood. We then descended; and she led us to the Monument of Lord Melville, a fine fluted Doric Column in St. George's Square, and along many of the streets in the new town, intersecting each other at right angles, and generally terminated by some public building, as a church, a portico, a temple, or a column. Lastly, and not least interesting, she pointed out, with his name on the door, the town house of Sir Walter Scott in Castle Street, telling us we had to lament the absence of this great man, as he was most easy of access, familiar, and most brilliant in conversation; and would have seen us kindly on the slightest introduction. We now attended the young lady to her house; and on shaking hands, she wished us to call tomorrow at noon, when she would procure us introduction to the Advocate's Library and other places worthy the attention of strangers. Pleased with her affable conduct, and the kindness we had altogether received in Scotland, we sought our hotel and dined, drinking to the health of our fair guide and the good people of Scotland, and highly gratified with our morning's walk.

After dinner we ascended Arthur's Seat, the loftiest hill in the neighbourhood of the city, being 814 feet high, and interesting both to the mineralogist and the botanist as well to the lover of the picturesque scenery. Passing along Regent Street, and under the southern side of the Calton hill, we turned to the right and went close behind Holyrood house. Near St. Leonards we mounted over a small brow, and got into a smooth secluded valley, as though far removed from cities and the busy haunts of men, shut out from everything by the back of the belt of Salisbury crags on one side, and on the other by the towering cliffs of Arthur's seat: flocks of sheep and cattle were peacefully grazing on the sides of the hills. The whole of this tract is called 'The Park' and was 'Once the lov'd haunt of Scotia's royal train', having been first inclosed by James the fifth when he built Holyrood palace. We now began to scale the smooth grassy slope of the hill towards the north and found it occasionally so steep (especially towards the top) that owing to the very dry state of the grass, we had some difficulty to keep upon our feet. When we attained the summit, we enjoyed a very broad and extensive view, similar of course to that from the Calton hill, but embracing a much wider range. It commanded both portions of the city with its valleys and eminences of roofs, its castle, its churches, public buildings, streets and houses, many of them, as it were, hanging in air. To the north was Leith and the Firth of Forth bounded by the shore of Fife, the Lomond and the Ochil hills; stretching westward was the high Grampian Chain, with Stirling Castle over the Forth, all indistinctly seen from the position of the sun; the Pentland hills intercepted the view to the southwest, but from their eastern end a very great tract of country was spread before us, comprehending a great part of Edinburghshire or Mid Lothian, and the whole of Haddingtonshire or East Lothian; in which the towns of Musselburgh, Haddington, North Berwick, Dunbar, Preston Pans, and other places upon the coast could be distinguished, together with the Bass and

May islands, and the dark flat ridge of the Lammermuir hills in the extreme southeast. The sun being in the opposite point of the heavens, gave a clearness and precision to this part of the prospect which no other portion of it possessed; and had our knowledge of the country been more general, it could have been amusing to identify the numerous villages, churches, gentlemen's seats, &c we so distinctly saw.

In our return, being Sunday and a fine day, we met and overtook many groups of the citizens in every part of our walk; the footpaths and fields below us seem thronged with well dressed people in every direction, enjoying the fresh air and a little relaxation from the cares of a life spent in the close smoky atmosphere of a densely populous city. Leaving St. Anthony's chapel on the right, we came in front of Holyrood house; and turning to the left up the Cannongate, crossed the North Bridge and reached our hotel a little before sunset, much fatigued.

Monday, 8th August　Having an appointment at twelve o'clock to accompany Miss Thompson to the Advocate's Library, we left our hotel immediately after breakfast, and went through Holyrood House, that the remainder of the day might be at her disposal. Instead of the direct road down the Cannongate, we crossed the High street, and taking the direction of the South Bridge, turned into the sinuous, serpentine, and descending street called the Nether Bow, making our way into the Cowgate and thence into the Cannongate near the bottom of the hill. In this walk we saw much of the singular structure of the old town; but the general idea of it has already been given. The narrow dirty streets, lofty houses, small shops crammed together and piled one above another, a swarming population, and the unpleasant effluvia which assailed us at every step, all tended to revive my recollections of Paris. Here also, as in that splendid city, the extremes of magnificence and wealth come in close contact with those of wretchedness and poverty. The character of the buildings and the general appearance of the streets of the old town, particularly the Cannongate, very much resemble Paris; and it is probable, from the frequent intercourse between the two countries, previous to the accession of the Stuarts to the English throne, that the style of its architecture has been borrowed from the French. Few of the houses appear to be of an older date than James the fifth or Mary, when many French customs were introduced. Walsingham, who wrote about A.D. 1440, speaks of Edinburgh as a mean place, and says the houses were only small wooden cottages covered with straw. About this time the Parliaments were removed hither from Perth and it began to increase in wealth and importance.

Holyrood house, the royal palace of Scotland, is a beautiful building of a quadrangular form: the western front consists of two lofty double towers, join'd by a gallery adorned by a balustrade, in the middle of which is a portico decorated with four Doric columns, which support a cupola in the form of an imperial crown. Underneath the cupola is a clock, and over the gateway are the royal arms of Scotland. Round the area in the inside is a handsome arcade. The more ancient parts were built by James the fifth, about the year 1528. It was destroyed by Cromwell's troops, and repaired and altered into its present form by Charles the second. Adjoining the palace, on its northern side, is the ruined chapel of the ancient Abbey of Holyrood, which was destroyed in 1546 by the regent Duke of Somerset. The chapel was subsequently restored and decorated by James the fifth; but was afterwards, in 1688, demolished by the fury of a mob.

We entered the Palace and were ushered into a long spacious gallery which occupies the north side of the quadrangle. It is filled with very large and coarsely executed figures and portraits of the Kings of Scotland, of various shapes and sizes, commencing with Fergus the first, who is here said to have lived 3300 years before Christ! and continuing in an uninterrupted series down to *our* James the second, being one hundred and eleven in number. The name with the period in which they respectively flourished, is painted under each of them; but it is obvious to the most superficial observer, not only that nine-tenths of the portraits of this kingly group must be spurious, but that the names and periods of those who lived during the first thousand years of the catalogue must be blended with fiction.

The Gallery was shewn by a different conductor to the one who went with us through the Chapel; and we were now transferred to a third, who led us through the suite of apartments occupied by the unhappy Mary Stuart, on the second floor of the towers at the north west angle of the palace. We were assured that they still remained in the same state and retained the same furniture as when she graced them; nor does their appearance belie the tradition.

We now returned up the Cannongate, which is truly a noble and spacious street, but the great height of the houses tends very much to diminish its real width. On the right hand, not far from Holyrood, is the oldest gaol in Edinburgh, still used as such, and nearly opposite, are some very old houses with curious Latin inscriptions and carved devices. We made our long way to No. 140 Princess Street, which we reached by the appointed hour, and waited on our gentle friend, Miss Thompson. The day was hot, and we sat with her an hour receiving refreshment of wine and biscuit. She produced a small and beautiful quaigh of oak, made out of one of the rafters of Kirk Alloway; it was tipped with silver, on which was written –

'Care, mad to see a man sae happy,
E'en drown'd himsel among the nappy.'

Her father is an enthusiast in Burns; and she shewed us also a common tin japanned tray, off which Burns eat his bread and cheese at 'auld wee Nannie's'. She now pepared to escort us to Mr. Millar's, whom we found a very pleasant and courteous man, and one of the principal booksellers in Edinburgh. He shewed us many splendid publications and books of plates; Dovaston had much conversation with him on Books, Music, &c. Speaking of our friend Bewick, Miss Thompson urged us to call on his friend Nicholson the painter, and accompanied us there: he was now in the Highlands, but his wife shewed us his exhibition rooms in which we recognized a portrait of our venerable friend among other men of genius of this northern Athens, Sir W. Scott, Jeffrey, Mr. Thompson, &c &c. We now returned to Mr. Millar's, and having spent, not lost, more time with that good man than we well could spare, we proceeded under the guidance of Miss Thompson, to the Advocate's Libraries. These were situate near the High Kirk, in very superb new buildings of great extent. We first saw that of the Writers, (attorneys) a long large room with many pillars and books in close departments, which we thought very extensive and grand, little dreaming what we had to see. Next we were shown the old libraries of the Advocates (Counsellors) a low suite of a perfect labyrinth of rooms, many of which had gaslights burning, now at noon: the extent and succession was astonishing, all filled with books, and having busts and statues in rooms that had no windows. A flight of stairs, however, lined with portraits, led us into a long spacious room of great splendour and elegance, supported on two rows of rich fluted pillars ornamented profusely in full luxuriance of decoration. In the midst was a dome, round the concavity of which was painted by Stoddart, Apollo and the Muses, each fostering the figure of her department. History had here Hume, Robertson &c, and Poetry had Shakespeare, Homer, Milton, and Burns, the latter painted in his leathern breeches, blue stockings and gaiters. This is by far the most considerable Library in Scotland, and is chiefly supported by the money paid by Advocates on their admission into the faculty. It has valuable collections of Manuscripts, prints, coins &c, of the former, a copy of the Bible, written in the eleventh century. The printed Books long ago were upwards of 60,000 volumes; it is one of the eleven public libraries entitled to a copy of every new work. One of the oldest printed books is a folio Bible on vellum, the incipient letters highly illuminated with the hand, and in the vacancies were rich drawings of stags and other animals. The date about 1470.

We were informed that the Advocates intend giving this superb edifice, magnificent as it is, to the Writers, and erecting a still more spacious and elegant library, as they have not room for all their books! We had occupied so much time in these noble apartments, that it was now past the hour of seeing the College Museum, which we wished to have examined; so, under the auspices of the indefatigable Miss Thompson (who now told us she had read our letter of introduction and that it was young Maclean's request to her father, that he would shew us everything we expressed any wish to see) we proceeded to call on the far famed Arch. Constable, whom Millar represented as a very witty man; but, alas! on reaching his place of business, we found he had left for his country house. We however got free permission during our stay, to have the run of all his book rooms, 'crypts', &c where we almost fear'd to encounter the ghost of Waverley or Capt. Clutterbuck. The warehouses were absolutely stuffed and choked with the multitudinous works of Sir Walter Scott. Here we bade adieu to our fair conductress with respectful and grateful thanks for her unwearied attention to two unknown strangers. The shortness of our stay forbade our availing ourselves of the opportunity we had, of seeing more of the society of this intellectual city; but if an opinion of the ladies might be formed from Miss Thompson, it would be most favourable. Her manners were unostentatious and therefore pleasing; heightened by a vein of natural unreserved freedom; yet without a film of levity. Millar joined her in regretting Sir W. Scott's absence (in Ireland) and said he was sure he would have been delighted with Dovaston. I asked his opinion, and the general opinion here, as to the real author of the Waverley novels: he said no one hesitated to ascribe them to Sir Walter, nor knew any other motive he could have, but a whim, for concealing his name.

After dinner we walked to St. Barnard's Well, at the northwest extremity of the new town. It is a mineral spring, on the bank of a small stream, and over it has been erected a pretty light circular temple with a dome supported by Doric pillars; in the centre is a statue of Hygeia, the goddess of Health. On our way there and back we saw another part of the new town which still increased our wonder at the splendour and opulence of this vast and superb city, by the high finish and uniformity of many a crescent, circus, and square, in perfect Grecian architecture and Attic chastity.

In the evening, we strolled among the commodious and elegant galleries that descend under and on each side the Bridge over the Norloch, and more than once completely lost ourselves among the subterranean flights of steps. While passing the shambles, a person stepped forward attired in a plaid apron, with a steel by his side, and, accosting us with modest courtesy, begged we would allow him the favour of sending us a lamb's fry to our hotel for supper. On our recognizing, by a cordial shake of the hand, in this honest butcher, the chatty companion of our ride from Dunkeld to Perth, he said with great good humour, 'Ye little kenn'd at Pearth, that I were ainly an Edinboro' flesher, when ye mistaed me for a gentleman'. To which Dovaston, with that smartness of repartee which is always at his command, said, 'No, Sir, your manners and conversation were those of a gentleman, so that we were not mistaken'.

Tuesday, 9th August The whole of this day was occupied in a visit to the ruined castle and chapel of Roslin, and to 'Scotland's vaunted Hawthornden', both of which lie about eight miles south from Edinburgh on the banks of the North Esk. We set out about nine o'clock in a slow coach, which during the summer, leaves the city every morning and returns in the evening. At the distance of about a mile, we passed on the left, the elevated

A Nineteenth-Century Tour 187

and extensive ruin of Craig Millar castle, once the favourite residence of Mary Stuart, when she wished to withdraw from the turbulence and clamour by which she was so much annoyed at Holyrood.

There was on the coach a master builder from Edinburgh going to Hawthornden on business, who communicated to us much local information, and finding we were bound thither also, offered to conduct us through a pleasant retired road from Loanhead, where we left the coach. He shewed us much disinterested kindness, and took a good deal of trouble in procuring us the keys of different gentlemen's grounds through which we were to pass, among which ought to be named the ornamented park, gardens, and conservatories, of Graeme Mather Esq. of Mavisbank. We had here and there proof, added to many we had before met with in the course of our journey, of the deeprooted dislike of the Scotch to Dr. Johnson; and also an allusion to a ridiculous story recorded by Boswell, of the Dr.'s courtship with Mrs. Porter, in which he told her, one of his ancestors had been hanged; to which she replied, that many of hers had deserved it. Dovaston, while admiring the magnificent oaks near the mansion at Mavisbank, said to me 'Here is another of the thousand contradictions to Dr. Johnson' – alluding to the contemptuous sarcasms so often repeated in his Tour, of the nakedness of the land. The builder instantaneously caught the remark, and with an arch leer at my friend, do 'D'ye talk o' Dacter Jaansoon? – Gin ye gang up i'th Highlands, ye'll see a pine tree thilk his forbear was hangit for a Reeble' (rebel). We cannot wonder at the wounded feelings of the Scotch, when we reflect that he replied to their modest intellect with supercilious haughtiness, and treated their liberal hospitality with brutal ingratitude. Though boasting of piety, he scorned their devout worship with intolerance, and insulted their forbearance with Christianity on his lips. In many cases he has recorded circumstances of downright falsehood; and thousands of venerable trees on the very roads he travelled, give the lie to his incessant laugh at their nudity of arboration.

Our conductor led us from Mavisbank up a steep shady lane (from one part of which, towards the east, he showed us 'Dreyden's groves of oak') to the classic and highly romantic Hawthornden. I soon recognized the notched gables of the ancient house, from my beautiful drawing of it by Spitta. It stands on the brink of a lofty perpendicular rock, overlooking a deep and secluded glen, through which the North Esk runs from the Pentland hills to the Firth of Forth. It is the residence and property of Captn. Drummond, a descendant of one of the sweetest and chastest poets of the period in which he lived.

At the west end of the house is a ledge of rock overhanging the glen, hollowed out into a stone balcony with stone benches and a solid wall left as a guard, over which there is a lovely and bewitching view of the sloping woods, projecting crags, and brawling river below. Close to the house on the south, being only separated from it by a small garden or court, is a ruined wall and the square tower of an ancient castle, some portions of which have probably occupied the site of the present mansion. In the centre of this court is a deep well, cut in the solid rock. Round it, and up to the walls, are nailed many of the 'White Apple of Hawthornden', one of which was pointed out as the original tree which has supplied England with scions of this celebrated fruit. In a cleft of a rock behind the house, the face of which has since been hewn smooth, is one of these which has a very singular appearance. The main stem grows out of the crevice at the distance of several yards from the ground; and the branches are trained in a diverging form round it in every direction, like the radii of an immense star. It was now profusely clustered with fruit, and appeared highly luxuriant and beautiful. Advantage has probably been taken of a self-sown crab-stock which thus offered itself for grafting upon.

Our conductor having business with Captn. Drummond, now left us; but he sent one of the servants, who led us down a staircase cut in the face of the rock just beneath the house, to the celebrated Caverns. In one part of the descent there was a chasm, made passable by boards. These steps lead to the entrance of the caves, which have been cut with vast labour out of the rock. The descent into the great chambers is by eight steps; but, on the first entrance on right and left, are two rooms; that on the right consists of a gallery, fifteen feet long, with a space at the end (twelve feet by seven) whose sides are cut into ornamented square holes, each nine inches deep, and seems to have been the pigeon house of the place, there being an entrance cut through the rock. On the left hand is another gallery, and through the front of this there is a hole facing the bridge, which seems intended as the means to draw in the boards, and secure the retreat of the inhabitants. The great cavern is ninety feet long and six feet high; at the entrance it is twelve feet wide, but narrows inwards to about six feet. A recess in it opens into the well already named, and into which we looked up and down; the roof is also pierced by a funnel for the admission of light and circulation of air. Narrow galleries branch off and communicate with the others, one of which is upwards of twenty feet long by five wide.

Tradition says, these subterraneous dens were strongholds of the Pictish kings, into which they retreated to escape the vengeance their deeds of pillage and bloodshed so justly merited. However this may be, it is highly probable they have been intended as an asylum for the neighbouring inhabitants, during some of the troublesome periods with which Scottish history abounds. Though perfectly dry and even comfortable, they are now tenanted only by pigeons, who have also built in the natural crevices of the rocks; and it was pleasing to see vast numbers of these pretty birds perched in the sunshine on the ruins and on the rocks, or wheeling about in graceful sweeps over the glen. The caverns are usually the point of attraction with strangers at Hawthornden; but the solemn and picturesque walks cut along the summits, sides, and bottoms of this beautiful glen, are much more deserving admiration. The vast mural fence formed by the red precipices, the mixture of trees and grotesque figures of many of the rocks, and the smooth sides of the Pentland hills seen from the top of the defile, are more striking objects to the contemplative mind.

Full of admiration, we passed through the garden down to the bed of the river, where we had a rich romantic view of the house and caverns above, precisely similar to that in the drawing already alluded to. Both sides of the glen consist of mural precipices richly mantled with luxuriant copsewood and larger trees and tastefully traversed by circuitous and irregular walks, frequently hewn out of the rock, overhanging the river, or concealed by the groups of trees; sometimes the Esk gurgles over the crags, and sometimes glides silently and sluggishly in deep dark channels. The whole of this secluded glen is indeed irresistibly enchanting; and the cool moist atmosphere and chastened light under the perpendicular and lofty rocks on the south side, were grateful and refreshing in so hot a day. It was delightful also to see here, the Hypnum proliferum and other mosses flourishing as luxuriantly as in the dank woods on a winter's day. This very unusual circumstance in summer, and after a period of excessive drought, attracted our notice, and led to a conversation on the laws of vegetable life, and on the peculiar organization which enables Cryptogamic plants to grow and produce their fructification in a season when the powers of all other vegetables lie dormant and suspended.

Such was our conversation as we sauntered heedlessly along in this delicious solitude: it was interrupted by the builder, who had followed us through the windings of the copsed path, to put us in the right road to Roslin. Before we had lost sight of Hawthornden, we had seen two figures standing on the rude balcony, and, as we thought, beckoning us to return; but we had disregarded them. He now told us he had informed Capt. Drummond of our being in the glen, and that he (Capt. D.) had politely left the house to speak with us; that at all events we must return, as there was no bridge in that direction; but as we were now not far from Wallace's Cave, he would first take us thither. We alternately ascended and descended several flights of steps hewn in the rock, without which it would have been absolutely inaccessible, for in many places, the precipices are not only perpendicular, but overhanging, and that to a great height. It has a more spacious opening than the caverns already described, and is said to have been the retreat of that hero amid his turbulent adventures. We now returned near to Hawthornden; and our kind Ciceroni, having procured the key of a locked up, light foot-bridge, admitted us over it, and returned to Captn. Drummond.

On our return to Edinburgh, Dovaston had the gratification to find at the post-office, a warm and spirited letter from our excellent friend Bewick, in reply to the one he wrote from Perth, saying, his house and his heart were open to us, and that we should have a Highland welcome when we should reach Newcastle. This decided our route for the remainder of the journey, and determined us to stay no longer in Edinburgh than might be necessary for visiting places in the neigbourhood. On enquiring what public conveyances there were to Stirling, we found a Steam packet would sail thither at six the following morning, and probably arrive in time to allow us to see the Castle and return in the evening by land.

Wednesday, 10th August We left Edinburgh at five o'clock, and walked to the Trinity Suspension Pier at Newhaven on the Forth, about two miles and a half to the westward, where we embarked, for Stirling, on board the Lady of the Lake, Steamer. This pier has lately been erected for the accommodation of steam boat passengers, and is the most elegant and convenient one I ever saw. It is seven hundred feet long, four feet wide, and is raised ten feet above high water mark, and fenced on each side by a neat iron railing four feet high. It consists of three equal portions united by strong frameworks of timber resting on the shore, but is without any other central support, thus forming a series of platforms, suspended by means of iron bars about two inches diameter, united by side plates and strong bolts, and having a similar appearance to the suspension bridge across the Dee above Llangollen. From the length of the spaces between the supports – upwards of two hundred feet – there is a considerable vibration. The pier head is sixty feet wide by fifty feet long, supported by a complicated framework of piles secured by strong beams at right angles, and protected from the weather by a boarded shed. Three broad and substantial flights of steps descend into the water, one in the direction of the platform, and one on each side of it, thus allowing the passengers of three vessels to embark or disembark at the same time. It is private property, and a toll of a half-penny is demanded from each passenger.

We were on board by six o'clock, and found a large and genteel company. The firth is here about seven miles broad, but gradually contracts to little more than a mile at North and South Queens ferry, where, in the middle of the channel, is a rocky islet called Inch Garvie, having a small castellated fort, erected during the late war with Napoleon. The rocks above North Queensferry are of basalt, and strongly marked with the columnar character. To the west of this point, the Forth receives the name of river, but again expands to the width of four or five miles, and appears in every direction completely landlocked, and like an extensive inland lake, on which our steam boat sailed like a floating volcano, leaving behind it a long, horizontal, and expanding line of dense smoke. Its banks are rich and varied, rising in pleasing swells richly adorned with the mansions and parks of nobility and gentry, towns and villages; and backed by the Ochil hills, here of no vast altitude indeed, but setting off the shores to considerable advantage. Some of the cits of Edinburgh who were on board, pointed out the names of most of the villas, &c; but it seemed an useless as well as troublesome task to note them down, as no separate descriptions could have been given of them, and they were all equally unknown to us.

When off Inverkeithing, some fine ranges of mountain scenery appeared; the Campsie hills to the west and the green Ochils to the north, the interval between them being filled up by the distant Grampian chain; among which we recognized Ben Ledi, Mealaonah, &c, with the top of Ben More, rearing his faint but lofty head behind the rest, a little to the north west of the Campsie range. As we advanced, the prospect became very magnificent – Ben Lomond and the Highland peaks that rise round Loch Katrine, Loch Lubnaig, &c, in the south of Perthshire, successively met our view; and though from their distance they were almost enveloped in the atmospheric tint, the eye could still trace the bold outline of their majestic forms and estimate the great elevation of their summits. Ben Arthur in Argyleshire was occasionally seen. In the various turns and windings of the river all the way to Stirling, they formed such picturesque groups and combinations, that we thought the background scenery of the Forth, the richest we had hitherto seen. The ever-shifting scenery of the nearer landscapes was in perfect harmony; verdant fields and darker woods, villas, cottages, and airy spires, interspersed with ruined towers, and the harder features of craggy rocks of different forms and stratificatons, now partially lighted up in glowing colours, and now cast into shade by the fleeting clouds, formed the varied and varying picture. The morning was fine with occasional showers, and the atmosphere more transparent than usual. The principal features were the Ochil hills, the heavy battlements of Stirling Castle, Culross and the ancient town of Clackmannan on the north and Borrowstouness on the south with a succession of villas and elegant mansions occupying delightful situations and forming altogether very enchanting scenery. The ancient tower of Clackmannan castle stands on a bold hill, and is said to afford one of the finest views in Scotland: it was once the residence of King Robert Bruce. On the shore near it are very extensive limestone rocks; and the whole district abounds in coal and ironstone.

The fine bay into which the Forth expands from Alloa to Queensferry is nearly twenty miles long, and of considerable breadth; and owing to the great contraction of both shores at the latter place, it forms one of the best roadsteads in the island. We passed, on the north shore, the small pretty town of Alloa, with its church and slender ornamented spire; and the Ochil hills which rose behind it possessed more of the character of the Welsh mountains than any others I had seen in Scotland – smooth, green, and lumpy, and generally barren of wood. In this part of the river are numerous productive salmon fisheries. From Alloa to Stirling, the Forth contracts into the ordinary dimensions of a river, and meanders in a very circuitous manner, through a fine alluvial plain, rich in corn and pasturage, and from the luxuriance of the crops, appeared to possess great fertility. The banks are low and flat, but fringed with fine timber and ornamented seats, and here and there a pretty wooded islet and a passing sail enlivens the view. The river is so excessively serpentine, that though the distance from Alloa to Stirling by land is only seven miles, it is more than twenty by water. We appeared to be sailing successively towards every point of the compass; and several times, after a circuit of a mile or more, were surprized to find ourselves brought back to within a few yards of the spot we had left behind. A reference to the map will shew that this is the general characteristic of this fine river from its source on the east side of Ben Lomond, where it winds among the mountains collecting its tributary streams, to its expansion into a bay at Alloa. Its whole length in a direct line would be about ninety miles, but so sinuous is its course, that following its various windings, the distance is not less than about two hundred and fifty. 'Stirling town and towers' which had long been seen at intervals, now, from our near approach, had a noble aspect; sometimes appearing on our left, sometimes on our right, and sometimes ahead, and the whole landscape was altogether changing and gliding before us like the shifting of theatrical scenes. This reach of the river is called the 'Links of Forth', from its chainlike appearance when viewed in certain directions.

When within about a mile of Stirling, we were obliged to leave the Steam boat, as there was not a sufficient depth of water to take her up. We landed close to the ruins of Cambuskenneth Abbey, one of the numerous religious establishments founded by David the first, and endowed with immense revenues. A very fine lofty and well built tower with a few detached contiguous parts, is all that remains of this once celebrated place. In our walk to Stirling we had to cross the river in a ferry boat: on arriving there, our first business was to ascertain if any coach went to Edinburgh in the evening; and we were fortunate in securing seats upon the mail at three o'clock.

After ordering dinner, we took a survey of the town in our way to the castle: it is built upon the ridge and sloping sides of the castle hill, which gives it an undulated appearance, and faintly reminded us of Edinburgh. The streets still present some venerable houses, indicatious of its former importance, when it was the cradle and the residence of royalty, and was a rival in dignity, even with Edinburgh. Its very large long church seemed also to have some claim to antiquity; but we were not very near it. The Castle itself, as a building, is not of much interest; the many important events connected with its history, the noble rock on which it stands, and the magnificent prospect it commands, are everything. The different buildings attached to it, and the varied features of the surrounding landscape, were pointed out to us by a civil and intelligent soldier who was one of the garrison. What remains of the old castle I could not well discover; but the present fortifications were erected by Queen Anne; this being one of the four castles stipulated for, in the Articles of Union, to be kept in permanent repair – the other three are, Edinburgh, Blackness, and Dumbarton. A number of barracks and other offices, governor's house, &c. &c., are within the walls, and altogether it appears a large establishment. On entering the court, the Palace first presents itself, and its appearance strikes the stranger with a sort of ludicrous surprise. There are on every side of it, around the windows, ornamented arches, each having an immensely thick and tall moulded pillar, very like a gigantic candelabrum, crowned with a monstrous grotesque figure, sometimes of a king, a beast, an imaginary animal, or a buffoon, very large; some mutilated and others entire. The edifice is lofty and well built; and the great room, now a barrack, is the scene of the final close of the lovely Lady of the Lake. It was the palace of James the fifth. Of the Parliament House, nothing but the bare walls remain: adjoining it, is the Chapel royal, now a storeroom and armoury. Mary Stuart was crowned here; and frequently retired to Stirling from the insults of her subjects. We saw the window by which she escaped, when confined by the regent Murray and the confederate lords, before she was sent to Loch Leven; and the schoolroom where Buchanan taught her son, James the sixth, whose minority was principally spent at Stirling. We were also shewn into a very close square court, called the royal menagerie, or lion's den; in two of the corners were oblong oval holes through which the beasts were fed.

We now parted from our military guide, and on the south side came to an arena, once appropriated for Tournaments, and close to which is a little eminence still called the 'Ladies' Rock', whence lofty dames used to behold the valour of the knightly champions.

From this spot we descended to a public walk, that, midway down, winds all round the castle hill. Hence the gaze upwards at the escarpments is very grand, the rock presents thousands of fissures and perpendicular basaltic columns of great diameter, mantled with verdant and flowing ivy and fringed with playful harebells. Many of these columns stand separate, and some seem pitched perpendicularly and stand apparently tottering, while others fallen and sloping, resemble Cromlechs; and a little farther on, are some, forming perfect square trilithons, reminding us of Stonehenge. On the northwest side the pillars are very magnificent,

– pil'd as by magic spell
Here scorch'd with lightning, there with ivy green.

It was by mere accident that we went along this romantic walk, which ought by all means to be visited; the numerous interesting objects which studded the vast plain below, bounded by the back-screen of the Highland mountains whose peaked summits pierced the sky, offer a combination of beauty and sublimity seldom equalled.

We now returned to the inn, where we met at dinner several intelligent gentlemen, about to commence a pedestrian tour through the Highlands. Conversation was becoming interesting and animated, when a blast of the mail horn suddenly cut it short; the horses were *to*; we mounted the roof of the coach and soon left Stirling behind us. At a short distance we passed through the town of St. Ninian's, and about a mile beyond it, crossed the Bannockburn, an insignificant stream near a village of the same name; but we could not ascertain whether we went over the site of the celebrated battle fought in 1314 between the Scotch forces under Bruce, and the English army under Edward the second – a memorable event in the annals of both kingdoms, but particularly of Scotland. This great and decisive victory secured her independence, fixed Bruce on the throne of that kingdom; and forms one of the most brilliant pages of her history; while their defeat by a comparatively diminutive army, made such a deep impression on the minds of the English, that for some years, no superiority of numbers could induce them to take the field against the Scotch.

We continued to drive through a pleasant country to Falkirk through the ancient forest of Torwood which afforded shelter to the followers of the renowned Wallace after the first battle of Falkirk in 1298, where they were defeated by the English under Edward the first, through the treachery of Cummin. Falkirk is a large and busy place, situated near the south shore of the Forth, and not far from the immense iron furnaces and foundries of the Carron Company, the most extensive of the kind in Europe. Just after quitting Falkirk, we had a sweet view of the plain extending down to the Forth, called the Carse of Falkirk, with the broad river and the Ochil hills beyond it, seen under the fine avenues of beech near Callander house. It was almost the only glimpse we obtained of this fine river on the whole line of road from Stirling to Edinburgh. Near Callander are said to be other remnants of the ancient forests, and also of the Wall of Antoninus, the northern boundary of the Roman territories in Britain.

Soon after entering the district of West Lothian, we came to Linlithgow, a place of some celebrity on account of the connection of its history with some of the most important events of the kingdom, and also of the noble remains of former magnificence with which it is adorned. Its present condition, however, as far as a hasty drive through it would allow us to form an opinion, shews a sad reverse. It consists principally of one long iregular street extending from east to west, gloomy, illpaved, and deserted, though the county town; the antiquity of many of the houses giving it a ruinous and decayed appearance. The magnificent square ruin of the Palace stands on a rising ground near the west entrance of the town, thickly embosomed in ancient trees. The eminence on which it stands, runs a considerable way into a fine lake, greatly enhancing the beauty of the situation. It was the favourite residence of James the fifth, and within its walls, his daughter, the unfortunate Mary Stuart, was born in 1542. The ruins appeared to be very extensive and in good preservation, though totally abandoned to decay. Contiguous to it is a very fine old church, adorned with beautiful Gothic windows and a handsome spire. In the centre of the town, and opposite the town house, (which as usual is terminated with a steeple) is a richly decorated fountain, having rich groined arches like the Catholic crosses, with two tiers of monster's heads, which on every side discharge jets of water into a reservoir below. This is in excellent preservation. As we drove through the long street, we observed more than once on sign-boards, the word Tawyer (tower) for flax dresser, now generally obsolete.

After leaving Linlithgow, the remainder of our ride to Edinburgh lay through a generally level and well cultivated district, diversified by numerous small hills, many of them clothed with wood out of which sometimes peeped a modern mansion or a dilapidated tower. Of the latter I shall only particularize the ruins of Niddrie Castle, seen on our right about twelve miles from the capital, memorable as being the first resting place of Mary (and that only for a few hours) after her flight from Loch Leven Castle, though a distance of not less than from twenty five to thirty miles. Though Edinburgh itself is so magnificent a city, the country even in its immediate neigbourhood, must not be named in competition with that round London – no crowded villages, and but few ornamented villas, mark the population and wealth which everywhere meet the eye for so many miles round the English metropolis. The residences of the Scotch nobility and gentry are generally on the rich wooded banks of the Forth.

We returned to Edinburgh about eight o'clock, and immediately repaired to the coach-office to enquire about a conveyance to Melrose. As this place lay nearly in the line of our route to Newcastle, we had reserved it, under the idea of taking it on our way thither, and to finish our long though delightful tour in Scotland with a view of its 'hallowed shrine'. A sad disappointment, however, awaited us. We found, after a long and fruitless enquiry at every office in Edinburgh, that no coach for the south passed through or near Melrose; and in short, to pass over unnecessary particulars, that we could only see it at the expense of two days and of getting forward in post chaises. We deliberated long in endeavouring to devise some more eligible plan, clinging to the idea that we would not leave Scotland till we had seen this far-famed ruin. Dovaston would willingly have made any sacrifice, but kindly referred to me the 'casting vote', so, after coolly balancing all the circumstances, I reluctantly gave it against Melrose. I began to feel anxious to be at home; and rich and magnificent as Melrose is represented to be, I did not think it prudent to devote to it the time and money it would have required. When we have travelled long and seen much, the keen edge of novelty imperceptibly wears away; and objects of ordinary interest and landscapes of considerable beauty, which at the commencement of a journey would have excited much attention, are passed by with comparative indifference. There were several other things in Edinburgh we were desirous to have seen, as the College and Museum attached to it, the inside of the High Kirk, Heriott's Hospital, &c, but as they were only of minor importance, we did not deem them, under present circumstances, sufficient to detain us. We therefore, without farther hesitation, engaged seats on the mail direct for Newcastle the following morning, there being no intermediate object sufficiently attractive to keep us upon the road

Thursday, 11th August We took our final leave of Edinburgh about eight o'clock, driving through Regent street and along the noble new road between the Calton hill and Holyrood; and soon afterwards passed two other ruins not noticed in the itinerary. A few miles from the capital, we saw on the right Pinkie House and Carberry Hill, both celebrated in history – the former for the fatal overthrow of the Scots by the Protector Duke of Somerset in 1547 – the latter as the spot where the imprudent Mary with Bothwell, attempted to make a stand against her insurgent nobles. The estuary opened very finely before us; but the haze in the atmosphere prevented the least reflexion of light from the surface, and gave to the vessels the appearance of being suspended in the air. We met upon the road, many masculine hard-featured women, bending under heavy burdens of fish and salt, which they carried on their backs in large creels or crates, and who strongly reminded me of the female peasants who supply Paris with vegetables &c. A good deal of Salt is made by artificial heat from the sea water along the shore of the estuary, and is thus carried to Edinburgh for sale. At Musselburgh, Preston Pans, &c, we saw many of the low open sheds where the process was going on. The waters of the North and South Esk are discharged into the Firth of Forth at Musselburgh – a bustling place, where considerable manufactures seemed to be carried on. In passing the village of Preston Pans, we saw, on the left, the site of the desperate battle gained by the Highlanders under their unfortunate Prince in 1747. It is a plain just below the village, almost close to the shore, and now covered with corn. Near it, is a square broad tower, the lower two thirds of which are of stone, and the upper part of white stone, looking like a modern house perched on the top of an ancient castle.

  We now left the coast, and went along an excellent wide and tolerably level new line of road through the centre of Haddingtonshire or East Lothian, to Dunbar. Haddington is a neat town with good streets and modern houses; its church is part of an ancient abbey, the remainder of which, with a fine lofty tower, is now in ruins and surrounded by venerable trees. The land in this district is very fertile, and in a high state of cultivation; the fields very large, and divided by good hedges. A considerable proportion of it was covered by waving corn, now ready for the sickle; the oat and barley harvest having already commenced. We were struck with the number of hands employed; in one field we counted between fifty and sixty reapers, in another, upwards of forty, chiefly women. Many labourers come down annually from the Highlands for the harvest. In consequence of the long drought, the pastures were quite burnt up; and hay was given in the fields to the cattle and sheep. The roads are universally made with trap or whinstone, which is judiciously preferred for its superior toughness and hardness, wherever it can be procured. After leaving Haddington we had a view of the conical hill of North Berwick Law, and of Bass island whose almost perpendicular basaltic crags rose from the sea, and long continued in sight. Approaching Dunbar, we saw far out at sea, the long flat topped island of May with its lighthouse, lying at the extreme entrance of the Firth of Forth.

Dunbar is a respectable and well built town; it stands on a rock of red sandstone which projects into the ocean, and forms a small bay or harbour defended by a battery. The houses are all built of this stone, and, with the soil of the neighbourhood and the rocky beach, give to the view an almost uniform red colour. The ruins of the ancient castle occupy a conspicuous station on a part of the rock that beetles over the sea; and are still considerable. Six or eight miles farther, at Dunglas bridge, the road crosses a very deep and dismal glen overhung with wood, where a river, that divides the counties of Haddington and Berwick, rushes down to the sea.

The Lammermuir hills (la-mer-moor, or the moor which reaches to the sea) are a series of very elevated, flat, and bleak moorlands, which run inland from the eastern coast for thirty or forty miles in a south west direction. They are principally of the millstone grit series, with some schist, and are intersected by various openings and valleys, which contain some sheep farms, with here and there a narrow strip of arable land; but the crops seldom arrive at maturity. Some idea may be formed of the general sterility of the district, from the fact, that one of the most wild and dreary of these farms, consisting of fifteen hundred acres, at the time of the Statistical Survey, was rented for £16 annum! Soon after we had passed the promontory of St Abb's Head, we began to descend into a cultivated country and a warmer atmosphere; and at and near the village of Ayton, saw such crowds of well dressed people, particularly young women, that the scene reminded us of an English wake. It was, however, no other than the celebration of the Sacrament; which we now found was by no means confined to Sunday.

Southwards from this point, the road winds in a zig-zag manner, round the craggy cliffs that rise immediately from the shore of the German ocean, often at a considerable height above it; the scenery having sometimes much wild grandeur. We were shewn a solitary public house by the roadside, in the hamlet of Lammerton, which is the last dwelling in Scotland in this direction, and the scene of many of those clandestine marriages of English parties which are solemnized in the summary manner of the Scotch law along the whole line of the Border from Graitney to Lammerton. Here, as at the former place, a comfortable parlour is provided for the accommodation of the southern fugitives; but we were told they are not very numerous, the confines of England being fifty miles more northwards than on the western coast. In passing through Lammerton tollbar, we left behind us, 'bonnie Scotland', where so many scenes of high gratification had been enjoyed, and many pleasing impressions formed, to which memory will often fondly cling. With some feelings of regret we bade

> Farewell to the land where the clouds love to rest,
> Like the shroud of the dead, on the mountain's cold breast,
> To the cataract's roar, where the eagles reply,
> And the lake her lone bosom expands to the sky.

A few miles farther brought us to the handsome town of Berwick upon Tweed; which we entered through an arched gateway of the fortifications. It is pleasantly situated on the north bank of the broad and rapid Tweed, on a kind of headland or peninsula between it and the German ocean. The houses are lofty; and the Court of Justice, with a market-place below, is a handsome structure of three stories high, with an ornamental tower and spire at one end, like those in Scotland. It is remarkable for containing a peal of eight bells, while the church has neither tower nor bells – a rather ludicrous kind of compromise between opposite national opinions, and something in the 'Vicar of Bray' style. On the land side, Berwick is defended by high walls, fortified and planted with cannon, and having a parapet walk on the top. The ingress and egress are through arched gates. On the northern side, is the uninteresting, shapeless ruin of an old castle.

On leaving Berwick, we crossed the noble bridge over the Tweed, which has fifteen spacious arches, and is upwards of eleven hundred feet long. On ascending the hill which forms the south bank, we had a commanding view of the town, the river winding from the westward, the bridge, and a handsome pier or mole which runs out about a thousand yards into the sea; and when we reached the summit, first saw the celebrated Lindisfarne, or Holy Island, lying about a mile from the shore, with its conical rock and castle at the south end, and near the village and church, the ruins of the Abbey. A bold headland, which approaches it from the south, forms with it a good sheltered bay; and beyond it, the open German ocean stretches as far as the eye can reach.

I had noticed that the peasantry generally on the eastern side of Scotland had a more comfortable appearance than those bordering on the Solway; and near Berwick, the women wore shoes and stockings; their cottages also were of a superior order; yet on entering England – 'merry England' – a more marked distinction in many things became immediately apparent; and even the road seemed to have its accustomed national character. We only first entered Northumberland a little to the north of Belford; the intermediate country from the Tweed, being, as well as Lindisfarne, an insulated portion of the county of Durham – probably in consequence of its originally forming part of the 'Patrimony of St Cuthbert'. We dined at Belford; and

A Nineteenth-Century Tour

on leaving it, had a prominent view of the once famed Bamborough Castle, a broad ruin seated on a steep rock upon the coast, and of very great antiquity. It was left, with very extensive estates in the neighbourhood, by Crewe, Bishop of Durham, about a century ago, to trustees, to be applied to undefined charitable uses: this is a redeeming feature in the character of this time-serving prelate – for charity covereth a multitude of sins. A portion of the funds are appropriated to the assistance and relief of mariners who are ship-wrecked on this rocky and tempestuous coast; apartment and bedding are always in readiness for thirty persons, and a constant patrol is kept every stormy night, which ranges above eight miles of the shore in parties, who are directed to the scene of distress by a cannon placed on the top of the tower, which is fired once, twice, or thrice, according to the situation of the wreck. Their orders are, to repair to the spot indicated by the signal with the utmost expedition, because it often happens that ships strike on the rocks in such a manner as to be capable of relief if immediate assistance is rendered. Machines are also in readiness to extricate ships out of their perilous situation; and thus, not only the crews, but the vessels are frequently saved.

A little before we reached Alnwick, we had a good view of Howick castle, lying a few miles on our left, not far from the coast. Alnwick, on account of its situation in a fertile valley, is not seen from the north, till the brow of the hill above it, is attained. The magnificent gothic castle of the Duke of Northumberland then appears to great advantage, as the south bank of the Alne, on which it stands, slopes in that direction. The extent of ground it occupies, as well as its general magnificence, astonishes the stranger: on the battlements and octagon turrets on every side, are numerous animated figures of warriors, heathen deities, &c, which from their bold and spirited attitudes, and the classic elegance of the sculpture, absolutely rivet the beholder's gaze. In the town of Alnwick, I saw nothing to require notice; but here, as at other places, the two minutes we were allowed to change horses were spent in rapidly committing to paper our brief notes, which we found it very difficult to write legibly, even to ourselves, while travelling so fast, and to defer them altogether to the evening, would have been fatal to many of them, as well as to their regular order. We were however now become comparatively indifferent about them; we had accomplished the main objects of our journey, and gleaned a much richer harvest than we had anticipated; and were disposed to indulge in a little relaxation from constant exertion.

A little beyond Alnwick, Warkworth castle, another fine seat of the Duke of Northumberland, was pointed out to us near the shore, beyond which was Coquet island. At Warkworth, is a picturesquely situated little hermitage hewn out of the solid rock overhanging the river. We had hitherto, with the exception of passing through the interior of Haddingtonshire, skirted the shores of the Forth and of the German ocean on the whole of our journey from Edinburgh, seldom losing sight of the sea altogether. Soon after leaving Alnwick, we did so for six or eight miles, and had afterwards only occasional glimpses of it at a considerable distance. We were generally eight or ten miles from it, and on tolerably high ground; the intervening country being neither flat nor hilly, naked nor wooded, but, pleasingly diversified with gentlemen's seats and ruined castles rising above the undulated wooded knolls and little shelves of rock, and altogether possessing more of an English character than any scenery we had seen in Scotland. The evening was fine and bright; and as the sun gradually sunk towards the horizon, his slanting beams fell upon the various features of the landscape, and tinged them with a rich and mellow glow. At Felton, a poor village, we crossed the river Coquet, whose banks were highly romantic and diversified with picturesque rocks and overhanging foliage. Near it, is a superb mansion and park belonging to a Mr. Riddell, a great sporting character; who, we were told, with one horse. (Dr. Syntax) had won thirty one gold cups – and probably, notwithstanding, had purchased them dearly enough.

The last objects we could distinctly see, were Morpeth and its vicinity, where is a large jail with clusters of very narrow windows, built round a spacious quadrangular area, in the centre of which were the foundations of another edifice of considerable magnitude. On the right, ascending the hill, are the ruins of its ancient square castle; and a little beyond, at some distance from the town, the high church of Morpeth, rising very picturesquely above some fine trees, with the rectory on the opposite side of the road. It was now so dusky that the objects were no longer distinguishable. We drove at an amazing rate, and were soon reminded of our near approach to Newcastle, by the great fires on the hills of slack or small coal, which is separated by screens from the large pieces at the mouth of the pits and thrown aside as refuse. The mass soon takes fire from the heat of the decomposing pyrites, and continues to burn for years. Not less than a hundred thousand chaldrons are thus annually wasted on the Tyne, and nearly an equal quantity on the Wear. After a journey of a hundred and twenty one miles performed in fourteen hours, we reached Newcastle at ten o'clock, and were set down at our old quarters, the Queen's Head in Pilgrim street, where, two years before, we had stopped on our arrival from Carlisle. The lateness of the hour prevented us from intruding upon the family of our friend Bewick; we therefore ordered beds and refreshment; and occupied the evening at our note-books.

Friday 12th August We rose early, and put ourselves into trim to walk up to Gateshead to breakfast; intending to devote the whole of the day to our kind and worthy friend Bewick.* When we reached his house, the family had breakfasted, though yet scarcely eight o'clock; but a second table was

---

* Thomas Bewick, (1753–1828). Naturalist and engraver, author of *'History of British Birds'*.

quickly spread before us, and our meal was heightened by the conversation of our cheerful host. He told us it was his birthday, having now attained seventy two; and that he had sat up for us the two last nights in consequence of Dovaston's letter from Perth. The first pleasure I received here was another letter from my beloved Eliza informing me of the continued well being of all at home. When the tide and effusion of heart at meeting had somewhat subsided, we settled down into calmer delight. His bright daughter Jane shewed us many boxes filled with blocks, principally *tale* pieces for his new work on Fishes, many of which were unsoiled by ink, having never had even a proof impression struck off. As far as could be judged these are all equal, some of them superior, to anything he has already published, and are full of incident and humour. He told us his inventive faculty and ardour were still as vigorous as ever, though his eyes began to fail, so that he was restricted from working more than two or three hours at a time and altogether by candlelight; but that his bodily health was generally good.

As this was the only day circumstances would allow me to spend in Newcastle, Mr. Bewick kindly offered to walk with us through the town, and shew us what was interesting. We left Gateshead about eleven o'clock, and returned to dinner at three. Newcastle was in early times, a place of considerable importance, being situated near the eastern termination of Hadrian's Wall. That emperor also built a bridge over the Tyne, on the very site of the modern one, as was ascertained from the number of Roman coins discovered in the foundations of the old piers. In a later period, both before and after the Conquest, the town abounded with religious establishments, of which but few remains now survive. Including the suburb of Gateshead, which being south of the Tyne, is in Durham, it numbers nearly 40,000 inhabitants; eight or ten thousand of whom are employed in freighting the coal down the river, and are called keelmen. These inhabit the narrow, dirty and ill-built streets of the lower parts of the town bordering upon the river; but the higher parts of it have a number of wide and respectable streets and public buildings. The church of St. Nicholas is much admired for the elegant architecture of its tower, built in the reign of Henry the sixth, and is 194 feet high, surmounted by beautiful gothic arches or flying-buttresses, which unite in the centre in the form of a crown. The other parts of the church are still more ancient: it contains a fine library and some curious manuscripts. Besides other churches, Newcastle has an infirmary, a lunatic asylum, baths, and several hospitals, one of which is appropriated solely for the keelmen, and is regulated by Act of Parliament.

From the bridge a bustling scene presented itself both on the quays and the river; the numerous steam packets, coasting vessels, keels, and craft of all descriptions moving in every direction, with the immense timber machines* elevated high above, and projecting over the water for the

---

* called Staiths.

purpose of shipping the coal from the tram-waggons that bring it from the pits; the dense and swarthy population on both shores; the noises and the eternally smoky atmosphere from the numerous glass and lead works; – formed a scene, interesting in a commercial point of view, but repulsive and disgusting as a residence. Many steam packets ply daily to and from Shields; and when I was last at Newcastle, I went there in one of them, saw Tynemouth Priory, the fine bridge at Sunderland, &c, and returned in the evening. In the Coal trade, Newcastle is the first port in the world; and has sometimes exported upwards of 600,000 chaldrons* in a year. London, and the counties on the east coast deficient in coal strata, are principally supplied from Newcastle and Sunderland.

After dinner our friend read to us large potions of a thick quarto volume of his own memoirs which he had drawn up at the earnest request of his daughter Jane, but which will not be printed till after his death. His countenance would often become animated and beam with benevolene when he touched upon passages relating to scenes of his early life, which he stopped to explain or illustrate. Dovaston, who remaind behind and spent six days with him after I had left, read the whole volume.

I shall conclude my detail of the delightful day I spent at Newcastle, with an anecdote of our worthy host, which was told Dovaston after my departure by a Mr. Fox whom Bewick had, with a few other literary characters, invited to meet my friend; and which I do the rather, as it is not inserted in his own Memoir. The Duke of Northumberland; when first he called for permission to see Bewick's workshops, was not personally known to our friend, yet he shewed him his birds, blocks, &c, as he does to all, with the greatest liberality and cheerfulness; but on discovering the high rank of his guest, he exclaimed, 'I beg pardon, my Lord, I did not know your Grace, and was unaware I was talking to so great a man.' To which the Duke replied – 'You are a greater man than I am, Mr. Bewick' – to which our friend, with that ready wit that never fails or offends – 'No, my Lord; but were *I* Duke of Northumberland, perhaps I could be.'

I had walked down to Newcastle before tea to call upon Mr. Read, and to take my place homewards for the following morning, in opposition to the repeated pressing intreaties of Mr. B. and his amiable family, from whom nothing but a feeling of duty would have compelled me to part so soon. As I was to set out at five next morning, I preferred sleeping at the inn, where I retired at a late hour, bidding both them and my fellow traveller a hearty farewell. Dovaston; being perfect master of his own time, lingered fondly at Newcastle, day after day, till the 18th assisting Bewick in arranging the new

---

* The Newcastle chaldron weighs about 52½ cwt. By calculation, made about twenty years ago, it was supposed that between 60 and 70 persons were employed by the coal trade on the rivers Tyne and Wear and that the capital employed in it, including that of the London merchants, was upwards of three Millions Sterling.

edition of his Birds which has since been published. He (Dovaston) liberally furnished him with the substance of his own valuable and copious notes, the fruit of his long and ardent study of ornithology; but a large portion of them came too late for insertion.

Saturday, 13th August Having now accomplished every object of my journey, and left behind my cheerful and talented companion, all that remained was to reach home with as little delay as possible – a matter, in these days of expeditous travelling, neither difficult nor laborious. I took few notes, and those of so little interest, that they might be altogether omitted, but for the sake of winding up the thread of the narrative: I shall therefore do little more than trace the line of my route.

I left Newcastle at five o'clock, and passed through Chester-le-street, a small, though very ancient place with a well built church and neat spire, to Durham. This city is situated on a singular low hill which is nearly encircled by the river Wear; its superb cathedral occupies the summit of the eminence, and is a noble object from every part of the surrounding country; particularly from another hill about two miles to the south-east on the road to Stockton, most of the city being here concealed by the fine woods which cover the precipitous banks of the river. The castle, or bishop's palace adjoins it on the north, and is a very old, extensive, and gloomy looking place, with turretted walls, and apparenty calculated more for security than comfort. The slope of the hill is in some places laid out in hanging gardens; and the opposite banks of the river are clothed with fine timber.

The great northern coal-field we had entered near Morpeth, extends southwards about six miles beyond Durham; for it was easy to trace it by the steam-engines and whimsies erected near the pits in every direction. On leaving it, we came to the magnesian lime district; the coal measures still running towards the south-west. We passed through Sedgefield, and before reaching Stockton on Tees – a pretty town with a very wide uniform street – entered upon the near red sandstone. At Yarm we crossed the Tees, and entered Yorkshire, passing through Thirsk, a dirty place with a fine old church, and its shabby pan-tiled shambles standing in the middle of an excessively wide street. This is the general character of all the small towns and villages I saw in Yorkshire; and being generally empty and quiet, their great width gives them a wild and deserted appearance. The occasional quarries mean the road, and the material laid down for its repair, shewed we were again upon the magnesian limestone. The general aspect of the country has a tendency to sterility, particularly in the more elevated districts; and even in the valleys, though the soil is apparently a rich, dark red loam, the wheats were very poor, and the trees and hedges had a stunted and unhealthy appearance. The view on either hand is bounded by hills – those of Craven, very distant and only occasionally seen on the west – and the nearer district of the eastern moorlands in the opposite direction. There was some improvement about Borough bridge – much more near Knaresborough, where the land is fertile and in good cultivation, with fine timber in the hedgerows. Knaresborough is a good sized pleasant town, with spacious market-place; but its streets seemed narrow for Yorkshire. I looked in vain for its celebrated petrifying spring, commonly called the Dropping Well. We next came to Wetherby, a small town, till lately belonging solely to the Duke of Devonshire, but now transferred in lots to numerous purchasers, who were repairing the old, and building new houses with so much spirit, that the chisel, the saw and the plane, seemed to be in universal requisition. I arrived at Leeds about nine o'clock after the close of a showery and rather stormy day. This overgrown smoky town numbers upwards of 50,000 inhabitants. It was the evening of market-day; and everyone knows or may conceive, the bustle occasioned by a large body of the working classes simultaneously receiving the reward of their labours for the past week, and laying it out in provision for the next. The night was very dark, and the dense population that crowded the streets and shops by gas light, gave to the scene the appearance of a subterranean city carrying on all its operations in full activity by artificial light.

Sunday, 14th August At eight o'clock this morning I continued my journey; and before I had well quitted Leeds, was surprised to find myself close to the lofty ivy-mantled tower of Kirkstall abbey; which, when I last saw it, was in a quiet well-wooded valley more than two miles from the town. So rapidly has Leeds increased that the streets and factories now extend to within a stone's cast of this magnificent and stately ruin; and the smoke and noise which have invaded its hallowed precincts, chase away those images and forbid those visions of the past, which monastic remains so naturally excite, when contemplated amid the verdant scenery of a sequestered valley, or on the bank of a softly gliding river. My route lay through the manufacturing towns of Bradford, Halifax, and Rochdale; but the intermediate country (excepting Blackstone-Edge) may be compared to one immense scattered town; and the population along the whole line of road is astonishingly great. Being Sunday, the streets and highways everywhere exhibited mixed groups of both sexes, whose coarse and boorish manners, reprobate habits, and uncivilized dialect and blasphemies, proclaimed their demoralized feelings, and shewed that the pecuniary advantages they had gained by their manufactures, enviable as they may appear, have been purchased at the expence of their simplicity and virtue – the only true sources of comfort and happiness to social man.

On arriving in Manchester, I transferred myself into another coach, which, passing through Harrington and Frodsham, set me down in Chester about ten o'clock. The following morning, Monday, 15th of August, I came by mail to Wrexham, and walked home to breakfast, where I was happy to find all well and to embrace again those nearest and dearest to my heart. The reciprocal congratulations which during the course of the journey I had frequent opportunities of witnessing in others when they left the coach or the steam packet, and were met at their own thresholds by their wives and children, I was now permitted by a kind Providence to experience, myself, in their fullest extent; and wrote the concluding pages of a journal rapidly penned under circumstances of hurry and fatigue, amid noisy company and ignorant curiosity – under the shade of my own peaceful roof, and surrounded by my own family.

The Tour now being brought to a conclusion, I shall only add a few lines relative to the changes made in the plan laid down at the commencement. The narrative was divided and separately paged under an apprehension that it might be too bulky for a single volume; nor has it been completed without the occasional intervention of a rough draft. Though it occupies more space, it has been drawn up in less time than I originally calculated upon, owing partly to the ample leisure which the winter evenings and my separation from friends and congenial society have afforded, but principally to an increasing anxiety to be at liberty to enjoy the beauties of the opening Spring. It has also been enriched by some additional communications from my excellent friend and fellow traveller, accompanied by a wish that they might not be specifically acknowledged; and by several drawings, copied at my request by my amiable and affectionate wife during the progress of the manuscript, though too late to be named in their proper place.

If those portions of Nature which have passed under review, lead to the contemplation and conviction of her Ineffable Cause, the great object of creation is accomplished, every blessing of existence enhanced, and the end of our being, here and hereafter, highly and expansively furthered: and with these plain precepts at heart, each individual through the pilgrimage of this world, may with happiness contemplate the Ultimate Home; and on arrival there, may say with me on the conclusion of this Tour, I return with a more expanded goodwill to all mankind, an increased sense of esteem to my immediate friends, a redoubled affection for the one who accompanied me, a confirmed love toward all my family endearments, and a higher sense of duty for his protection to the Great Father of all, the Author and Giver of all good things.

Index

Aberfoil 38, 46, 83
Abernethy 176
Achnacraig 101
Ailsa 44
Aldgeth 25
Alloa 191, 192
Alnwick 199, 200
Annan 14, 18–19
Ardentinny 44
Ardgowan 87
Ardincaple, Point of 98
Ardkinglas 53
Ardlamont Point 90
Ardmaddy Castle 99
Ardnamurchan 105
Ardtornish Castle 101, 123
Aros 100, 101, 102, 123
Arran, Isle of 45, 90, 91
Arrochar 41, 42, 43, 49, 50
Aviemore 161, 163, 166
Ayton 197

Balfron 84
Balloch 37
Balquhidder 72, 73, 74
Bamburgh Castle 199
Bannockburn 194
Bass Island 177, 181, 182, 197
Beauly Abbey 159
Belford 198
Belleville 162
Ben Arthur (The Cobbler) 41–42, 43, 49, 57, 82, 84, 191
Ben Cruachan 39, 41, 59, 61, 62, 65, 97, 99, 105, 126, 143
Ben Lawers 41, 62, 143, 165, 173

Ben Ledi 71, 74, 76, 191
Ben Lomond 29, 33, 37, 39, 44, 46, 81, 84, 85, 181, 191, 192
Ben More 41, 66, 68, 97, 143, 191
Ben Nevis 99, 105, 124, 128, 131, 133, 139–145, 147, 153, 161
Ben Uaish 145
Ben Vane 41
Ben Venue 62, 76, 78
Ben Vorlich 41, 71, 72, 73
Berwick Law 177
Berwick-upon-Tweed 198
Bewick, Thomas 100, 175, 185, 189, 200–203
Birkenhead 6
Birnam Hill 170
Blackness Castle 192
Blackstone Edge 10
Blair Atholl 163, 164, 166
Blair Castle 164
Boreray 93
Boroughbridge 204
Borrowstouness 191
Bow Fell 13
Broomielaw, the 86
Brougham Hall 12, 13
Bruce, Robert 24, 69, 102, 191, 194
Buachaille 113
Bualmaha, Pass of 38
Buchanan, George 84, 193
Burleigh Castle 176
Burns, Robert 20–23, 150, 179, 184, 185
Burnt Island 177
Burnt Islands 89, 90
Burscough Priory 7
Burton 9
Bute, Kyles of 87, 89

Index

Cadzow 29
Caerlaverock 19
Cairn Dearg 143
Cairndow 53, 54
Cairngorm 161
Cairn Scourach 149
Callander 45, 72, 74, 75, 81, 82, 84, 194
Cambuskenneth Abbey 192
Cameron 148
Campsie Hills 29, 82, 83, 84, 191
Canna 104
Cannobie Lee 18, 19
Carberry Hill 196
Carlisle 6, 10, 12, 14, 15–16, 19, 27, 200
Carluke 29
Carrick Castle 44
Carse of Falkirk 194
Carse of Gowrie 172, 173, 174
Cartland Crags 29
Chatelherault Woods 29
Chester 6, 204
Chester-le-Street 203
Clackmannan 191
Cladich 62
Cloch 44, 86
Clydesdale 27
Coilantogle Ford 76
Coll 105, 121
Colonsay 95, 106, 107, 143
Coquet Island 199
Corpach 139, 145, 146
Corryvreckan 95, 96, 97
Craignethan 29
Craignish, Point of 95
Crinan, Canal of 91, 93, 95, 99
Cromdale 160
Cruefell 18, 20, 23
Culloden Moor 160
Culross 191
Cumberland 14, 18, 19

Dalguise 166
Dalmally 61, 62, 63, 67
Dalnachardoch 163, 164
Dalveen Glen 26
Dalwhinnie 163
Dorishmore 95
Dornoch 18
Douglas, Margaret 24–25
Dowally 166
Drumclog 28
Drumlanrig Castle 26
Drymnen 92, 93, 123

Duart 100, 101, 123
Dumbarton 36–37, 39, 45, 46, 49
Dumbarton Castle 36, 46, 86, 192
Dumfries 14, 16, 20–24, 33
Dunbar 182, 196, 197
Dunderave Castle 54, 55
Dundrennan 16
Dunglas Bridge 197
Dunglass Castle 36, 45
Dunkeld 159, 162, 165, 166–170
Dunolly Castle 99, 100, 125
Dunoon Castle 44, 86
Dunottar Castle 169
Dunstaffnage Castle 100, 125, 170
Duresdon 27
Durham 203

Eamont 13
Easdale 97
Edinburgh 162, 177–186, 190, 192, 195–196
Egg 104, 105, 121

Falkirk 194
Farlton Knot 9
Felton 200
Fingal's Cave 109–113
Fintry 82, 84
Firkin, Point of 39, 48
Firth of Forth 177, 181, 182, 187, 197
Fort Augustus 133, 135, 139, 146, 149, 150
Fort George 158
Fort McClain 135
Fort Ross 158
Fort William 101, 124, 125, 127, 128, 131, 133, 139, 144, 146, 147
Foyers/Fyers, Falls of 152–153
Freeburn 160

Gair/Gare Loch, the 44, 87
Gateshead 200, 201
General's Hut, the 152, 153, 154
Glasgow 25, 28, 29, 30–35, 45, 82, 84, 85, 96, 88, 124, 125
Glen Aray 58–59, 63
Glen Coe 5, 99, 143, 146
Glen Croe 43, 50, 53, 54, 85
Glendow 150
Glen Essachosen 58
Glen Falloch 41
Glenfinglas, Forest of 68, 76
Glen Fruin 46–47
Glengarry 149
Glen Gloy 138, 147

Glen Kinglas 53, 57
Glen More 161
Glen Morison 154
Glen Nevis 144, 145
Glenorchy/Glenurchy 39, 45, 63–64, 65, 66
Glen Roy 131, 135, 137, 138, 139, 147
Glen Spean 138
Glen Stewart 19
Glen Turit 138
Glen Urquhart 154
Glouton Fall 59
Goat Fell 90, 95
Gometra 106, 107
Gourock 44
Grant, Sir James 158–159, 160
Great Cumbrae/Cumbray 44, 87
Greenock 44
Gretna Green/Graitney 12, 16, 17, 197
Gylen Castle 99

Haddington 182, 196–197
Hamilton 29
Harribee Lee 16
Hawthornden 186, 187–189
Helensburgh 45
Helvellyn 13
High Hesketh 14
Holy Loch 87
Holyrood House 183–184
Howick Castle 199
Hume, David 181, 185
Hunter, Dr. William 33

Inch Cailleach 38
Inch Garvie 190
Inch Keith 181
Inch Kenneth 106, 107
Inch Murrain 37
Inglewood Forest 14
Inishail 63
Inish Eraith 63
Innis y Cloch 127
Inveraray 45, 53, 54, 55–58, 65, 67, 85, 131, 133
Invergarry Castle 149
Inverkeithing 191
Inverkip 87
Inverlochy Castle 133, 139, 147
Inverness 131, 143, 146, 147, 149, 153, 154, 155–160, 162, 167
Inveruglas 39, 48, 49
Iona 45, 104, 106, 111, 115, 116–121, 123, 124

Johnson, Dr. Samuel 93, 107, 123, 151, 171, 187
Jura 95, 96

Kames Bay 89
Kendal 7, 9, 10
Kenmore 66
Keppock 135, 138
Kerrera 98, 99, 125
Keswick 13
Kilchiarn 126
Kilchurn Castle 62, 63, 64
Kilmallie 146
Killearn 84
Killiecrankie, Pass of 164–165
Killin 45, 65, 66, 67, 70
Kilpatrick 36, 45–46
King's Pass/King's Seat 165–166, 168
Kingussie 162
Kinloch Moidart 92
Kinneff 169
Kinrara 162
Kinross 176, 177
Kintyre, Mull of 42, 90, 91, 95
Kirkstall Abbey 204
Knaresborough 204

Lammermuir Hills 183, 197
Lammerton 197, 198
Lanark 28
Lancaster 8, 9
Langdale Pikes 13
Largs 87
Latherhall 7
Latter Findlay 147
Lead Hills 26, 27, 28, 65
Leeds 204
Leith 177, 181, 182
Lennie/Lenny, Pass of 74, 85
Lincluden Abbey 24–25
Lindisfarne 198
Linlithgow 194–195
Lismore 100, 125, 126
Little Cumbrae/Cumbray 87
Liverpool 6, 8
Loanhead 187
Loch Achray 76, 81
Lochaber 147
Loch Alvie 162
Loch Awe 39, 61, 62, 64, 65, 85
Loch Beauly 157
Loch Craignish 95
Loch Creran 126

Index

Loch Dochart 68–69, 71, 72
Loch Earn/Loch Earn Head 45, 70, 71, 72–73, 75, 81, 163, 176
Loch Eil 127, 131, 145, 146
Loch Ericht 163
Loch Etive 61, 100, 124, 125
Loch Fyne 53, 55, 59, 90, 93, 95, 127
Lochgilphead 93, 102, 105
Loch Goyle 44
Loch Inch 162
Loch Katrine 46, 68, 74, 75, 76, 77, 78, 79, 80, 81, 85, 191
Loch Laggan 143
Loch Leven 176, 177, 193, 195
Loch Linnhe 139, 143
Loch Lochy 146, 147, 148, 149
Loch Lomond 37–41, 43, 46, 48, 49, 59, 85
Loch Long 42, 43–44, 49, 50, 53, 54, 87, 127
Loch Lubnaig 74, 191
Lochmaben 23–24, 27
Loch Moy 160
Loch-na-gar 163
Lochnell, Point of 125
Loch Ness 147, 149, 151, 153, 154
Loch Oich 146, 148
Loch Palney 166, 168
Loch Rannoch 143
Loch Restal 53
Loch Striven 87, 89
Loch Sunart 104
Loch Tarbert 91
Loch Tarf 151
Loch Tay 5, 45, 66, 70, 85
Loch Venachar 75, 76, 81
Lomond Hills 182
Longtown 16, 17
Lorn 97, 98
Lowther Hall 12, 13
Loudon 28
Lowther Law 27
Luib 66, 68, 69–70
Luing, Sound of 96, 97
Luncarty 170
Lunga 97
Luss 38–39, 46, 47, 48

Manchester 204
Mavisbank 187
May Island 183, 197
Mayburgh 13
Mell Fell 13
Melrose 5, 99, 195
Menteith, Lake of 83

Milnathort 176
Mingarury Castle 104
Monadhliath Mountains 160
Montrose, Marquis of 164
Moray Firth 143, 156, 158
Morpeth 200, 203
Moss Flanders 83
Muck 104
Mull 97, 99, 100, 101, 102, 104, 105, 106, 107, 115, 122, 140, 143
Musselburgh 182, 196
MacGregor, Rob Roy 38, 39, 82, 83
MacLean, Donald 92, 93, 94, 95, 178, 179, 185

Neilson, Mr. John 30, 45, 85
Netherby 17, 18, 19
Newark Castle 45
Newcastle-upon-Tyne 180, 190, 195, 200–203
New Lanark 22, 28
Niddrie Castle 195
Nithsdale 20, 25, 26
North Berwick 182, 197

Oban 62, 99, 123, 124, 125, 127
Ochil Hills 176, 182, 190, 191, 194
Ogilvy, Sir George 169–170, 174
Ormskirk 6, 7
Owen, Robert 22, 28
Ossian 58, 61, 63, 67, 93, 94, 99, 138, 150, 162

Paisley 36
Penrith 10, 13, 14, 18
Pentland Hills 182, 187, 189
Perth 162, 169, 170, 171–176, 183
Pinkie House 196
Place Fell 13
Port Appin 127
Port Glasgow 45
Port Menteith 82
Port Patrick 22
Preston 7, 8
Prestonpans 182, 196

Queensferry 177, 190, 191

Raschachans 73
Renfrew 36, 124
Rennie, John 8
Ribchester 7
Roseneath 44

Rossdhu 47
Rothesay 88, 89
Rothiemurchus Forest 161
Rowardennan 39
Rum 104, 105, 121
Ruthven Castle 162
Ruthwell 19

Saddleback 13
St. Abb's Head 197
St. Columba 115, 116, 118, 119, 166
St. Fillans 67–68
St. Helens 8
St. Kilda 93
St. Ninians 194
St. Sunday Fell 13
Scarba 95, 96, 97
Scaw Fell 13
Scone 100, 170, 173
Scott, Sir Walter 5, 16, 17, 21, 81, 126, 164, 182, 185, 186
Sedgefield 203
Seil 97
Shap 11, 12
Shap Fell 10, 12
Shuna 97
Sidlaw Hills 173
Skiddaw 10, 13, 18, 19, 20
Skye 90, 104, 121, 123, 144, 146, 149
Slate Islands 97
Smollett, Tobias 37
Solway Firth 14, 16, 18
Solway Moss 17
Staffa 45, 86, 93, 99, 103, 104, 106, 107, 112, 113, 115, 116, 121, 124
Stalkir Castle 127
Stibra Crags 13
Stirling 27, 46, 83, 182, 190, 191, 192–194
Stockton-on-Tees 203
Strathblane 84
Strathearn 176
Strath Fillan 66, 68, 72
Strath Nairn 160

Strath Spey 161, 166
Strontian 102
Stuart, Charles Edward 148, 160, 196
Stuart, Mary 16, 84, 176, 184, 193, 194, 195, 196
Sunderland 202

Tarbert, East/West 42, 90, 91
Tarbet 41, 42, 48, 49
Thirsk 203
Thornhill 26
Tinto Top 27
Tiree 56, 105
Tobermory 102, 103, 121, 123
Toward Castle 87
Toward Point 86, 87, 88
Treshinish, Point of 105, 106
Trossachs, the 45, 46, 68, 74, 76, 77–81, 85, 152
Tyndrum 64, 65–66, 67

Uist 93
Ullswater 13, 74
Ulva 106, 107
Ulverstone 9
Urquhart Castle 154

Vale of St. John 13

Wade, General 47, 60, 151, 154
Wallace, William 24, 28, 189, 194
Warkworth 199
Warrington 8
West Felton 6
Wetherby 204
Whinfield Park 13
White Pike 13
Wishawtown 29
Workington 16
Wrexham 6, 69, 92, 204

Yarm 203
Yornoch 26